Newcastle
City Council

Newcastle Libraries and Information Service

☎ 0845 002 0336

Due for return	Due for return	Due for return

Please return this item to any of Newcastle's Libraries by the last date shown above. If not requested by another customer the loan can be renewed, you can do this by phone, post or in person.
Charges may be made for late returns.

SHANE WARNE'S CENTURY

SHANE WARNE'S CENTURY

MY TOP 100 TEST CRICKETERS

SHANE WARNE

MAINSTREAM
PUBLISHING

EDINBURGH AND LONDON

First published in Great Britain in 2008 by
MAINSTREAM PUBLISHING COMPANY
(EDINBURGH) LTD
7 Albany Street
Edinburgh EH1 3UG

ISBN 9781845964153

A catalogue record for this book is available
from the British Library

Typeset in Champion and Concorde

Printed in Great Britain by
CPI William Clowes Ltd, Beccles, NR34 7TL

CONTENTS

FOREWORD

Sir Michael Parkinson

IF I EVER SAT DOWN TO make a list of the 100 best cricketers I have observed in a lifetime (60 years or more) watching the game, I would put Shane Warne at the top of my list. Like Tiger Woods and Muhammad Ali in other sporting occupations, he didn't so much dominate the game as redefine it.

As a cricketer, he belongs in a select category that includes Donald Bradman, W.G. Grace and Viv Richards – players not simply masters of their craft, but also able to dominate the opposition by the force of their willpower as well as their abundance of talent. When Warne was given the ball – particularly against the Poms – the pulse rate of the game quickened, the crowd sat forward in expectation, the bars emptied. What the batsman knew was that his great gifts as a bowler – the prodigious spin, the accuracy and the ability to be both an attacking bowler as well as a frugal one – was only part of what they had to deal with. No cricketer of my acquaintance brought to the game his capacity for dominating opponents and exploiting their frailties – both technical and psychological – with such precision and intelligence. He once told me the story of one international player who was so dominated by Warne's mastery that he sought psychological help. Upon his return to the Test match arena, he was confronted by Warne, who, instead of the expected sledging, greeted him with the polite enquiry: 'What colour was the psychiatrist's couch, mate?'

Shane Warne brought a sense of theatre and drama to cricket, and some of it spilled over into his private life. For a time, he became celebrity-tabloid fodder. Moreover, the wear and tear on his body caused him to refine his bowling action and to rethink his repertoire. He survived it all to have taken more Test wickets than any other bowler at the time he left the game. When he departed the field of play, it was as if the floodlights had been switched off. Perhaps his most significant contribution was that he changed the tempo of cricket. When he first appeared, the game was dominated by fast bowlers, and spinners were considered an endangered species. By the time he had retired, he had not only shown repeatedly what we had been missing, but demonstrated, as *Wisden* put it: 'That a man could take wickets by seduction as well as extortion.'

He is an agreeable, if not exhausting, companion, and I am delighted to be his friend. The 100 Test cricketers he has chosen in this book should also be delighted by the knowledge that they have been selected by one of the greatest of them all.

INTRODUCTION

NOTHING KICKS OFF AN ARGUMENT MORE quickly than claiming that a particular singer, a TV cop or even a flavour of crisps is better than another. For every viewpoint there will be somebody else in your group who holds the opposite view and isn't afraid to express it. Over the years, in bars, dressing-rooms, departure lounges – anywhere and everywhere – cricket and cricketers have split opinions and created debate. In the end, they are opinions and not right or wrong.

When I wrote an article in *The Times* of my top 50 players, and a brief summary of each, the feedback was amazing. In Pakistan, they thought I'd put Waqar Younis too far down the list. In Australia, they wondered why Mark Taylor was above Steve Waugh. In South Africa, they thought I'd snubbed Allan Donald and in India they revelled in Sachin Tendulkar's position at the top of the tree.

The idea for this book came from all those emails and letters. I thought it would be a good idea to explain some of my selections in more depth and, to get people talking for a little bit longer, go the full hog and pick 100 players: *Shane Warne's Century*. I'll admit that some of the positions have changed. A few of the guys I chose in 2007 are now out of my 50, but still in the 100. One or two have gone up and some have gone down. That's the great thing about lists – no matter how long you have, there is always a bit of fine-tuning to be done. I'll back that up with a challenge: when you've finished reading this book – and not before – write down your top ten records of all time and put the sheet of paper somewhere safe. Do the same thing a few months later, and then compare the two.

I'll be amazed if the lists are exactly the same. It has taken several months to put my 100 names in place and if the publishers had not imposed a deadline I would still be tinkering now.

I want to stress that this is purely a personal choice. There is no right or wrong. I've put Mark Waugh above his brother, for instance. But there are a few general things I can say straight away to try to make sense of my selections. First, I've gone on battles, influences on the game, bowling to them or facing them with the bat, rather than figures alone. Yes, I've checked a few things, but I've made sure that the record books are a servant rather than a master. Statistics do not always tell the full story; there are plenty of examples of that in these pages.

I guess there is also a bias in the book towards match-winners and players who have entertained and the aggressive style they played, not to mention the input they had on their opponents or what impact an opposition player had on us and me as a bowler. No apologies there. The game needs characters who can excite crowds. We are facing stiff competition from other sports these days. I have also taken into account areas such as longevity of career – that's one reason why the incredible Courtney Walsh is so high – and consistency of performances all over the world and in different conditions. A truly great player can adapt to different pitches and conditions. Brian Lara is a good example: he has struck big hundreds in England, Australia and the Indian subcontinent. Test cricket has been my biggest consideration because I still feel that is the supreme form of the game and a true test of your character, technique and mental strength. But a few of my hundred have probably made more of a mark in one-day cricket, and I even took Twenty20 performances into account. Again, though, the best players can adapt to all formats.

A few of the names might turn heads. Arjuna Ranatunga is one; it's pretty well known that we aren't on each other's Christmas card list, but I can see that he has made a contribution to Sri Lankan cricket. Though I say it through gritted teeth, he deserves to be here. At the other extreme are some great mates such as Robin Smith, Stephen Fleming, Jonty Rhodes and Michael Clarke. Maybe they will want to know why they aren't a few places higher.

I have tried to take friendship out of the equation and to be as objective as I can.

Those are my guiding principles. Let the arguments begin . . .

Publisher's note

At the end of each entry, brief career records have been included. These are given for each player's speciality only: wickets and strike rate for bowlers; runs and batting average for batsmen; runs and dismissals for wicket-keepers; and batting and bowling figures for all-rounders. There are a few exceptions. If a player predominantly known for one discipline has contributed significantly in another, details have been included; for example, Anil Kumble's Test batting record has been given, in recognition of his contribution as a batsman despite being considered an out-and-out bowler.

1

·······

SACHIN TENDULKAR

SINCE THE AGE OF 16, WHEN he made his Test debut, Sachin Tendulkar has known nothing but pressure. You have to see him in India to realise and understand the weight of expectation on his shoulders and the way that his life is restricted by the adulation of his fans. The way he conducts himself and handles the fame and everything that goes with being Sachin is a great example to all sportsmen. On the field, he has never put himself before the team. Every aspect of his game is absolutely first class. He is very tough mentally, with a solid technique, and can play strokes all around the wicket. He doesn't score runs every innings, of course, but he hasn't suffered long troughs of poor form at any time in his career. In fact, for the best part of nearly two full decades, he has scored runs in different conditions and opposition attacks all over the world – more than eighty hundreds in Test and one-day cricket combined. Cricket has been fortunate to have a wonderful player and a first-rate ambassador, and to me he plays the game in the right spirit.

The great Sir Donald Bradman said that Tendulkar at the crease was the closest in style he had seen to himself. That statement caused a great deal of interest in Australia and around the world. Tendulkar and I had the honour of being invited to Sir Donald's 90th birthday. It was fascinating to see the pair of them together, both small men, talking about different grips and bats and approaches to batting. There was enormous mutual respect between them. Some of the conversation was quite technical, but Bradman was sharp as a tack. He was amazed when Tendulkar told him that he had been coached as a boy, because Bradman thought that he batted like a natural.

Tendulkar was even more surprised when Bradman told him that he had prepared for a day's cricket by spending hours in the office before play in the morning. In those days, even the greatest players had jobs outside the game.

Tendulkar has a touch of genius about him. But I wonder if people appreciate the amount of time he spends working on his game. Sachin plans well before every tour. Before our tour to India in 1998, he had the nets deliberately roughed up outside leg stump so that the practice bowlers would be able to replicate my spin from around the wicket. Another example: before the last Test of the series in Australia in 2003–04, he thought he was vulnerable when cover driving because something was slightly awry with his technique. The cover drive is a bread-and-butter shot for most batsmen, but Tendulkar decided for the final Test at Sydney that he could not afford to play it. He stuck to his game plan for hour after hour and scored 241 not out, with not one cover drive – amazing discipline. That is mental strength.

In this book, I will say frequently that footwork is the key to being able to play spin and for that matter all bowling. I make no apology for repeating myself because it is just that important. Tendulkar is the best in the business. Being quick and decisive means that he either goes all the way forward or back on the crease, but doesn't get caught in two minds. That helps his shot selection. He rarely sweeps. Once a batsman is in the right position, anything is possible: defend, attack or leave alone. I have found it difficult at times to deceive him because he reads the length and the spin so quickly! That is an advantage of being brought up in a land of so many slow bowlers, at least traditionally. I thought that his reflexes would start to slow over time, and perhaps the grind of playing so much has begun to take its toll with injuries, but even as recently as 2008 he scored 150s in Sydney and Adelaide – those innings brought back a few memories while I was watching on television, very happily retired, thank you.

For me, his success has been a case of having a plan and concentrating on every delivery, trying to stay confident and building up pressure with accuracy but also giving the ball a good rip. They might think of him as a god in India – and look how grounds fill up when word spreads outside that he is coming in to bat – but he is an opponent, and he can make mistakes. My view was always that if I bowled well enough for long enough, I would have a chance at knocking him over – it only happened five times. There was such a small margin of error when bowling to Sachin. Even when he was scoring hundreds in India, I didn't think that I bowled badly; he just played extremely well, and a few people have commented that our battles in 1998 were some of the most intense cricket they have seen and enjoyed. I really did relish the challenge. Glenn McGrath and Jason Gillespie had some success against Sachin. They liked to cut down run-scoring opportunities by bowling just outside off stump and quite full – again, it was a case of doing the basics well and having a plan, and plan B, C, D, E . . .

Over the years, we have become very good friends. We came into the game at roughly the same time – he was a year or so ahead of me – and he played in my debut at Sydney. Actually, not only did he play, but he scored 148. By then the phenomenon was starting to take hold. It worked both ways, because the papers would praise him but also blame him sometimes if his innings did not win matches, as though he was responsible for the rest of the side – what a joke that is. Stories about him having to put on a disguise to be able to go into a cinema are true. He just accepts that life will be like that and gets on with it instead of fighting something he cannot change. All good things come to an end, and we should make sure we really appreciate Tendulkar whilst he is around and playing well. We will all miss him when he is not around any more!

SACHIN RAMESH TENDULKAR

BORN	24 April 1973, Mumbai, India
TESTS	147
RUNS	11,782 in 244 innings at 55.31 with 39 hundreds/49 fifties
WICKETS	42 at 52.66
ONE-DAY INTERNATIONALS	417
RUNS	16,361 in 407 innings at 44.33 with 42 hundreds/89 fifties
WICKETS	154 at 44.12

2

· · · · · ·

BRIAN LARA

BRIAN LARA WAS ONLY JUST PIPPED by Sachin; it was very hard to split them. There is actually very little to separate them. At his best, Lara was probably more destructive a batsman than Tendulkar but not as consistent. He has played monumental innings – 400 not out and 375 in Test cricket and the all-time record of 501 not out, playing for Warwickshire during the most prolific spell of his career. Tendulkar was more consistent, whereas Lara was a 'mood' player. It helped that Tendulkar was playing for a side that was generally on the rise, whereas the West Indies, in Lara's time and through no fault of his own, were slipping down the ladder.

Whether you love him or hate him, Lara was a bloke who captured your attention straight away. He was an awesome player to watch when on song, with his high back lift and his all-round presence at the crease. He had a lovely strut and a swagger; he also had a lot of natural flair. He was a great player, and he wasn't afraid to express that in his approach. Without being a big or bulky guy, he imposed himself on bowlers. He had a massive presence; I guess that Viv Richards must have had that same demeanour at the crease. You just knew you were in the company of somebody who was better than the rest, who wasn't going to just hang around; he wanted to stamp his authority, straight away. Lara scored runs all over the world. And it was the way he got his runs and scored, that's what captured everyone's imagination, as well as his ability to play genuine match-winning innings for his team, a number of them against Australia.

Probably the biggest compliment to him was the way captains used to think of the 'Lara factor' when it came to setting a target. If a bloke is capable of scoring triple-hundreds quickly, then it is bound to distort calculations. The rate of scoring was another consideration. Even more than Tendulkar, Lara could hit boundaries in clusters. He just found a groove and batting almost became too easy. A lot of his hundreds were big ones – raising his bat for the century was often just the start. Like a lot of small men, he cut and pulled really well, but he was also strong on the front foot. His shots always found the gap and his placement was a real strength. Glenn McGrath had the most success against him – their ongoing individual battle was one of the great contests of my time. Glenn's plan was to bowl around the wicket and try to nip the ball away. He wanted Lara to hit the ball on the rise and give a chance between the keeper and gully. I had a great seat at slip to watch.

The first time he made a real mark on Australia was at Sydney in 1993 when he was still trying to earn a regular place in the team. He dominated partnership after partnership to the point where I said to Border, half jokingly, that we were bowling for a run out. In the end that is how we got him, but not before a great 277 and a career had been blasted into motion. All the previews of the game suggested that the pitch would turn but there wasn't a lot of joy for either Greg Matthews or me. As the decade wore on, Lara practically carried the West Indies batting. In 1998–99 we drew a series 2–2 which I'm convinced we would have won 4–0 if Lara hadn't been playing. He scored a double-hundred in the second Test at Jamaica, then a hundred in the third and fourth matches. And the way he played those innings from the first ball was amazing to watch.

I remember on one occasion Brian complained about 'verbals' in the middle, which he knew were part of the game. Captaining the side as well as being the only significant run-scorer was a lot to ask. His mood could swing from day to day. It is a bit of a cliché, but people really do know their cricket in the Caribbean. They like to party at the games, but they also watch closely, and opinions flow as strongly and easily as the rum at the kiosks. Lara gave them something to be proud of, and when he wasn't playing as brilliantly as he could, supporters wanted to know why. I am sure he would have been even more successful had he been around ten years earlier to slot into a line-up with Gordon Greenidge, Richards and Clive Lloyd. Some of the responsibility would have been lifted.

I really enjoy Brian's friendship, and we have become good mates! We had some great battles on the field, and looking back I'll admit that things got quite intense, but we struck up a good friendship that I am sure will last, and we both have a huge respect for each other. He likes to come to Australia, and he has been generous with his time in helping my charity, the Shane Warne Foundation. In fact, in 2007 I had the pleasure of playing with him in the All Stars team at the Hong Kong Sixes. We had a pile of fun, and it was a relief to see him from a different angle, not with the ball in my hand staring down from 22 yards. We all miss the batting maestro and that dashing blade. He was a 'once in a generation' player.

BRIAN CHARLES LARA

BORN	2 May 1969, Santa Cruz, Trinidad
TESTS	131
RUNS	11,953 in 232 innings at 52.88 with 34 hundreds/48 fifties
ONE-DAY INTERNATIONALS	299
RUNS	10,405 in 289 innings at 40.48 with 19 hundreds/63 fifties

3

· · · · · · ·

CURTLY AMBROSE

IF YOU PLAY CRICKET FOR ANY length of time, you have to be prepared for a few injuries. And have the mental strength to ride the highs and lows. The game, as a bowler, and especially a quick one, puts unusual strains on your body. In my case, I grew to expect pain in my shoulder, from all the rotation, and my spinning finger. Bowlers in general have trouble with their knees and backs mainly from the constant pounding on the hard turf and carrying their body weight.

The Caribbean in 1995 was where Australia became the number-one side in the world, taking the mantle from the West Indies. At the same time, there was no way they were going to give up their crown lightly. Going into the third game, we were 1–0 up with two to play. The West Indies were determined to fight back, they were roused, they were nasty and the damp, emerald-green pitch was perfect for their pace bowlers.

Ambrose was an annoying bowler; he had the height, the pace, the aggression and the consistency to trouble the best in the world. But what set him apart was his ability to find that extra gear and work over a new batsman. We always thought the best way to deal with him was to keep him calm and see him bowl from the non-striker's end. He was a really accurate bowler, and as long as you did not take many runs from him, he would be fairly happy. Hit a couple of fours, though, and he turned into a different proposition, moving up at least one gear as if his pride had been offended. He took those shots personally, and that is all it would take to wind him up. In Trinidad, things went beyond that. He had a major

21

disagreement in the middle with Steve Waugh – at one point, their captain, Richie Richardson, had to restrain his giant fast bowler as Curtly and Waugh went eyeball to eyeball. Ambrose was like an angry bear with a sore head, and all he wanted to do was make sure the West Indies finished that game level in the series.

Amazingly, the match was over inside three days (despite losing more than three hours to rain on day one), with each innings lasting an average of little more than forty overs. Curtly was Man of the Match with overall figures of nine for sixty-five. If he had played many more matches on pitches like that, I think a few batsmen would have contemplated early retirement.

Do not let me give the impression that he needed conditions in his favour to be a threat. It is just that when they were, he could be as close as there was to unplayable because of his accuracy, height and pace. Glenn McGrath was the same. I rank Curtly just a shade higher – only just – although he was not the quickest of the West Indies bowlers. His height and bounce made him very awkward. He was like a ruthless machine with a nasty streak. Unfortunately, I never really got to know him away from the game. I think he wanted to maintain his reputation among opponents as a strong, brooding character. Best, he thought, for us to see him with a scowl on his face rather than a smile. In his own dressing-room, he was said to be a practical joker, and outside the game he was very easy-going, happy strumming his guitar with some mates, slamming down the dominoes in another Caribbean pastime or shooting Gaskets.

I came across other examples of the devastation he could wreak. Early in my career, he took seven wickets for one run in an incredible spell at Perth in the 1992–93 series. And these were good wickets, including tough guys such as Allan Border and David Boon. I played another 137 Test matches after that but never encountered an instance of a bowler doing so much damage in such a short space of time.

In Perth in 1997, we had already retained the Frank Worrell Trophy, and I wonder if the frustration of losing the series had simply got to him, although the West Indies actually won the game by ten wickets. Ambrose had a lovely, smooth and rhythmical approach, but towards the end of our second innings he suddenly developed a no-ball problem, over-stepping by a couple of feet from around the wicket. Batting was already difficult on a dodgy, cracked pitch, but it became a very unpleasant experience. I seriously wondered whether this guy was deliberately trying to hurt us. One over lasted as long as 15 balls because of his back foot overstepping the front line. Although he played on until 2000 – and could have continued for longer had he wanted – that was his last Test match in Australia. It was a shame that he left on a sour note as far as our spectators were concerned. Better to remember him for the days when he got things very, very right, than wrong, hey?

CURTLY ELCONN LYNWALL AMBROSE

BORN	21 September 1963, Swetes Village, Antigua
TESTS	98
WICKETS	405 at 20.99
ONE-DAY INTERNATIONALS	176
WICKETS	225 at 24.12

4

• • • • • • •

ALLAN BORDER

THE FIRST FEW GAMES IN TEST cricket can make or break anyone's career, so I owe so much to Allan Border for the way he treated me when I first came into the Australia side. I wonder if I would have survived without him. From the very start, I felt he had unshakeable faith in me, and not just because of his words of encouragement. Words can be cheap, but Border actually backed me to do a job, even when I was unsure that I was up to the task.

The way he made me feel and backed me was a huge influence and gave me confidence. My breakthrough came in my third Test match, in Colombo in 1992, when Sri Lanka needed thirty-six runs to win with four wickets in hand. I was staggered when Border brought me on to bowl, with poor figures already. I thought the match could be finished in a couple of overs, so A.B. showed enormous faith in me at a crucial stage. I have never forgotten that. I bowled a maiden – a big achievement for me at that stage of my career – and took three wickets in thirteen balls in all without conceding a run. His gamble paid off, and I felt I had contributed to an Australian victory.

Sorry A.B., I've written two paragraphs there without mentioning your batting. No Australian has scored more Test runs, and he averaged over 50 in his 156 games. Even this long after his retirement, an innings might still be described as being 'Allan Border-like' and people around the world will know exactly what that means. His name is a byword for grit and determination and toughness. He came into the side at a time when the Kerry Packer revolution had temporarily weakened the mainstream Test team, making his debut in an Ashes series which Australia lost 5–1 on our own soil. Hammered by the Poms – these were not great days for Australian cricket – Border not only held his own, but made runs, and he used that savage experience to toughen himself: first into a batsman who gave the bowlers no hint of encouragement and then into a captain who set us off on the march to recover our position as the best side in the world. People forget how low we had sunk when he took over from an emotional Kim Hughes.

I have never thought it a coincidence that Mark Taylor and Steve Waugh, who both later took the captaincy baton from Border, came into the side under Allan. His positive influence rubbed off on all of us, and I think it is fair to trace the incredible success we had in the years around the turn of the decade back to Taylor and Waugh's predecessor – one Allan Border. There are some players who reassure the rest of the side just by being part of it, and for as long as he lined up as an Australian cricketer, Border fitted into that category.

Nobody I played with or against taught me more about the game. Border was a streetwise cricketer – he had to be to come through those dark days. He taught me a way to use sledging to my advantage. He thrived on confrontation, and if he felt his focus was going for some reason, he would spark a little disagreement with an opponent to wind himself up. That might mean turning to short leg and saying: 'What are you looking at?' He knew there would be a response, and that would get him in a contest and help him to switch on.

The Ashes brought out the best in him. After losing in England in 1985, he put so much time and effort into winning back the urn four years later. He instilled a ruthless approach, which I encountered on my first tour in 1993. We were playing a warm-up game at Worcester before the first Test, my first chance to bowl to Graeme Hick. My instinct was to try to get him out to go into the series with a psychological advantage. Border saw the bigger picture. He instructed me to bowl nothing but leg-breaks, even if it meant Hick carted me around the park – which he did. The point was to save my variations and the element of surprise for when it mattered most.

On that tour Border played what was, in its own way, one of the most amazing innings I ever saw to score an unbeaten 200 at

Headingley. There was nothing flash about it at all, but I have rarely seen a batsman so completely in control of his own game or so devoted to just grinding down the bowlers. He never looked like getting out in nine or so hours at the crease, breaking down the sheer will of the England team. Graham Gooch resigned as captain straight after the game. Border's captaincy style was a more of a lead-by-example approach, but when he spoke, the team listened, and let me tell you when he gave you a rocket, wow it was personal and in your face, but it was spot on. And his all-round fielding, both of slips and mid-wicket, was second to none.

Of course, his place among the greats was secured while I was still at school. Border was the guy who captained our first World Cup win in 1987. As I watched that game on television, I could never have dreamed that I would be playing in the same team as him one day. A few years ago, Cricket Australia established a Player of the Year award to take in performances in Test and one-day cricket over the preceding 12 months. They called it the Allan Border Medal. That says it all.

ALLAN ROBERT BORDER

BORN	27 July 1955, Sydney, Australia
TESTS	156
RUNS	11,174 in 265 innings at 50.56 with 27 hundreds/63 fifties
ONE-DAY INTERNATIONALS	273
RUNS	6,254 in 252 innings at 30.62 with 3 hundreds/39 fifties

5

GLENN MCGRATH

NOBODY UNDERLINES THE OLD SAYING THAT cricket is a simple game more than my old buddy Glenn McGrath. All of the top players have an X-factor about them and the ability to change gear. In McGrath's case, you might look at footage and struggle to find that precious, extra something to explain his fantastic record. People miss it because it is so, so obvious. He just looked after the basics more consistently than anybody else: line, length – with the odd variation and just enough movement to take the edge – and an uncanny knack of taking the big wicket. Also, don't underestimate how smart a bowler he was, with a great plan for each batsman, and his execution was first class. He knew that if he executed often enough, and didn't give the batsman a bad ball to allow him to relieve the pressure, then eventually he would wear him down. For any aspiring young bowler, there has never been a better role model.

I used to love bowling in tandem with McGrath. In terms of style, we were completely different, but we could both wear down batsmen into making a mistake and challenge their patience and techniques.

Over the years, he consistently showed his ability to get the big wicket. He used to pride himself on knocking over the main danger man after targeting him. He had an incredible record against Mike Atherton and was as likely as anyone to get Brian Lara. It took a lot of practice before he began to tick like clockwork, but once he reached that stage in 1995 and gained confidence and some momentum, there was no stopping his strong, high, repeatable action. Batsmen reckoned they knew what he was going to do, but I can count on the fingers of one hand the number of occasions one of them successfully took him on over the course of a few spells in an innings.

Off the field he could be a pest. There is no other word for him. His sense of humour would embarrass an eight year old, and he wasn't very good at sitting still to concentrate on just watching the game. As our long-term number 11, he had plenty of time to get up to his tricks in the dressing-room. He liked a practical joke and he found an accomplice in Jason Gillespie. There was nothing nasty about him, or anything even approaching it. He might sprinkle a sachet of sugar in your hair, leave something in your shoe or squirt you with a water pistol. McGrath always found that sort of thing hilarious. It takes all sorts to make a good dressing-room, and he helped to create the right dynamic and had a great attitude to life and cricket.

It was his clowning around on the morning of the 2005 Edgbaston Test that caused shock headlines. I was chatting to Nasser Hussain and Darren 'Boof' Lehmann, who were doing some TV work, in the middle when I heard this groaning noise and looked back to see McGrath on the floor. I think I shook my head, turned back to Nasser and probably muttered something uncomplimentary. Of course, it turned out that he had wrenched his ankle on a cricket ball and couldn't play in the game. That stroke of misfortune has come to be seen as the turning point in the series, and I agree. I don't want to take too much away from England, because we all need a bit of luck now and again, but it is certainly fair to wonder whether the Ashes would have changed hands but for that twist of fate; we are allowed to wonder – it's my book after all!

Pigeon had what us sportsmen call 'white-line fever'. This is when a bloke's character suddenly changes, as though a major virus has just taken a grip of him when he crosses the white line onto the field. There were times when the umpires needed to step in and have a word with him. Again, it wasn't nasty. When he growled at a batsman 'I'm going to rip your head off', it was the hollowest threat imaginable. In the slips, we would laugh amongst ourselves.

He didn't really need the words because his bowling on its own was hostile enough. He first seized his chance in the West Indies when our plan was to match their fire with fire. We decided to bounce their lower order instead of hanging back in the hope that they would spare us the same treatment. McGrath relished the challenge. He used the bouncer wisely and cleverly throughout his career, and he was bang on target when he did drop short, unlike some bowlers who waste their energy with balls that soar harmlessly over a batsman's head. We had lost Damien Fleming and Craig McDermott to injury, but McGrath stepped up to the plate and stayed there until he retired in 2007.

It was an honour to play with Glenn and to retire at the same time was a privilege. Regaining the Ashes 5–0 was a lovely way to depart the international scene.

Despite all the mountains of evidence to the contrary, he really thought he could bat. Before going out to the crease, he would practise his shots in the dressing-room, take his time and then stroll out. We would try and wait till he was out of the dressing-room before we all rushed to get changed and ready to field. Looking back, I really take my hat off to Pigeon. The way he went about his cricket was totally professional, with a lot of passion and common sense. We have developed a very close relationship. I was so sad for Glenn and his children when I heard the news that his lovely wife, Jane, had lost her brave battle with cancer. She showed amazing courage, and for Glenn to play cricket at the highest level and deal with his wife's illness must have been so difficult. I don't think anyone in the team could imagine what he was going through.

Love ya, Pigeon, and, mate, you are the definition of a champion!

GLENN DONALD McGRATH

BORN	9 February 1970, Dubbo, New South Wales, Australia
TESTS	124
WICKETS	563 at 21.64
ONE-DAY INTERNATIONALS	250
WICKETS	381 at 22.02

6

· · · · · ·

WASIM AKRAM

WHEN I LOOK BACK OVER MY career, I can see that I was fortunate for so many reasons. One of them might not be obvious; when Wasim Akram bowled the fastest spell I ever saw, I was not in the middle to face it. Instead, I was part of a quiet Australia dressing-room, as Wasim came out after tea on the second day at Rawalpindi in 1994 and gave Steve Waugh a real going-over. I have no idea what prompted him to hit top gear in the fifth session of the innings, but he found some extra reserves and just looked awesome. He is the best left-arm bowler I ever faced or witnessed, a complete practitioner who could go over and around the wicket and move the new – and old ball – either way at great speed. There was nothing he couldn't do, except, I suppose, to bowl right-handed, but he didn't need to. He had tremendous skill and was very clever.

Wasim was one of the real greats of the past 20 years. We had lots of chats about the game, and I can appreciate the effort he put into reaching the consistent standard that made him one of the most awkward bowlers in the world. He was also a good batsman, scoring a double-hundred in Test cricket, and he was the best captain of Pakistan I came across. As a one-day player, he might rank even higher, because his fast, swinging yorker could be unplayable at the end of an innings and his approach to batting was perfectly suited to the later stages of a match – as long as the ball was placed in his arc so he could swing his arms through the line.

He suffered a lot of injuries through his career but from my experience did not lose a lot of pace between the first time I faced him and the last. Even if he did not bowl at express speed all the time, he had that very quick ball up his sleeve and his bouncer could be deadly because it was so well directed. And like the greats he had that extra gear when he needed it or when the game was on the line. He never wasted a ball by letting it soar harmlessly over the batsman's head. In fact, he was very crafty all round. When he bowled around the wicket, he would run in from behind the umpire so you only saw him at the last moment, close to his delivery stride. He cut back his run early in his career, but he still generated pace from a very whippy arm action and perfect wrist position. There was no wasted energy, and he could bowl long spells, making it difficult to see him out of the attack as you would some of the other fast bowlers with longer approaches. And he loved bowling.

One of the most impressive things about his record is his consistency all over the world. His record is pretty good everywhere because he had the skill to bowl on any surface. I remember seeing him in Melbourne a couple of years before my own debut when he took 11 wickets. He was the toughest bowler to start your innings against because he came quicker on to the bat than his approach suggested, and his late swing was the real key. He got a lot of batsmen out, in general either bowled or lbw, and his economy rate was incredible.

He was still effective later in his career. I remember a one-day international at the Docklands Stadium in Melbourne in 2002 on a really cold day when he produced a brilliant outswinger to get rid of Adam Gilchrist first ball and then removed Ricky Ponting two balls later. By that stage, they had Shoaib Akhtar as well as Wasim and Waqar Younis in the bowling attack, but with all of that talent in the side they never achieved what they could have. We found the key to doing well against them was to make sure we played consistently. Pakistan could be hot and cold, although Wasim's displays were more consistent than most.

He learned a lot from Imran Khan, a mentor he almost revered. I think that young players coming into the Pakistan team looked upon Wasim in the same way that he saw Imran. He could lift them just by his presence. Captaining Pakistan has been a poisoned chalice – in one year alone they went through five different skippers – but Wasim never went about it as though he thought he was a temporary choice. I liked the way that he gave spinners a good run and was prepared to back young players no matter how little experience they had coming in to the side.

Despite all of his experience, he says he is reluctant to go into coaching because he does not have the patience for anything more than consultancy work, fine-tuning bowlers and talking to them about specific areas of their game. He is a big believer in the importance of practice and puts down his success with reverse swing to hard work and commitment to the team. He also thinks there is a problem with over-coaching. In Pakistan probably more than anywhere else, players come from outside whatever system is in place and go straight into the side. It is great when natural ability is allowed to flourish, and I also agree with Wasim's assessment of team meetings: that anything going on for too long is counter-productive and a waste of time.

WASIM AKRAM

BORN	3 June 1966, Lahore, Pakistan
TESTS	104
RUNS	2,898 in 147 innings at 22.64 with 3 hundreds/7 fifties
WICKETS	414 at 23.62
ONE-DAY INTERNATIONALS	356
RUNS	3,717 in 280 innings at 16.52 with 6 fifties
WICKETS	414 at 23.62

7

· · · · · · · ·

MUTTIAH MURALITHARAN

HOWEVER MANY WICKETS MURALI HAS AT the end of his Test career, the figure may never be beaten. People thought I was mad when I first said that he could push all the way to the 1,000 mark. Maybe that will prove to be an overestimation, but not by much. Although injuries are starting to take their toll a little bit, with medical science being what it is, and Sri Lanka's determination to keep him going for as long as possible, he could still make that magic number and sit there for ever at the top of the list. I say this because Murali has been unique – nothing about other bowlers prepares you for the challenge. And because he has not been in the same side as other great bowlers, he is used to sending down 40 per cent or so of Sri Lanka's overs in every innings. On that basis, the law of averages says that he should take four wickets at least in each innings. It is rare for an attack to lean so heavily towards one bloke. Put it this way: if he gets numbers nine, ten and eleven plus one top-order batsman every innings, that's four in an innings.

No matter what anybody thinks about his action, he presents challenges that any serious batsman loves to tackle. However unorthodox the delivery itself, what he does with the ball is special. There are stories of him turning it off straight into the side of the net at practice. He can spin it that far. I know that everybody will have an opinion about his action and wonder what I think as a fellow spinner. But to me the debate is now redundant. Let's move on. It doesn't matter whether or not the ICC changed the law to a 15 degree bend in the elbow to accommodate him. The plain fact is that he's been cleared to play, and we all know where we stand. He has been great for the Sri Lanka team.

Time spent complaining is time and energy wasted, especially in the dressing-room. It is better to watch him and admire the way he bowls and ponder the way he does it and come up with a way of trying to counter his skills. There are chinks in his armour. For such a good bowler, he tends to be very, very defensive. It was interesting to watch him in the Indian Premier League (IPL), where he seemed to think of his role as being to simply contain runs rather than take wickets. With batsmen looking to take risks, you might have imagined he would come away with loads of stumpings and top-edged catches, but that was not the case. Whether that stemmed from instructions or a lack of confidence, I don't know. But it did seem to be a slight waste of his ability.

He does not like playing in Australia, where he feels that the crowds are against him. Purely on a playing level, I think our batsmen have dealt with him pretty well. The numbers back that up. In all Test cricket, Murali averages roughly 22 overall. That figure rises to 36 against Australia home and away, and 75 just in Australia. I think our players read him and are prepared to go after him and attack. Michael Clarke's footwork was superb in the 2007 series, and Murali had no answer. There must be a reason for our success against him, and I think it comes from our decision to be more aggressive. If you can get rid of the close catchers around the bat, that removes some of the possible dismissals straight away. Again, being defensive, he is quick to push mid-on and mid-off back to the ropes when a batsman looks to get after him, whereas other spinners would be happy to see them taking that risk and back themselves to force a mistake.

When Allan Border faced him for the first time many moons ago, he missed five balls out of six because he could not get his body attuned to facing an off-spinner when the action, which was new to him, looked as though it belonged to a guy bowling leg-breaks. Gradually, batsmen adjusted so that by the mid and late 1990s most of our players were able to read him from the hand. That takes away a lot of the trouble, because it means you can be more decisive with your footwork, get to the pitch of the ball and play with a straight bat. Murali wants batsmen to sweep, cut or stay at the crease and try to play him off the surface, because he knows that the spin and dip he generates will not leave long to adjust. As a general rule, I think that the better a bowler, the more aggressive you have to be. Poking and prodding around hands over the initiative and sooner or later you will get something that is simply unplayable or has your name on it. I am not saying batsmen should try to hit everything, but there is more chance of the bad ball coming along by looking for the ones and twos and rotating the strike. A bowler cannot set up a batsman for a particular dismissal if he is only getting two or three balls in a row at the same guy.

Sri Lanka always made a decision to back Murali in every way they could whenever eyebrows were raised, which you have to admire. Personally, I do not think it is good for the game when the decisions of the umpires are being challenged. I guess my real concern about his action is that, as a role model, he is bound to be copied by kids who do not have the same condition in their elbows and wrists. Murali's elbow may well lock, but other people's will indisputably bend beyond the 15 degrees. Administrators have to keep an eye out and make sure any problems are solved early before bowlers get to the higher levels.

On a personal level, I have always found Murali to be a really nice guy, with a great sense of fun, and he is very, very competitive. He is the joker in the Sri Lanka team. We got to know each other more closely after the terrible tsunami on Boxing Day 2004. Anybody who could help wanted to do something, and Murali gave so much of himself in the days and weeks that followed. His status in Sri Lanka meant that he could cut through red tape and make sure that aid got to the areas most in need. Nine months earlier, I had taken my 500th Test wicket at the Galle ground flattened by the tragedy. It was very emotional to go back, and to see the faces of kids in the area, who had lost their parents and possessions but were still smiling and optimistic, stands as one of the most humbling experiences of my life. All in all, whatever your opinion is of the great off-spinner, it's a real challenge to face him, and the way the ball leaves his hand and dips and fizzes is truly a great skill.

MUTTIAH MURALITHARAN

BORN	17 April 1972, Kandy, Sri Lanka
TESTS	120
WICKETS	735 at 21.95
ONE-DAY INTERNATIONALS	310
WICKETS	475 at 22.85

8

········

RICKY PONTING

I STILL WONDER WHETHER PEOPLE IN England know how highly we rate Ricky Ponting back home. He was earmarked very early as a potential Test player, and after a couple of inevitable stutters, he has blossomed into one of our great batsmen and a serious contender for a place in any all-time Australia XI. I also think that the experience of losing the Ashes in 2005 has helped him to become a better captain. He learned a lot on that trip. Injuries went against us, but he never once complained, and I think the way we took our defeat in a sporting way left an impressive mark. It says a lot about Ponting's skill and determination that his personal form never once took a knock that summer, and he is still young enough to be able to smash all the Test aggregate records by the time he calls it quits. As for his leadership, he is one of a select group to have led Australia to a 5–0 Ashes win. Again, he batted brilliantly through that campaign, averaging more than 80.

I first saw him bat as a 16 year old when he was at the Academy in Adelaide. I knew of him thanks to his reputation as a great talent from Tasmania with a mullet and a liking for greyhounds and horses, but he still took me by surprise. He was such a scrawny, skinny kid, so light on his feet. This will sound like hindsight, but it was pretty obvious that he had a special talent. And I remember him making his Test debut as a 20 year old in Perth; he fitted in as though he was born to play for Australia, scored 96 and then got a terrible lbw decision. I started to feel quite old the day he captained me for the first time, but I also felt proud that a guy I had helped in those early days had come so far in the game.

It is interesting that whenever a really good young batsman starts to come through nowadays he is described as being the best since Ponting. Michael Clarke had that tag for one and is now Ricky's vice-captain. In his early days, Ponting could be vulnerable against spin. He didn't always pick the turn, and I think maybe he got himself confused and lost his instinct. But as well as being a really strong natural talent, he also works hard, and he managed to iron out those problems. He has now scored hundreds against all of the other nine Test-playing countries on different surfaces. Like all batsmen, he can be vulnerable early, before his feet are moving, but once he finds his timing and starts to pick up the length, look out bowlers. He is so hard to bowl to, as he is such a great player of the short ball, and you pitch up at your peril; he is a wonderful attacking number three.

He is also a versatile batsman in that he usually scores at a good pace but can also put those shots to one side if he needs to cut out risk. His century at Old Trafford in 2005 to save the game was a great innings. You also see his range of strokes in the way he plays one-day cricket. He can knock the ball around during the middle period, when he scores deceptively quickly, but if he is still there for the last five overs, he can go all the way up to fifth gear. The way he played in the 2003 World Cup final against India in Johannesburg was a great example. By the end of the match, he just kept whacking the ball sweetly over long on as though he was driving a stationary golf ball off the tee. You could see the Indian bowlers starting to flag well before the game was over, and he finished on 140 not out.

As well as being the best batsman in the world, he is also one of the leading fielders, even now – he is as quick as the best of the greyhounds he owns. There is nothing flash about Ponting, and I think the nights he enjoys best are the ones at the dog track. I gave him the nickname that stuck: 'Punter'. He loves a flutter on the dogs and horses and is a real greyhound fanatic. He could be a bit more high-tech in the days of the Internet, though you have to remember that Tasmanians are about ten years behind everyone else so he may not have logged on yet. Only joking. His other passion besides dogs is golf. He plays off about two, and strikes the ball well; for a little fella, he hits it miles.

He could be a bit fiery in his younger days, and he still has a wiry strength about him. He doesn't stand on ceremony or worry about reputations if he feels strongly about something. And that is something to admire in this day of media savvy sportsmen. But the only time I can remember when his frustration really got the better of him was at Trent Bridge in 2005 when Gary Pratt ran him out with a throw from cover. What annoyed him was to look up and see Duncan Fletcher grinning from the England balcony. I guess Fletcher was bound to be happy after seeing a player such as Ponting on his bike, but I don't think it reflected on him too well overall. Pratt became a specialist fielder, and that surely goes against the spirit of the game. Overall, to have watched Ricky Ponting come from Tassy as a 16 year old to become captain of Australia and now the number-one batsman in the world makes me feel great. And the way he goes about his business as a player and as a friend: long may it continue. Good luck, bud.

RICKY THOMAS PONTING

BORN	19 December 1974, Launceston, Tasmania, Australia
TESTS	119
RUNS	10,099 in 199 innings at 58.37 with 35 hundreds/40 fifties
ONE-DAY INTERNATIONALS	301
RUNS	11,113 in 280 innings at 43.24 with 26 hundreds/64 fifties

9

· · · · · · ·

MARK WAUGH

MARK WAUGH WAS ONE OF MY best buddies in the Australia side. We just hit it off straight away. We came from the rival states of Victoria and New South Wales, and we went at it tooth and nail when we played against each other in the Sheffield Shield, our domestic four-day game. But we had a lot in common: we both enjoyed a game of golf and a punt – 'Junior' more on the horses and me the roulette wheel. We both started our Test careers at roughly the same time. He was great company off the field but on it he was a guy you would pay to watch – more so than any other Australian batsman in my time, which is saying something given the competition for that particular tag.

Batting just looked so easy and graceful when Mark was in the middle. He was a different type of player to his brother; Mark had the more flair of the two, and Steve had better concentration. I think the key was his natural sense of timing and great hand-eye coordination. That gift helped to make him a brilliant fielder as well as a lovely, fluent batsman. Mark was always handy with the ball, too, whether spin or pace, and loved bowling the short ball. I remember him actually opening the bowling for us in a Test match at Lord's in 1993 when Craig McDermott picked up an injury.

That was an amazing game, my first Test at the great venue. England were in disarray and our batsmen simply took them to the cleaners. A punter had placed £10 at odds of 1000–1 that all of our top-four batsmen would score hundreds. Mark Taylor, Michael Slater and David Boon reached that landmark only for Mark to be dismissed for 99. So that one single, that little nudge into the on side or whatever, cost somebody £10,000. As a gambler himself, Mark would have shed a tear had he known. But to have been around him in the dressing-room a few minutes later, you would never have known that he'd gone for 99 in a Lord's Test. He had to wait eight years to get his name on the honours board for reaching three figures.

Mark Waugh was the best player of spin in his time in the Australian team. (I would say Michael Clarke has taken over that role now.) You always have a bit more respect for those who give you trouble, even if it is not something you like to admit. Mark played with soft hands, so he did not give a lot of catches to the fielders close in, and he never allowed himself to get tormented or bogged down if there was a bit of turn in the pitch. Playing his state cricket at the SCG (Sydney Cricket Ground) would have given him invaluable experience of coping in spinning conditions. He really put pressure on the spinner. Any hint of a bad ball was dispatched to the boundary, and he also smashed good balls, too, as he was so quick on his feet.

One innings in Bangalore in 1998 was sheer genius. It was like playing against an India side from the 1970s when the job of the seamers was to take the shine off the new ball and let the spinners get on with the work. Sourav Ganguly opened the bowling, and the Indian team included three specialist spinners in Anil Kumble, Harbhajan Singh, who was only 17 at the time, and a slow left-armer called Venkatapathy Raju. Mark stayed out there for more than six hours to score one hundred and fifty-three not out and we ended up close enough to their first innings four hundred and twenty-four to be able to go on and win the game. Those who criticised him for a supposed lack of application ought to remember this match. His brother was injured, so our batting was not at full strength, but Mark took responsibility despite having a gastric problem himself. People underestimated his competitiveness and passion because of his laid-back approach, but he was very, very competitive.

Another example of his commitment is just as vivid, from the critical game against the West Indies in Jamaica in 1995, which we needed to win to take the series. That was when he put on 231 with Steve in the critical partnership of the game against a pace attack of Curtly Ambrose, Courtney Walsh, and Winston and Kenny

Benjamin. So the idea of him somehow being unable to bat under pressure just does not stand up to scrutiny. I think that people held it against him that he could make the game look ridiculously easy, forgetting that he practised as hard as the next man. He was a great player to have in the team because he exuded this sense of calm and had a very good sense of humour. He could defuse tension with a quick one-liner.

His opening partnership with Adam Gilchrist must go down as the greatest in the history of one-day cricket. They complemented each other perfectly with their left–right balance and different scoring areas, which made life awkward for a bowler trying to find consistency. Mark's one-day average is only a couple of runs below his Test figure, and he had a couple of incredible periods of scoring hundreds. His 173 was the highest score by an Australian at the time. Even in that innings there was nothing brutal about Mark. He stroked the ball as though he was batting with a wand, and he still believes to this day that he would have made 200 with a decent bat. His stats don't give you a true indication of his greatness. And that's why I've judged him on how he got his runs, not his stats and average.

MARK EDWARD WAUGH

BORN	2 June 1965, Canterbury, New South Wales, Australia
TESTS	128
RUNS	8,029 in 209 innings at 41.81 with 20 hundreds/47 fifties
WICKETS	59 at 41.16
ONE-DAY INTERNATIONALS	244
RUNS	8,500 in 236 innings at 39.35 with 18 hundreds/50 fifties
WICKETS	85 at 34.56

10

·······

IAN HEALY

WHEN I PICKED MY TOP FIFTY players for *The Times* in 2007, a few people seemed to be surprised that I ranked Ian Healy above Adam Gilchrist, as if that was some sort of insult to Gilchrist. It wasn't anything of the sort. Healy was simply the best wicket-keeper I played with or against in international cricket. He was also a really good batsman – bearing in mind this was in the days before Gilchrist raised the benchmark. He had excellent footwork and worked hard at improving his game: his favourite drill was to throw a golf ball against a brick wall for hours and catch it.

The partnership between a keeper and a spin bowler is one of the most important in the game. It tends to go unnoticed. Healy, from his prime position, was very quick to spot things with batsmen, such as where they were looking to score their runs or their balance at the crease. After an over or two, I would also ask him how I looked in my delivery – whether my action looked right. Very often, as he knew, it was just a case of me getting a bit of reassurance; he was great to talk tactics with.

It is hard to pick one catch that stands out, but I would have to go for his dismissal of Ken Rutherford, of New Zealand, in 1993. The ball pitched outside leg stump and spun across the batsman, taking it out of Healy's line of sight. A pretty substantial nick made the angle even more difficult, but Healy reacted like lightning to be able to make the ball stick in his gloves. And a stumping? We're agreed on this one. He was immaculate all the way through the 1993 Ashes, but at Edgbaston he managed to fetch a ball from quite wide outside off stump all the way back to the wicket to stump Graham Thorpe before Thorpe could recover.

Heals was a hard and dedicated trainer, and he put a lot of effort into maintaining his standards. At some grounds he would go into the basement with his golf ball, and he was even known to practise in squash courts. We used to find him in action in the strangest places, but they do say that all keepers have their funny little ways or have a weird streak!

Speaking of which, one of the things that made me laugh loudest during my career involved Heals. It was the Old Trafford Test match in 1993 when he completed a typically plucky hundred when the team needed it. Unfortunately, when he went to celebrate his 100, in his excitement he couldn't undo the chin strap of his helmet so that by the time he'd managed to remove his headgear the moment had gone. He also had a great a sense of humour . . . well, we laughed. In South Africa in 1994, A.B. was struggling to find his timing in the morning session, and at lunch when A.B. was resting Heals grabbed his hat and put it on ice. We cracked up laughing when A.B. came back; he said: 'What the hell is this?' and Heals said 'You are on fire, skip,' and suddenly A.B. started laughing with us.

On the field, Heals was very quick with a one-liner. He believed that Test cricket was played 90 per cent in the head and saw nothing wrong with trying to get into the mind of a batsman with a bit of friendly banter.

Because of the likes of Gilchrist, Healy's batting can get overlooked when people look at the records these days. He was a different type of player who would not take an attack apart in the same way but could be as tough to shift as an oil stain on your carpet. That made him a great buffer after the top six because he could stay in with the last specialist batsman. He was super competitive and I would class him as a keeper/batsman, whereas I would say Andy Flower, Kumar Sangakkara and Gilchrist are batsmen/keepers. Against England at Brisbane in 1998 he helped to get us out of trouble alongside Steve Waugh. That was a good example of when you get your runs being important. He got his most of the time when the team needed them.

As a Queenslander, he loved playing at the Gabba. A couple of years earlier, he made his highest Test score on the ground: 161 against the West Indies. At the time it was also the best by an Australian wicket-keeper. Heals was truly a great team man and always gave 100 per cent, never gave in, was a strong senior player and sang our team songs after a victory with great passion. He was generally the last to leave any team function, party or celebration in the dressing-room. Kept, Heals!

IAN ANDREW HEALY

BORN	30 April 1964, Brisbane, Australia
TESTS	119
RUNS	4,356 in 182 innings at 27.39 with 4 hundreds/22 fifties
DISMISSALS	366 catches and 29 stumpings
ONE-DAY INTERNATIONALS	168
RUNS	1,764 in 120 innings at 21.00 with 4 fifties
DISMISSALS	194 catches and 39 stumpings

11

....

COURTNEY WALSH

STRANGE TO THINK THAT I OWED my early promotion into the Australia Test side to guys such as Courtney Walsh. How could a young, inexperienced leg-spinner in Australia benefit from a bunch of strapping fast bowlers knocking over stumps and batsmen in the Caribbean? Well, in the early 1990s our selectors decided that if we were ever going to topple the West Indies we would have to come up with something different, something they had not really seen for a while. There is a long history in Australia of wrist-spin against the Windies, going back to the likes of Arthur Mailey and Bill O'Reilly. It seemed to be the way forward, and to the surprise of everybody in Australia, including myself, I was the bloke earmarked to have a crack at the West Indies, and it was fun bowling to their batsmen.

To me, Walsh does not really get the credit he deserves. When people talk of the great West Indian quicks, you hear the names of Malcolm Marshall, Mikey Holding, Andy Roberts, Joel Garner and Curtly Ambrose. I didn't have the pleasure – if that's the right word – of facing all of those players, but their records place them in the highest class. However, I feel that Courtney deserves to be up there, too, for his incredible longevity and sheer haul of wickets. To play for 17 years is amazing, especially for a fast bowler who ended his career in an era when international cricket was being squeezed into every gap in the calendar. He was also the first of his type to reach 500 Test wickets.

Courtney must be a medical freak. He never seemed to get injured yet he bowled long spells day after day. Don't forget that he also managed to cram in a very successful county career with Gloucestershire around his commitments with the West Indies, so it was not the case that he held back and saved all his energy for the big occasions. He was a dream of an overseas player and kept himself fit by bowling. The muscles he needed to do his job were perfectly tuned. It also helped that he had a lovely simple, smooth and economical action so that not a lot could go wrong with it. You can break down the biomechanical bits and bobs, but it comes down to this: Courtney simply loved bowling and was very clever.

Apart from his stamina, his great trick was the way he could get a ball to hold its line so it would leave the right-hander off the pitch. He used the crease very intelligently in his delivery stride so that he sowed uncertainty in the minds of batsmen by changing the angle. You needed very sound judgement and confidence to go against the instinct to play at a ball that seemed to be coming into the stumps when facing Courtney. His height also meant that he could get that steepling bounce that batsmen hate and made him very effective on uneven surfaces. He had an effective bouncer, which always seemed to be quicker than his stock ball – about three yards quicker! When the wicket did a bit, it was amazing to watch him bowl to a left-hander, as he had the ability to seam it both ways.

We always think of Walsh and Ambrose in partnership with the new ball, although when I first played against the West Indies, Walsh tended to join the attack first change. Yes, they were that strong. Later in his career, as the production line of West Indian quicks started to break down, he became a stock and strike bowler in one. With his experience and natural fitness, he was able to perform those roles, and he had a lot of knowledge to draw upon, but I wonder if he would have been even more effective with better back-up in the final part of his career. He began when the West Indies could pick from up to ten fast bowlers who were all good enough to play at the highest level, but I think his ability to keep going longer and better than people really had a right to expect meant that the true decline of the state of cricket in the Caribbean was not always obvious.

He was heroic against us in the 1999 series when he bowled at least as well as Ambrose to take twenty-six wickets in the four Tests. At 36, he was the oldest bloke on either side, but he still bowled more than 200 overs. The West Indies rested him for the one-day series that followed, and I've never known a break to be so richly deserved. On his home island of Jamaica, they even declared a 'Courtney Walsh Day' after he took his 400th wicket in the previous game. He accepted everything with his usual grace and humility, as if wondering what all the fuss was about.

A top-class bowler, then, but I wouldn't want him a lot higher in the batting order than number 11, unless Glenn McGrath happened to be in the same side. I remember our World Cup semi-final in Lahore in 1996. Australia were out of it almost all the way through, but we fought back to set up a really tense finish. The West Indies needed five to win, with Walsh on strike as the last man and Richie Richardson, who was looking nicely set, at the other end. All that Courtney needed to do was to get a single off Damien Fleming and leave it to Richardson to smack the winning runs. But the big man had other ideas. True to the Caribbean spirit, he opened his shoulders, went for a big, beautiful drive and heard the rattle of stumps behind him. He is a gentle giant and a real credit to world cricket. He played in the right spirit, always with a smile, and he was good fun to play against.

COURTNEY ANDREW WALSH

BORN	30 October 1962, Kingston, Jamaica
TESTS	132
WICKETS	519 at 24.44
ONE-DAY INTERNATIONALS	205
WICKETS	227 at 30.47

12

·······

MARK TAYLOR

THERE WAS NOTHING FANCY ABOUT MARK Taylor. He had wonderful leadership skills and excellent communication, but his main weakness was his terrible dress sense – the shirts he used to wear were horrendous, although Steve Waugh's were worse. Tubby was the best of the four captains I played under. That judgement is very difficult for me, as I have learned a lot under all my captains. Taylor had the advantage of inheriting a good, tough side, which he then had the man-management and leadership skills to take to the next level. Australia very clearly went for the right man at the right time.

Taylor was an instinctive captain. Communication was his big strength, allied to his superb tactical brain. He was happy to listen but was very much his own man when it came to making decisions. There was a great example of his courage at Old Trafford in 1997 when everything about the first-day conditions and the greenish pitch would have told a captain to bowl first and leave the seamers to capitalise. But Taylor looked beyond the first session, reckoning that the pitch would deteriorate so that runs on the board would be worth more in the long run. We won the game.

You can examine his decision a bit deeper to see how it lifted the players' confidence. It also sent a message to the batsmen: yes, it is going to be tough going for that first couple of hours, but I believe that you are good enough and brave enough to withstand England's bowlers and give us the platform to win the Test. Being an opener himself, he wasn't asking the rest of the top six to do anything he was not prepared to go through himself. Was it a risk?

I guess so. Had we bowled first, we might have won even more convincingly. But if you look at the facts rather than the ifs, buts and maybes, you can only say that Taylor's courage and conviction – and the players' backing of him – was right.

This was a difficult time for him as a batsman. He had proved to be a very good Test opener alongside first Geoff Marsh and then Michael Slater – theirs was a real chalk-and-cheese partnership that consistently confused bowling attacks. Taylor was a very solid player, but in the build-up to the 1997 Ashes he'd been going through a terrible run. Had he not been such a good captain and slip fielder, there is every chance that he wouldn't have made the tour. Then, in the first Test at Edgbaston, he scored one of the bravest hundreds I saw by a teammate. Not brave in that the ball was whizzing past his ears, but in the character he showed to hang in when he wasn't hitting the ball fluently. When he raised his bat, there were genuine cheers from the dressing-room, and again when he walked back in afterwards. At that time he probably thought everyone was against him – even his own players.

I suggested a few years ago that as players we could have done more to rally around him during that year, even just grabbing him for a beer and saying 'Mate, how you going?' but he was the captain. It was hard for everyone. Again, it comes back to his fantastic captaincy. Your leader has to be positive at all times. However badly he was batting, he never looked like a bloke under pressure in the dressing-room or around the hotel. Most of us only realised later that he was shattered and could have used an arm around his shoulder. In a similar situation, he would have been there for all of us.

It all comes down to being a bloke of dignity and integrity. He really is the type of guy who should be involved in helping to run the cricket side of the sport worldwide. Like Stephen Fleming, another great captain, he has the respect of every cricket-playing nation because he has no hidden agenda. Those two would be able to make the difficult decisions on issues such as dubious bowling actions and the crisis in Zimbabwe and Bangladesh, etc., without their motives being questioned. He cares deeply about the game and its values.

I should also stress that he was a top-class batsman at his best. After that hundred at Edgbaston, he went from strength to strength in the middle. He equalled what was then the record score for Australia: 334 not out against Pakistan. Everybody expected him to keep going the next morning to overtake that best score of Sir Donald Bradman, but he decided to declare overnight because it was the best option for the side. The game petered out into a high-scoring draw, so he could easily have taken up a few more minutes. Most captains would have carried on in that situation without any eyebrows being raised.

His greatest triumph came when we finally beat the West Indies in 1995. They had not lost a series for 15 years, an amazing record that will probably never be broken, given the amount of cricket played these days. The funny thing is, we did it even though Taylor lost all four tosses. That was an area of captaincy in which he might have been better! Another interesting statistic from that series: he held more catches than wicket-keeper Ian Healy.

Taylor was a great slip fielder and, as I said, a very solid top-class opening batsman. He was a fantastic player of the short ball, and was absolute dynamite at slip for us spinners. It was a pleasure playing and learning under Mark Taylor, one of the good guys in the game.

MARK ANTHONY TAYLOR

BORN	27 October 1964, Leeton, New South Wales, Australia
TESTS	104
RUNS	7,525 in 186 innings at 43.49 with 19 hundreds/40 fifties
ONE-DAY INTERNATIONALS	113
RUNS	3,514 in 110 innings at 32.23 with 1 hundred/28 fifties

13

·······

ANIL KUMBLE

ANIL KUMBLE HAS THE AGRESSION OF a fast bowler. And I love that. He has the height and he certainly has the competitive temperament. They talk about the quicks breathing fire, but Kumble could set a house ablaze with his passion and commitment on the field. Off it, he is even-tempered and a great credit to his country, with a very clear sense of what is right and wrong. Indian cricket owes him so much, and I think he will be one of those cricketers who isn't really missed until he is gone and the size of the hole he leaves in the team suddenly becomes clear. It is not just a matter of losing however many wickets he finishes with – it will be well over 600 – but he has also been one of their most important senior players, a guy who is prepared to take the pressure away from the youngsters.

Having been in Jaipur for the Indian Premier League recently, I know there are plenty of talented young guys coming through, and the one-day team has changed over the last couple of years. There should never be any shortage of cricketers in India, and the game there is now more popular than ever. But I think the selectors need to make sure that they don't lose too many very experienced players from the Test team in a short space of time, because Kumble, Tendulkar and Rahul Dravid have all been around for a long time. It is a pity that Kumble in particular was not captain sooner.

As a wrist-spinner I can empathise with him a lot. We have had loads of chats down the years about batsmen, variation of deliveries, pitches, schedules and so on. We always agree that nobody outside our little group really understands spin bowling – especially selectors and umpires! I'm sure you could get a bunch of any profession together and they would start whinging like a group of old women. We are no different. There is competition on the field but surprisingly few secrets off it. He has shown me his grip for the flipper, and I showed him my leg-break.

Kumble is quicker than most spinners, and he doesn't turn the leg-break as much as many of us. He really comes into his own when the bounce is uneven. His height accentuates the differences, so he is very difficult to play confidently. Pitches give you natural variation. You can bowl the same ball from the same part of the crease and with the same revolutions, but if it lands in two slightly different spots, it will turn by different amounts and vary in bounce. A lot of teams have treated Kumble as an in-swing bowler because of his pace and googly, but his career has never dipped for any length of time – given that we are all entitled to a bad game or two somewhere along the line – so I don't think any side has ever completely worked him out. He uses the crease to mix his angle, and slight changes of pace mean that batsmen can be too early or a shade late on the ball.

Strangely, perhaps, his record in Australia, where the pitches offer quite a bit of bounce, is a lot worse than overall. But we played a game in Chennai in 2004 when he ripped through us in the first innings and took 13 wickets in the match, a lot of them with a top-spinner that we struggled to pick. I asked him afterwards which he preferred. 'All of them,' he said, a typical bowler's remark. A striker will tell you there's no such thing as a bad goal. Well, there is no such thing as a bad wicket, either. Unfortunately, rain washed out the whole of the last day in Chennai when the game was really well poised.

There is a lot of romance about spin in India. At times they played three or even four spinners together in the 1960s and '70s but Kumble has taken twice as many wickets as any of the famous quartet of Bedi, Venkat, Chandrasekhar and Prasanna. Alright, he has played more games, but he deserves to rank in that class if not above them for his longevity, and his average also stands up to comparison. Chandra, too, bowled his wrist spin at almost medium pace but from a longer approach. Bedi, the great left-armer, is seen as having the perfectly smooth approach. He would applaud a batsman if he played what he thought was a good shot. Kumble only growled at you.

Few achievements have given me as much pleasure as his maiden Test hundred against England at the Oval. He was playing in his 118th Test match and was only two months away from his 37th birthday. He had always been a handy number eight. Pace did not frighten him, and he could perform even when he was in pain. I even remember him bowling in the Caribbean once despite a fractured jaw.

His greatest day came against Pakistan in Delhi in 1999 when he took all ten wickets in an innings. The more you think about that, the more incredible it becomes. To achieve that feat, the ball has to be turning, in which case the guy at the other end ought to be capitalising as well. And on this occasion his partner was no mug – Harbhajan Singh, who did so much damage to Australia a couple of years later. I talked to Kumble about the match not long after, and he told me about the chaos that followed. He had to walk out of the dressing-room with his head in his hands for protection from all the well-wishers wanting to give him a pat – and that was only to get to the press conference. A true gentleman of the game and a good friend, he continues to impress and remain at the top of his profession.

ANIL KUMBLE

BORN	17 October 1970, Bangalore, India
TESTS	130
RUNS	2,456 in 171 innings at 17.66 with 1 hundred/5 fifties
WICKETS	616 at 29.33
ONE-DAY INTERNATIONALS	271
WICKETS	337 at 30.89

14

·······

GRAHAM GOOCH

GRAHAM GOOCH WAS THE ENGLISH EQUIVALENT of our Allan Border, and that is almost the highest praise I can give to a cricketer. He probably didn't inspire his players in the same way as a captain, but that's from an outsider looking in. However, he tried to hold things together personally with his batting and integrity when a lot was going wrong for his side. Fortunately for us, and unfortunately for him, the task proved too much and he finally retired, with the Ashes pendulum swung back towards Australia in a big way. I competed against him in two series, and if it hadn't been for Gooch, I know for a fact that those England defeats would have been even heavier. Although I played for another 12 years after our last meeting, I can honestly say that I never came across a tougher opponent from England, and that's right up to when I retired.

During the 1994–95 series at home, we used to guess in our dressing-room who would be the next of their blokes to go home injured. They were falling like flies – and bear in mind that as Australians we know a thing or two about flies. The funniest part of all was that Gooch, at 41, just went on and on, while players 15 years younger were suffering all sorts of fitness trouble. He was like the Iron Man. I now realise from playing in my late-30s myself how difficult it must have been, especially knowing deep down that he was fighting a lost cause. He certainly couldn't have been playing for glory by that stage of his career. Like Border, he just had an ingrained pride for his country and a personal pride in the way he performed. His never-give-up approach, I think, rubbed off on some.

I remember playing in Brisbane in 1994–95 and my deliveries were coming out well, but Gooch was batting well, too, and after he reached fifty I turned to him and said: 'Well played, Mr Gooch.' He looked back and replied in that kind of nasal, high-pitched voice: 'You might have got the others out, but you won't get me.' At the start of my career against England, Goochy thought that I called him Mr Gooch sarcastically, trying to make a point about his advancing years. That wasn't the case. I guess I'm up for a bit of sledging, but in this case it really was the genuine respect of a rookie bowler towards a bloke who had the admiration of everyone in our dressing-room.

Ian Botham told me that he was once walking back from a night out as the dawn was breaking, only to pass Gooch in the lobby of the hotel setting off on his morning run. It's a great tale because it gets to the heart of both of them. But I think that Gooch has had a bad rap for being dull and boring. He isn't anything of the sort. He is excellent company over a beer and dinner, and is a very funny man, actually.

Gooch had really struggled against Terry Alderman in the past, but we didn't have that kind of swing bowler when we played in England in 1993, and, personally, I found it very hard to break down his defence. A lot of opening batsmen grope around against spin, and leggies were almost an extinct species in England back then. Gooch had been up and down the order during his career – he started at number five for England but was best suited to opening.

It was his temperament as much as anything that saw him through, and although he was very patient, he never got into what I think of as blocking mode, where you could bring everybody in because his mind wasn't free enough to respond to the bad balls and put them away. He scored two hundreds in the 1993 series but moved down to number five because he thought it was a problem position. All that resulted in was making the opening spot a problem position instead. They brought in a young guy called Mark Lathwell, who wasn't in the same class, and after two games went back to Plan A with Gooch opening again. There were simply too many holes in the top six for him to be able to plug. I think deep down he would have loved younger players such as Lathwell to force him out of the side with their weight of runs, but that never looked like happening.

Gooch's was the wicket, and he was such a wonderful player. It was hard work bowling to him, but one dismissal at Edgbaston gave me special pleasure because I had talked about it in the bar the night before with A.B. Gooch played with Border for Essex. They knew each other's game and personality inside out, and Border was a shrewd judge of technique, mindset and how to bowl to someone. The idea was to go around the wicket and try to spin it out of the rough because Goochy put his foot straight down the pitch when trying to pad away, not to where the ball pitched. The ball came out well and ripped big time to hit the stumps, and I saw Gooch raise his eyebrows as he walked off. Sorry, mate, but it was a 'ripper'.

That series also saw one of the strangest wickets I ever witnessed. Gooch was battling beautifully, as usual, at Old Trafford when he defended a short ball from Merv Hughes, turned round to see the ball heading for his stumps and instinctively punched it away. He was out handled the ball, a very rare dismissal, and it was only later that Merv realised he wouldn't be credited with the wicket. Fifteen years on, he still moans about the injustice if anybody is foolish enough to raise the topic.

Over the years since, we have worked together and shared a few dinners, etc., and I've discovered what a great person Graham Gooch is. You can learn a lot from listening to him and the way he approached batting.

GRAHAM ALAN GOOCH

BORN	23 July 1953, Whipps Cross, Essex, England
TESTS	118
RUNS	8,900 in 215 innings at 42.58 with 20 hundreds/46 fifties
ONE-DAY INTERNATIONALS	125
RUNS	4,290 in 122 innings at 36.98 with 8 hundreds/23 fifites

15

· · · · · · ·

MATTHEW HAYDEN

HISTORY WILL REMEMBER MATTHEW HAYDEN AS one of Australia's great opening batsmen, a towering bloke who stood over bowling attacks like a colossus and helped to break down barriers between Test and one-day cricket in the way he sought to attack from ball one. But that is only part of the tale. Hayden also gets high billing in my list because of the determination he showed in his career to recapture his place after being twice dropped when the competition for batting places was fiercer than at any other time I can remember. Like his mate and opening partner, Justin Langer, Hayden deserves every success that international cricket has brought his way.

I like to think it is an Aussie trait that both of them battled it out when there were so many other really good openers around at the same time – guys such as Mark Taylor, Michael Slater and Matthew Elliott. Greg Blewett came in and had some success as well. In the case of Hayden he broke through in his third spell in the side in India in 2001 with a hundred in the first Test and a double in the third. That series in India in 2001 gave him the confidence and self-belief that he had the technique and game plan to succeed at international cricket.

Openers are not generally reckoned to be the best players of spin, and to look at the muscular Hayden you wouldn't think of him as having a light touch in his hands or feet. But he grew in confidence on the slower pitches as the series developed and decided the best way forward was attack, either blasting balls straight or sweeping. That is a sure-fire way of getting rid of the close fielders and creates a margin for error in defence. With his huge stride, he worked out that he could sweep almost anything on length unless the ball was genuinely short – in which case it was a long hop waiting to be pulled.

With his great stamina and powers of concentration, batting for a long time was never a problem. And I think his incredible concentration came from his second love: fishing. He has caught some monsters in his time. Mind, we almost lost him a few years ago when his boat was blown over off the Queensland coast and he had to swim more than a kilometre to safety with Andrew Symonds and another mate. Only the previous day sharks had been spotted in the same stretch of water. Guys who were less fit would have been in trouble. He reckoned that if he could survive that ordeal, he could overcome anything that bowlers sent at him.

Hayden is into his outdoor pursuits in a big way; his nickname should be 'Nature Boy' not 'Haydos', or 'Dos'. Which reminds me of a weird celebration in South Africa when he was not long into the side. We had won a really tight game at Port Elizabeth, and Hayden and Jason Gillespie decided to smear Vegemite on their faces and act out a sequence as warriors pretending to hunt animals in the dressing-room. It looked pretty impressive, but nobody wanted to go near either of them for the next few days before the smell of the Vegemite wore off. People do some pretty odd things in the high atmosphere of winning big games of cricket but that takes the gold medal.

In a way I think that his sheer bulk might have worked against him. In the early days there always seemed to be questions about his technique. He did not look an elegant player, a bloke you would watch and think he was stacked with natural ability. But the point was that he scored runs for fun with Queensland. There could not have been a lot wrong, and his self-belief and strong religious faith enabled him to plug away, knowing that he would be rewarded in the end. Confidence was never a problem. The story goes that on the eve of his debut for Queensland he asked whether anybody had ever scored a double-hundred in their first innings. He kept making big scores until finally the selectors had to pick him.

He thought a lot about the game, spent hours in earnest conversation with Langer and always looked to improve his game.

After the 2001 Ashes, when they first came together, they made a conscious effort to be more aggressive and to dominate bowlers. In one-day cricket – and even in Test matches when he was set – Hayden looked to take a couple of steps down the pitch to disrupt the bowler's length.

He also has very big hands and anything that hits them tends to stick. He is a great guy to have in the gully because he looks so intimidating when new batsmen come in – probably looks like two players. And he isn't shy to chip in with a few words, either, to reinforce how hard it's going to be for the batsmen. But he is also a very sporting player. A couple of years ago, there was some debate about a low catch he took off my bowling to get rid of Jacques Rudolph in Johannesburg. The umpires consulted and television replays were inconclusive – as they usually are for low catches. Hayden gave his word that it carried, and despite all the boos around the ground, the players on both sides could be sure that what he said was the truth. He always contributes around the group, and for him to come back in the team and dominate and set the tone for an innings was a pleasure to watch. I hope he continues to improve in all facets of the game.

MATTHEW LAWRENCE HAYDEN

BORN	29 October 1971, Kingaroy, Queensland, Australia
TESTS	94
RUNS	8,242 in 167 innings at 53.51 with 30 hundreds/27 fifties
ONE-DAY INTERNATIONALS	161
RUNS	6,133 in 155 innings at 43.80 with 10 hundreds/36 fifties

16

·······

ADAM GILCHRIST

THERE IS NO DOUBT ABOUT ADAM Gilchrist's contribution to cricket, and to Australian cricket in particular. Gilly was not the first batsman/ keeper, or even the first to go after the bowling from the start of a one-day game, but in both cases he took the skill to a new level.

One of the biggest tributes to him today is that every side wants an Adam Gilchrist. England have tried all sorts of players in their one-day team without realising that the search is a waste of time. A player such as Gilchrist comes along once in a blue moon, and we should enjoy the way he plays the game and his skill and not try and compare young players that come into international cricket with one of the greats. The fact is that Gilchrist was good enough to have played as a pure batsman in the top six. Without the burden of keeping wicket as well, his scores might have been even better, and bear in mind that it was only in the last two or three years of his career that his average dropped below fifty.

He will be remembered mainly for his destructive batting at number seven and at the top of the order in one-day cricket. I think that will irk him a bit because he took his wicket-keeping very seriously. In his own mind he was a keeper first, batsman second. In a sense he was unfortunate to follow Healy, who was an outstanding keeper. I actually think Gilly's wicket-keeping improved, and that's all you can do as a player.

He had a difficult debut in the 1999–2000 season, replacing Healy on his home ground in Brisbane, because Healy wanted to retire at his beloved Gabba. The timing proved spot on, and the fact that Gilchrist was already a regular in the one-day side meant that he knew all about the pressure brought on by big crowds and could make an impact straight away. He scored 81 and went on from there with an incredible innings in his next Test, against Pakistan in Hobart. We needed three hundred and sixty-nine to win and were five-down for not very many, but he played fearlessly with Justin Langer to see us home. That was an important victory in our development, because we proved to ourselves that we could win from any position, not just save a game. Our success and self-belief stemmed from there. Gilly gave us depth and a wonderful attacking batsman at number seven.

From time to time, somebody would suggest that Gilchrist should move up the order. Given the talent we had in the side at the time, I thought that seven was the perfect spot. He had a big psychological impact on the opposition. Once you get five-down as a bowler, you think the hardest part of the job is done, so the sight of Gilchrist walking out would be a big knock-back. Because he scored runs so quickly, it did not matter too much if there was only one specialist batsman left or he had to bat with the lower order. At Johannesburg in 2002, he managed to score a double-hundred from number seven. It was an amazing assault on South Africa's bowlers.

He had his weaknesses, like the rest of us. England had a lot of success in 2005 when they went around the wicket and moved the ball away from him. That was a good plan, and Freddie Flintoff executed it perfectly. Another option was to bring on spin early, before he was settled. I often wondered what would happen if teams opened the bowling with a spinner against him in one-day cricket. It would have been a brave call, with only two fielders outside the ring.

Towards the end of our careers, I thought that a few people were looking to drive a wedge between the pair of us. Rumours of a rift were just rubbish, and I never understood the motivation of those who were peddling the line. We did not hang around together away from the game in the way that I mixed with Michael Clarke, Darren Lehmann or Merv Hughes, but we got on well without being best buddies. Do people seriously expect all 15 or 16 members of a squad to do everything together? We did not agree on quite a few things about the game, such as the best tactics and approaches, but none of these are issues that split a team. We had a lot of respect for each other as cricketers.

We have had some great times down the years. I remember after the 1999 World Cup final at Lord's, long after everybody else had left the ground and gone home, we went back out into the middle and relived the Pakistan dismissals, placing beer cans on the pitch where each wicket-taking ball had landed. There was another funny moment in Dunedin when the tour social committee decided that everybody should buy a bad-taste shirt for one of the others on the next night out. Gilchrist decided to go into a charity shop where a reporter saw him buying a frilly blouse. The next day, the paper carried a story about cross-dressing in the Australia camp. I think overall Gilly was a special cricketer, and just as with some of the other great players, the public and everyone involved in the game will miss him now that he is retired.

ADAM CRAIG GILCHRIST

BORN	14 November 1971, Bellingen, New South Wales, Australia
TESTS	96
RUNS	5,570 in 137 innings at 47.60 with 17 hundreds/26 fifties
DISMISSALS	379 catches and 37 stumpings
ONE-DAY INTERNATIONALS	287
RUNS	9,619 in 279 innings at 35.89 with 16 hundreds/55 fifties
DISMISSALS	417 catches and 55 stumpings

17

·······

JACQUES KALLIS

THE FIRST TIME WE CLAPPED EYES on Jacques Kallis, I think most of us in the Australia side were pretty sure that we would be seeing a great deal of him in the years ahead – especially the bowlers. Even at the age of 21, the South Africans thought so much of him that he walked out to bat at number three in the intimidating atmosphere at the Wanderers in Johannesburg, otherwise known as the Bull Ring. We won the game comfortably, but I remember this young kid batting with incredible maturity for nearly three hours in the second innings. The ball turned and senior guys such as Hansie Cronje, Daryll Cullinan and Jonty Rhodes were getting out at the other end. Occasionally, you see a young player who seems to have natural ability as a stroke-maker, but I cannot think of many who looked as sure of their method as Kallis so early in their careers.

His technique is first class. There is barely a chink in it, and his statistics put him up there with the best. He will finish his Test career with a batting average of well over 50 and a bowling figure around the 30 mark. His current record is nearly identical to Ricky Ponting's, and he has almost 250 Test wickets as well. Even if he never delivered another ball in his life, he would probably be considered the best South Africa player of the post-apartheid era and one of their all-time great all-rounders. Perhaps that is why he has never been viewed as a potential captain. With guys such as Graeme Smith and Herschelle Gibbs around, it is not as though the batting has been a one-man show. Kallis over the last few years seems to have become a lot more conservative in his approach to batting. He has all the shots, and my advice to him would be to try and take on the bowling a little more and impose himself on the game – stamp your authority.

This might sum up what I am saying regarding Jacques: it would take Kallis an average of 58 balls more than Ponting to score a hundred. There is a time when you do your side a favour by hanging in, and I don't want to be seen to be knocking a guy who can play that role to perfection. Yes, if I wanted to save a game, Kallis would be high on the list of batsmen I would choose for the task. But there are other times when he hasn't used the full range of his shots and taken the game away from the opposition.

I can think of one instance straight away when his concentration and defence helped South Africa to save a game. That was at Melbourne in the 1997 Boxing Day Test when he scored one hundred and one in almost six hours in the fourth innings. He batted more than twice as long as any of his teammates, and we tried all sorts of ways to unsettle him, but he wouldn't be disturbed from his own little bubble. That was when he was at his best, when he didn't have to think about trying to win the game. It was his maiden Test hundred, and whatever we said to him out in the middle – nothing too harsh, I'm sure – we were quick to shake his hand afterwards and say well played. He is a very good player and a nice man away from the field as well. His record against us overall was a lot better in Australia than on his home pitches.

He is very strong, and I think that probably puts pressure on his knees in his heavy delivery stride, restricting his bowling. At one point around the turn of the decade, he was the best all-rounder in the world without any doubt. Although he didn't sprint to the wicket, he could be genuinely sharp. In fact, with three all-rounders of the quality of Kallis, Shaun Pollock and Lance Klusener in their one-day side, they had a great balance – the one thing they lacked was variety. To me, Kallis is an amazing all-round player and has showed his skills in all parts of the game: catching at slip, batting and attack bowling. South Africa should appreciate him whilst he is playing, as he will be a tough player to replace.

JACQUES HENRY KALLIS

BORN	16 October 1975, Cape Town, South Africa
TESTS	119
RUNS	9,657 in 209 innings at 57.14 with 30 hundreds/48 fifties
WICKETS	230 at 31.30
ONE-DAY INTERNATIONALS	274
RUNS	9,541 in 261 innings at 45.21 with 16 hundreds/66 fifties
WICKETS	239 at 31.53

18
· · · · · · ·

MERV HUGHES

A GREAT FRIEND, VERY GOOD BOWLER and the bravest and most courageous cricketer I have played with or against – that is Mervyn Gregory Hughes. The image I will take most from the 1993 Ashes is not Mike Gatting's puzzled face at Old Trafford, but of Hughes sitting in the dressing-room at the Oval after the last Test, staring out like a zombie and covered in ice packs to keep down the swelling after his last input into a memorable series. You had to wonder whether he would ever be able to rouse himself from his seat. But he always found a way. He had ice on both knees and on his shoulders, groin and back. And you know something? If we had been called out to take a couple more wickets, Hughes would have been the first through the door of the dressing-room.

For Allan Border, he was a dream. Hughes would take the ball in any situation, from the flattest of pitches in the searing heat of India to a green seamer at Lord's – and he certainly deserved a few of those. However difficult the conditions, you knew he would give you six balls of effort and aggression. Opponents saw a bloke who never, ever gave a hint that he was beaten and who symbolised the pride of being chosen to play for Australia. He ranks so highly in my list, above players of greater natural ability who finished their careers with more impressive statistics, because he was just inspirational to the rest of the team.

I'm taking nothing from his skill as a pure bowler, because he did have lots of skill and tricks. Behind his signature moustache and his clowning and pantomime-villain act, he was a really good performer in his own right. Without a huge knowledge and understanding of the game, he would not have been asked to become a Test selector a few years ago. I just think it was his resilience, character and sheer determination that put him ahead of the rest. Going back again to that game at the Oval, I remember him limping back to the boundary at the end of an over but somehow finding it in him to sprint back in for another four or five minutes later. In all he bowled nearly three hundred overs in the six Test matches in the series, every one of them at full pelt.

His image was great for the game, and the crowds took to him all over the world. He played up to the comments. At one time, he was nicknamed 'Sumo' – and instead of grumbling about it he posed for photographs in a T-shirt with 'Sumo' on the front. He also did a shot dressed as the Terminator in leathers on a bike with a machine gun and ammunition over his shoulder. He could laugh at himself. Whenever he did those stretching exercises on the boundary, the spectators behind him in the stands would follow suit as though he was their aerobics teacher. Whatever he says, he loved the attention.

Those dark eyes also gave him a classic, nasty fast bowler's stare, which he used to his advantage, especially against young players who were trying to make their way in Test cricket. And he loved the game so much that he stayed on to play for his grade side long after his international days were up. Actually, that 1993 series probably did for him at the top level because even at the start one of his knees was giving him a lot of grief. Every morning he took two painkillers, then a couple at lunch and two more at tea to help him through. And when they finally operated, they found a piece of dead bone that had come away, roughly the size of a 20 cent coin.

Beating England is the highlight of any Australian career and he could step down knowing that his job had been done. However, he actually prefers the 1989 win in England, because the squad was described as the worst to leave Australia. That view had changed by the time they went home 4–0 winners. I think Hughes thrived on proving people wrong and loved a challenge. Of all the English batsmen he liked to dismiss in 1993, his favourite was Mike Atherton, because he really rated him as a player. Merv took me under his wing on that tour, one Victorian keeping an eye on another. Allan Border called him 'Fruitfly' after the great Australian pest. But he is also a really funny speaker as I know from our time doing engagements together.

Even when he was not taking wickets, he had control over his bowling. He didn't just bowl a bouncer to look aggressive. If he thought a batsman was vulnerable on the back foot, he would go full on. And a lot of the sledging was to keep himself pumped up, not just to get at the batsman. He also had his superstitions. I remember in England he was offered a lot of money to shave off his moustache, but he turned it down because he thought it would bring bad luck. It says a lot about our great sport that a bloke such as Hughes could be successful without having to compromise his character. He had a massive heart and was the centre of many Australian victories, his sheer personality helping the team. Never underestimate how good a bowler and lower-order batsman he was. He was a fantastic cricketer, and he is a great mate.

MERVYN GREGORY HUGHES

BORN	23 November 1961, Euroa, Victoria, Australia
TESTS	53
WICKETS	212 at 28.38
ONE-DAY INTERNATIONALS	33
WICKETS	38 at 29.34

19

·······

ARAVINDA DE SILVA

I HAVE NOT PICKED ANY OF my 100 on a single performance alone, but Aravinda de Silva's contribution to the 1996 World Cup final has pushed him towards the upper end of my list. That game was probably the biggest disappointment of my cricketing life, along with losing by one run to the West Indies in Adelaide in 1992–93. We were hot favourites to win, having come from behind to beat the West Indies in the semi-final and we felt we had the wood on Sri Lanka after our series in Australia a few months earlier. It wasn't to be. De Silva not only hit a hundred, but took three wickets and held a couple of catches; there have been other hundreds in World Cup finals before and since but nothing to match that all-round effort. It is amazing to look at his record, remember some of his innings and then consider that in Sri Lanka a few people still reckon that he didn't quite live up to his potential. Well, I can't think of too many others from that country to win Man of the Match awards in World Cup finals. He was a stroke-maker of the highest class and the best Sri Lankan batsman I have seen, with great respect to Mahela Jayawardene and Kumar Sangakkara, who are piling up the runs today.

At our team meetings, we spent more time chewing over de Silva than any of his teammates. The trouble was that he had a little bit of genius about him – not on a level with Sachin Tendulkar or Brian Lara, but enough to be able to hit good balls to the boundary or to give the impression that he had a couple of shots for every delivery. It is hard to plan for talent like that, so the onus was on the bowlers to think on their feet and assess the way he was going ball by ball.

His best shots were probably the cut and the pull – not surprising given that he was only about 5 ft 4 in. tall – but he also liked to use his feet and get on the front foot to drive. That could be a weakness if he went to hit balls that weren't quite there, especially when the pitches were a bit bouncier than those he was used to at home. Hitting through the line left him vulnerable if there was anything in the surface or overhead conditions made it difficult for batting.

Looking back to 1996, it is easy to remember Sanath Jayasuriya as being Sri Lanka's star of the tournament. He turned a lot of heads, but de Silva was the main man on the big occasion in Lahore. We had not set a big enough target, but their pinch hitters, Jayasuriya and Romesh Kaluwitharana, both went early, and de Silva pulled them around by playing a more orthodox innings, timed to perfection so that he was there at the end to see them home. The ball was very hard to grip because of heavy dew, which helped de Silva as he managed to pick off the runs. So much went wrong for us that day, it isn't funny. I heard another story quite recently that Mark Taylor was thinking of moving to slip when Arjuna Ranatunga came in, decided against it and saw Ranatunga edge his first ball through that region. Pinch hitting might have won Sri Lanka a few games on their way to the final, but not on that occasion. The only redeeming feature of the match for us, looking back, was that it took a brilliant innings to ultimately win the game for Sri Lanka, and they deserved to win.

I said earlier that de Silva had taken three wickets. They included Taylor and Ricky Ponting, two of our best batsmen at the time. His off-spin was seriously underrated, at least in one-day cricket. One good reason why Sri Lanka have been such a good one-day side, especially on their own pitches, is the ability of their batsmen to chip in with a few overs. De Silva was not one of their five designated bowlers, but he would often appear after the halfway stage when the ball was getting soft. He bowled very slowly. With another guy of similar style at the other end, not only was it hard to score runs – you had to put your own pace on the ball rather than dink and nudge it away – but the overs ticked down quickly. You could be in trouble before you knew it. India were a bit like that as well, with guys such as Virender Sehwag, Yuvraj Singh and Sachin Tendulkar getting through a stint between them.

Relations between the sides became quite tense for a few years. Things would have been far warmer if de Silva rather than Arjuna Ranatunga had been in charge. During Sri Lanka's tour to Australia in 1998–99, when all sorts of rubbish was flying around, de Silva took over for the final Test when Ranatunga had some sort of injury, and bridges began to be repaired almost straight away. That is not to say that he was a walkover. He just had a better idea of the way the game should be played. And he was a charming bloke himself, a lovely little man. I've heard that the Kent boys were close to tears when he left after his time as their overseas player. He also loves fast cars, so we often chatted about cars over a quiet glass.

It is good to see that he is still involved with cricket in Sri Lanka, even though he has some business interests. He has been working with the Under-19s and is looking at ways to improve the game at school level, which is probably far more important to the Sri Lankan system than anywhere else in the world. That is where their players come from; in fact, it hasn't been so unusual for the very young talent to go almost straight from school into the national side. They've got themselves a great teacher now.

PINNADUWAGE ARAVINDA DE SILVA

BORN	17 October 1965, Colombo, Sri Lanka
TESTS	93
RUNS	6,361 in 159 innings at 42.97 with 20 hundreds/22 fifties
WICKETS	29 at 41.65
ONE-DAY INTERNATIONALS	308
RUNS	9,284 in 296 innings at 34.90 with 11 hundreds/64 fifties
WICKETS	106 at 39.40

20

·······

RAHUL DRAVID

INDIAN PEOPLE LOVE TO GIVE THEIR cricket heroes a nickname. As these things go, Rahul Dravid being known as 'The Wall' is pretty much spot on. 'The Fortress' could also describe Rahul. Because once Dravid was set, you needed the bowling equivalent of a dozen cannon firing all at once to blast him down. True, he is not a batsman to destroy you in a mad half-hour like a Lara or a Gilchrist, but he can grind you down and test your patience bit by bit until you lose concentration and forget your plan. Honestly, that is the way it seemed after a full day's play in the Indian heat if Dravid had batted any length of time.

He grew in my estimation as the years went on. Believe it not, I thought that I had the better of him for a few years in the 1990s. He didn't seem to be as comfortable against spin as some of the other Indian batsmen, unusually for a guy who was obviously very accomplished at the crease and had an unflappable temperament and great stamina. But the thing with Rahul is that he improved, and that's a sign of strength.

Even in 2007, my final year at Hampshire, members would ask me about a Dravid innings for Kent at the United Services ground in Portsmouth. A lot of people have described it as the best county game they have seen. The pitch was starting to turn, and I thought I was bowling pretty well. But Dravid scored 137 out of 252 in the first innings and then won the match with 73 not out in the second. He just picked up the length quicker than anybody else in the match and used his decisive footwork to go all the way forward or all the way back. And his shot selection and timing were brilliant. He is not a stocky man, and when you see him display that kind of lightness on his feet, you wonder whether he could have been a ballroom dancer. I remember my little lad Jackson being at the ground – he was only one year old but even he managed to totter up and clap when Dravid reached three figures. It was about the only thing that made me smile that day.

When summing up a player, you have to look at where they scored their runs, the quality of the bowling attacks and their influence on the game. A lot of that is taken into account in the ICC ratings, and for Dravid to sit up there alongside the likes of Ricky Ponting, Sachin Tendulkar, Brian Lara and Jacques Kallis means that he didn't just notch up the easy runs – it was the way he was at the crease: calm and determined and very focused. He did not try to be someone else; he was and still is his own man.

I thought that he could and should have captained India earlier and more often than he did. He was not as upfront as Sourav Ganguly, but he was more attuned to the spirit of the game, and I think that his sides were just as tough and more united. And he also had the respect of the team. He was a gentleman, basically – not a man to push himself forward into the limelight, but when the call came, he did a good job and never allowed himself to be swamped by the incredible complications of Indian cricket politics. I saw a bit of their series in England in 2007 because I was over there playing for Hampshire. To win in conditions that are very different to those in India was a huge achievement. Only two other Indian captains had ever done that.

He must have been a great player to bat with because he was so reliable and unselfish. I guess the great example of Dravid's skill is the Calcutta Test in 2001 when our unbroken sequence of 16 wins came to an end. He put on 376 for the fifth wicket with V.V.S. Laxman, and while Laxman took a lot of the credit, he could not have done it without Dravid, who very quietly put away the bad balls with that wristy elegance of his and kept the strike ticking over. And his encouragement and determination rubbed off on V.V.S. They swapped positions between three and six after the first innings, and I think Dravid felt he had something to prove, judging by his gesture towards the commentary box after completing his hundred. It was very rare for him to become so agitated. Usually, he was the calmest bloke on the ground.

That innings might have been a turning point. He became super consistent after that and scored a double-hundred when India beat Australia in Adelaide in 2003. I was taking a rest from the game for most of that year courtesy of the ICC and looked on as a spectator rather than a bowler. That, as I learned, was the best way to watch Rahul Dravid.

RAHUL SHARAD DRAVID

BORN	11 January 1973, Indore, India
TESTS	122
RUNS	10,098 in 216 innings at 54.88 with 25 hundreds/52 fifties
ONE-DAY INTERNATIONALS	333
RUNS	10,585 in 308 innings at 39.49 with 12 hundreds/81 fifties

21

·······

DAVID BOON

IF YOU WERE BUILDING A PERFECT model of the bloke you would want to wear our Baggy Green Cap, he would bear a pretty strong resemblance to David Boon: tough, uncompromising, defiant and proud. Like Allan Border, he knew the hurt of losing an Ashes series, and if he wasn't strong-minded before then, he was certainly hardened by that experience. He was the best number three I played with until Ricky Ponting – another gum-chewing Tasmanian – started to blossom a few years later. As far as Boon was concerned, crisis was simply another word for 'opportunity'.

By the time I came into the side, he had more than earned his stripes against the great West Indian quicks, and his bravery went unquestioned. He is not the tallest bloke but he had the presence of a giant. He looked after me a little bit in my early days, and I will be forever grateful for that. He has a deep voice and is one of those guys who uses words economically but knows that everyone will listen when he speaks. With that natural authority, he became a great captain for Durham (and Tasmania) when they wanted somebody to bring a young team together in county cricket. He put them on the road to success, and I know that a lot of people up there at the Riverside trace the good times back to the inspired appointment of Boon. Australia also recognised his shrewd cricket brain when they made him a national selector.

They treat him like royalty in Tasmania. He was little more than a kid when he played in their first successful side in the late 1970s, and he went on to become an elder statesman. A couple of years ago he agreed to come out of retirement to play in a grade Twenty20 match in Hobart to try and get some publicity for the competition and a decent turnout on the gate. The crowd flocked to see their hero but typically of Boon he treated it like a proper, full-on game and decided to open the batting rather than come in later, even though he had not played for Tasmania since 1999. He saw it as his job to go out there and face the new ball; he had opened the batting for Australia before finding his best position at three.

We used to call him the 'keg on legs' at short leg because of his barrel chest and his fielding position. Usually it is the newcomer who has to crouch in there under the helmet close to the bat, but Boon made the place his own because his reflexes were so good and he wouldn't flinch if the hard ball came his way. There were never too many alternative volunteers, and I can't think of anybody else in that spot who would have taken the catch that completed my hat-trick against England at Melbourne in 1994. He was the best in that position out of anyone I saw. The ball whizzed off Devon Malcolm's edge in a split second, but he still reacted incredibly to dive to his right and hold the chance. Although his figure might not have looked too flattering, he was quite athletic and quick over the turf.

I've spent many a happy hour talking about cricket over a cold tinny or two with Boon, so it was probably appropriate that I recently took over from him as the ambassador for VB beer. That really was a tough act to follow. Part of the marketing promotion is a small plastic figurine cast in your image which speaks random catchphrases such as (in my case) 'I think the baked beans just kicked in'. They are given away with slabs of beer, and the 'Boony Doll' seems to have become a collector's item. I've heard that people will pay up to £100 a time on eBay.

Stories like that are testament to the continuing popularity of Boon, but it is important for everyone to remember that he would not have become such an enduring character unless he was a top-class batsman. There are numerous examples of great innings that he played for Australia. He always seemed to get described as pugnacious, and I guess my overriding memory is of him cutting and pulling or getting up on his toes as the quick bowlers fired it in around his helmet.

He was very proud of hitting the winning runs in the 1989 Ashes series. Wins against England always mean a little bit more than the rest to an Australian, and Boon was as patriotic as they come. He was the best leader of the team song that I played with. When he got up in the dressing-room and started 'Under the Southern Cross I stand . . .' it made the hairs stand up on your neck. On my first Ashes tour in 1993 he struck hundreds in three successive Tests, all of them in the first innings when you want the runs in the bag to be able to dictate terms throughout the rest of the match. I swear he nearly cried when he saw his name on the famous honours board at Lord's after scoring 164 not out. Four years earlier he had been out for 94.

Never a bloke to make a fuss, he announced his international retirement only the day before his final Test, against Sri Lanka in 1996. He thought it was time to go, even though he had scored a hundred in the previous match. At that point only Allan Border had scored more runs or played in more Test matches for Australia. That pair could have been chiselled from the same granite rock. David Boon was more than just a very good batsman. He is a great Australian.

DAVID CLARENCE BOON

BORN	29 December 1960, Launceston, Tasmania, Australia
TESTS	107
RUNS	7,422 in 190 innings at 43.65 with 21 hundreds/32 fifties
ONE-DAY INTERNATIONALS	181
RUNS	5,964 in 177 innings at 37.04 with 5 hundreds/37 fifties

22

·······

MARTIN CROWE

AS WITH A FEW OTHER GUYS in this book, I only came across Martin Crowe late in his career. He was such a stylish and elegant player, with a touch of grace and the same skill as the best Indian players of picking up length very early. He had the full range of shots off his front and back foot, and seemed to play spin and pace equally well. These days he is known as an interesting thinker of the game who does not hold back on his opinions of players. You can't sit on the fence in the media, and with Crowe's record, he can back up what he says and thinks. Even if people don't agree with him, he creates debate with his opinion.

Some of my mates who played for Australia in the 1980s used to say that our team talks before New Zealand games were dominated by two blokes: Richard Hadlee and Martin Crowe. Both of them had a lot of responsibility on their shoulders but still managed to be successful. Unfortunately, Crowe suffered terrible knee-injury problems, and eventually they just gave up on him. He stopped playing Test cricket at the age of 33. By the end, he was almost hobbling around on the field, but when he retired, he was recognised as the best batsman that New Zealand had produced. One year, he managed to score 4,000 runs in all cricket, helped by a spell at Somerset through the summer.

He was ahead of his time with his idea for something called 'Cricket Max'. Although he loves Test cricket as much as the rest of us, he realised that cricket needed a really short version to keep the game vibrant and flourishing. Basically, it was twenty overs per side split into two sections of ten overs per innings. There were a few other little gimmicks, such as a 'Max' zone positioned at both ends. A ball hit in that region on the full would earn twelve instead of six to encourage straight-bat shots. Looking back, it isn't all that different to Twenty20, but for whatever reason he couldn't find enough interest for his idea.

I came across him in his own country during a three-match series in 1993. We played a warm-up game at New Plymouth, where he scored plenty, and I didn't bowl to him much during the first few Tests, but I admired his skill and elegance and in particular his timing. He was very similar to Mark Waugh. I had a good battle with him in the final Test in Auckland. He liked to treat me as a straight bowler to negate my top-spinner and flipper, then look to pick my leg-break. He loved to pull and sweep – a shot that can be risky unless it is executed with very good timing. I well remember the googly I bowled to him. He misread it and was caught at bat pad, and I enjoy reminding him of it.

New Zealand actually won that game, but the pitch was pretty dodgy: my first innings figures were 15–12–8–4. During that series, he was the only one of their batsmen who seemed confident. It was one of the best spells I ever bowled, and it needed to be to dismiss Marty. He put a lot of time into preparation, but when it came down to it, his game against spin boiled down to trying to force the bowler to drop short. He did not rate off-spinners very much at all. His main hitting zone was into the leg side, so he could just play with the turn. He saw wrist-spin as being more dangerous, but he always had a plan.

More than most players, he liked to find his rhythm at the crease. He tried to put himself in his own little world in which there was nothing to worry about except his own game. He looked to shut out external factors such as the crowd, the conditions – probably a good idea given some of the surfaces he played on at home – and the opposition. Merv Hughes thought that he had some success against Crowe because he could draw him from his comfort zone with those big, dark stares and a few verbals. Crowe got annoyed and wanted to retaliate by making sure that he punished every bad ball that came along, but this meant that he sometimes became a bit uptight.

Cricket is a game for the mind as much as technique, and I

remember Merv telling me a story about one of Crowe's dismissals. Merv had just been hooked for four, and Border shouted to him from the slips to cut out the short stuff. Merv being Merv, the next ball, of course, was a bouncer. Crowe was slightly caught by surprise but still went through with one of his favourite shots, only to see it fly to our man at square leg. Border was flabbergasted – it sounds like a joint plan hatched by the two of them but was really nothing more than Merv trusting his instinct. Overall, Marty was a wonderful player and a good tactician who thought outside the square. To watch him bat and go about playing his great array of shots was enthralling. I'm sure he is missed by all.

MARTIN DAVID CROWE

BORN	22 September 1962, Auckland, New Zealand
TESTS	77
RUNS	5,444 in 131 innings at 45.36 with 17 hundreds/18 fifties
ONE-DAY INTERNATIONALS	143
RUNS	4,704 in 140 innings at 38.55 with 4 hundreds/34 fifties

23

········

KUMAR SANGAKKARA

KUMAR SANGAKKARA SAID THAT HE TOOK up wicket-keeping because he used to get bored in the field waiting for the ball to come along. He wanted to be in the game at all times. Nowadays, he concentrates on batting only, and I reckon that he's decided to use up the brain power he saves through not keeping wicket by batting for longer. Writing this now, I would put him in the top ten in the world purely as a specialist batsman, maybe even in the leading five or six. The fact that he can still keep wicket if the situation demands makes him an outstanding option for Sri Lanka to have up their sleeve if they ever want to go with an extra batsman or bowler for a must-win one-off game.

He is like Adam Gilchrist in that he can get in the side purely for his batting, though Gilchrist never relinquished the gloves. Sangakarra is a different type of player, a more traditional, orthodox figure who sets out to bat for long periods rather than change a game inside an hour. That means he is not as destructive, but he wins games by grinding down bowlers, and his scoring rate, by normal standards, is perfectly acceptable. He can bat anwhere in the top six, and the fact that Sri Lanka have put him as high as number three is a tribute to his technique. I think he would find it difficult to fill that role if he was still keeping wicket, but his form since he gave up the gloves has been phenomenal.

An innings that he played in Hobart in 2007 stands out. True, Sri Lanka were losing heavily, so I suppose you could say that the pressure was off, but he scored one hundred and ninety-two and was on course for a third double-hundred in successive matches – the other two had been against Bangladesh – when Rudi Koertzen gave him out to a questionable decision, caught via shoulder and helmet. Rudi is a sound, honest guy and actually apologised to Sangakkara afterwards. It was still a thrilling innings, and one shot when he stepped across the stumps to flick Brett Lee behind square was just phenomenal.

There is a bit of class about Sangakkara. I think it comes from his nimble footwork. He is light on his feet, and he looks as though he strokes rather than hits the ball. Batting never looks like an effort to him. He picks up length quickly and plays the short ball very well. There is not really a technical weakness in him. He is equally good against spin, swing and pace. If anything, he tends to slash through gully, which applies to most left-handers. In the same way, an in-swinger can get him lbw or bowled, but more often than not, as I said, his footwork is good enough to stop him ending up having to play around his front pad.

In the early days, he tended to lose concentration and could become too fired up in the middle, but that cannot be offered as a criticism any more. Australians have been quite a big influence on his career; I know that Ian Healy has helped him with his wicket-keeping. He also stepped up a level when Tom Moody became the Sri Lanka coach. Moody is a big one for taking players out of their comfort zone, and Sangakarra is exactly the kind of guy to benefit from that approach. He looked at the way that Ricky Ponting, Jacques Kallis and Rahul Dravid were starting to carve out big runs two or three years ago and challenged himself to sit in that company.

As a wicket-keeper, he needed to be very good to be able to deal with Muttiah Muralitharan, especially with Murali able to bowl the doosra. Again, the hard work paid off. Sangakarra could probably read Murali better than any opposition batsman, but that was only part of the battle, because there was no guarantee how far the ball would turn off the pitch. They always worked well together as a pair, with that combination of Murali's grin and rolling eyes and a few words and a chuckle from Sangakkara behind the stumps to help to grind away confidence after a play and a miss or a nick. Like most keepers, Sangakkara was always happy to offer a bit of advice from his perch about how you ought to be batting or how you were going to get out.

The mental side of cricket fascinates him. He is one of the brightest blokes in the game, and if people listening to his interviews think he is articulate, it is worth remembering that English is not even his first language. If Mahela Jayawardene was not such a good captain, Sangakarra would be the obvious candidate to lead Sri Lanka. Every article about him seems to point out that he gave up legal training to concentrate on cricket and now studies in between commitments. He could easily go into law when he retires and become a formidable opponent in court because of his intelligence, charisma, will to win, memory and attention to detail. His summing up at the end of a case would be brilliant, and I can imagine him having a clear sense of what is right and wrong. However, he is exactly the sort of bloke who should be encouraged to stay in the game in some form or another.

KUMAR CHOKSHANADA SANGAKKARA

BORN	27 October 1977, Matale, Sri Lanka
TESTS	73
RUNS	6,127 in 125 innings at 55.19 with 16 hundreds/26 fifties
ONE-DAY INTERNATIONALS	224
RUNS	6,736 in 211 innings at 36.60 with 10 hundreds/42 fifties

24

·······

BRETT LEE

I THINK THERE ARE TWO PHASES to Brett Lee's career. In the first, for a couple of years or so from 1999, he was the fast, dynamic young bowler who backed up the accuracy and movement of Glenn McGrath and Jason Gillespie. His pace, along with Adam Gilchrist's batting, gave us something extra, and the pair, both new to the side, helped to take us to another level. More recently, since McGrath retired, Brett has become the leader of our bowlers, and he has thrived on the extra responsibility. Actually, I think he has loved it. He is now at an age that he can still hit the 90-mph mark but has the craft and experience to go with it – to know when to deliver a quicker ball and how to use his variations in seam, swing and position at the crease. He has blossomed into the bowler that we thought, nearly ten years ago, he would become. Whatever the ICC rankings say, I think he is probably the best fast bowler in the world at the moment, with Andrew Flintoff second.

His game may have come on, but in personality he is still the same bright-eyed kid who first burst onto the scene after knocking over batsmen in state cricket. Out-and-out fast bowlers rarely emerge, so whenever word gets round about a newcomer on the block, people take notice. It was the same a few years ago when Shaun Tait broke through with his 'slingy' action and express delivery. These guys are like gold! And with Lee, the timing was impeccable, because India just happened to be touring Australia in 1999. They enjoy pace least of all and met the cyclone head on in his Melbourne debut. Lee took five wickets in the first innings and seven in the match, a performance which set him up for a dream first year in Test cricket.

He was smart enough, though, to recognise the pitfalls ahead. He suffered back trouble early in his career, and he knew the importance of keeping up with the fitness work so that his stomach muscles were always strong. Very few fast bowlers can go through year after year without a serious problem somewhere along the way, and there were always players waiting to take their opportunity in the Test side when and if Lee broke down. Guys such as Andy Bichel and Mike Kasprowicz were fantastic back-up for Australia, and it was never an issue having them in the side, because they were so wholehearted. It meant that Lee sometimes had to bide his time to get back in the side, even though we knew there was that extra class about him.

Unlike Shoaib Akhtar, he never gets carried away with simply bowling fast. With Shoaib, I always think there is this thing about him getting to 100 mph. He is a really dangerous bowler, for obvious reasons, but Lee seems to have a tighter control of his game. He keeps his focus on the batsman at the other end, not the speed gun. There was a lot of media interest in Lee's first Test, in Perth against the West Indies – would he be able to crack the 100-mph mark on our quickest pitch? It would have been easy to get carried away with all that hype, but he simply bowled the way he knew and came away with seven wickets. The way he filleted the lower order was an example of Lee at his most effective. Having a bowler like that who can remove the tail is a great asset – anything fast, full and swinging is very difficult for those guys coming fresh to the crease.

Back then, he kept his job selling suits at a shop in Sydney. I think he has bought the shop now, though, ha, ha. They love him in India probably even more than they do in Australia because of a hit record he had over there, and he has taken part in a Bollywood film. He is thinking of going down that route when his career comes to an end. Music has always been his second love. He kept us entertained on tour with some of his guitar playing. Like cricket, music runs in his family, because his older brother Shane, a handy one-day player and talented batsman in his time, is also musical. Their band Six and Out have made a few records, and to my untrained ear they sound pretty good.

Although he had been playing Test cricket for six years, I think the 2005 Ashes was the start of a breakthrough for Brett. Those were big games, and he had a major role to play when McGrath was injured and Gillespie lost his form. He almost helped to pull off a win at Edgbaston with the bat and then at Trent Bridge when, between us, we had England seven down before they could get the 129 they wanted. By the time of the rematch in 2006–07, his control of line and length was really good, and he has taken three, four and five wickets in innings regularly since then. He doesn't need the new ball in order to be effective, because his action and pace mean that he is able to exploit reverse swing. He has been a top one-day bowler for a number of years, but his overall importance was underlined when he won the Allan Border Medal – our Player of the Year in all formats – in 2008.

BRETT LEE

BORN	8 November 1976, Wollongong, New South Wales, Australia
TESTS	68
WICKETS	289 at 29.58
ONE-DAY INTERNATIONALS	173
WICKETS	303 at 22.95

25

·······

ANDY FLOWER

ANDY FLOWER WAS THE BEST OF the Zimbabwe players I came up against. At face value, that might not seem to be saying a lot, because we only faced them in a single Test match, in Harare, during my career. But we played against each other in a number of one-day matches, and I knew his game well enough to recognise that he was a very good cricketer. He was the first of the batsmen/wicket-keepers to break through in the 1990s, making him a forerunner of Adam Gilchrist, even though their styles and roles were completely different. At one point, he even stood at the top of the batting rankings, an incredible achievement for a player with so much responsibility on his shoulders. And this was in the days of Sachin Tendulkar and Brian Lara. Zimbabwe relied on him for their runs, but he also had to concentrate on every ball in the field because of his position as the keeper. And, on top of that, he also had a couple of stints as captain and led them to their first-ever Test win. Given his enormous input, it isn't surprising that he gets so upset and angry at the way the game has collapsed in Zimbabwe over the past few years. We all do, and it's a shame the ICC has let it slip.

I first came across him on an Australia B tour in 1991. We had a strong side, with Mark Taylor as captain and Steve Waugh, Tom Moody and Michael Bevan also in the top five. Flower was yet to make his Test debut, but he batted at number four and kept wicket. He looked a pretty composed player against pace in those days but hadn't fully developed his game against spin. That was to come later, and he became one of the best in the world at working the ball around. Dave Houghton captained the Zimbabwe team we faced back then, and I know that he was a big influence on Flower.

These days, more and more batsmen look to reverse sweep and even reverse pull. Andy Flower really was the first player to do it consistently well. Nowadays, you get guys such as Kevin Pietersen playing a full switch shot. As a bowler, I did not mind batsmen shaping to reverse. To me, it meant that they did not think they could score runs in orthodox ways. There was only one time when I felt I was really struggling to come up with a plan and that was a game against Glamorgan when a bloke called Darren Thomas scored a hundred in something like 50-odd balls. I tried fast balls, slow balls, straight balls, and I might even have tossed in a bouncer. That was a case of a batsman having his day.

Flower was consistently successful with the reverse sweep. He did not go overboard, just using it every now and then, and for a particular reason. He wanted to make the captain change his field to block the scoring options for that shot, which then opened a gap somewhere else. Flower was very clever like that. He was great at taking the ones and twos during that period of the fifty-over game when fielding restrictions are finished but the all-out assault is yet to start. Very often, when I looked up at the board, Flower had more runs than I thought.

Whereas Gilchrist came in at number seven with the job of counter-attacking, Flower's role was to build an innings, often from a shaky start. He finished with twelve Test hundreds, including two really big innings in India, giving further weight to his reputation against slow bowling. In the early days, people thought he was playing beyond his level, probably because he was a functional rather than a stylish batsman. There might have been a bit of snobbery about this point of view, too; how could Zimbabwe have such a fine talent? By the end of his career, though, he was recognised as being a top-quality performer. His wicket-keeping was steady, but with his importance to the batting side of things, he probably didn't have time to give it the attention he would have wanted. I remember a one-day game in Harare when he had to battle through virtually on his own. He finished ninety-nine not out with a couple of sixes in the last over against Andy Symonds; none of his teammates got to thirty.

As a bloke, Flower is full of integrity. It was a brave gesture to wear the black armband to symbolise the end of democracy in Zimbabwe during the 2003 World Cup. He did not make a big song or dance about it; he just made the point and let others think about what it meant. He is a guy who everyone should listen to when he talks about cricket and the world in general. He is not one of those bar-room bores who foists his opinions on you as though there isn't another side to the story. Basically, he is just good with people, a solid, no-nonsense bloke with a nice dry sense of humour. His character will stand him in good stead now that he has gone into coaching as an assistant to Peter Moores with England. Deep down, I'm sure he would love to go back to Zimbabwe one day when things improve to try to get their cricket back on track. Because of his achievements, he will command respect from all sides.

ANDY FLOWER

BORN	28 April 1968, Cape Town, South Africa
TESTS	63
RUNS	4,794 in 112 innings at 51.54 with 12 hundreds/27 fifties
DISMISSALS	151 catches and 9 stumpings
ONE-DAY INTERNATIONALS	213
RUNS	6,786 in 208 innings at 35.34 with 4 hundreds/55 fifties
DISMISSALS	141 catches and 32 stumpings

26

· · · · · · ·

STEVE WAUGH

WHEN I RANKED STEVE WAUGH SOMEWHERE in the 20s for my list in
The Times, it caused a bit of a stir in Australia, though Waugh
himself was fine. People tried to suggest there was a problem
between us when in actual fact we are friends. They also accused
me of jealousy because he succeeded Mark Taylor as captain and I
was appointed vice-captain. That wasn't right, either. So it is nice
to have an opportunity to write about Steve in a bit more depth and
maybe set a few things straight once and for all. First – and most
importantly in a book in which I'm trying to evaluate cricketers
– there is no doubt about his ability as a batsman. He was a tough,
uncompromising player whose captaincy was all about leading by
example. We had incredible success under his leadership, and I'm
not disparaging him by saying that he inherited a side that was used
to winning under Mark Taylor and included some top players. I
hope that can be taken at face value and not as some backhanded
criticism.

To me, Waugh was at his best when he was trying to save a match
or the game was skipping away; that's when he found something
extra. It was like he would send a message to the bowler that said
'you're not getting me out, no matter what you send down'. He was
a good all-round player, and he knew his game. One of his strengths
was being aware of the shots he thought he could play without risk
and not going outside the parameters he set himself. He might have
struggled against the short ball, but then again he didn't get out to
bouncers too often, and he never gave up his wicket easily when
the ball was flying around his ears. One of the best innings I saw

him play was a double-hundred against the West Indies at Jamaica in 1995 against an attack of Curtly Ambrose, Courtney Walsh and the two Benjamins in a game we needed to win to clinch the series. I also think of the great Test match at Old Trafford in 1997, his best game for Australia, when he scored a hundred in each innings after Taylor had decided to bat first in difficult conditions. As in Jamaica, Waugh's strong temperament shone through, and he played with a lot of pain in his hands in the second innings.

Over his career, he averaged more than 70 in England and almost that figure in the West Indies. As captain and vice-captain for a period, we spent a lot of time together talking about cricket. I was his deputy when we won the World Cup in 1999, a great effort after a low-key start to the tournament. It was interesting to be in those selection meetings and various other discussions and listen to his views on the game. There is no doubt that we had different outlooks, but these were matters of opinion rather than cases of being right or wrong. I am pretty aggressive about the way I play the game; Waugh took a more conservative approach, and he wasn't a big risk taker. You could see that in the way he batted. However, square of the wicket, he and Robin Smith were the best in the business.

As his batting went from strength to strength, his bowling tapered off, but the presence of Steve and his brother Mark gave the side a great balance around the early and mid 1990s, especially in one-day cricket. They offered some different options. In his early days, Steve worked really hard on his bowling and could be an effective guy to have at the death in 50-over cricket with his yorkers and variations of pace. He had the right temperament to bowl in those closing stages. Steve is a proper all-round sportsman. He is good at soccer, tennis, table tennis and so on, but not so strong at Aussie Rules or fashion – he and Mark Taylor had the worst dress sense of any players I played with. Needless to say, he was always very competitive when we played those other games on tour. He was also the king of the one-liner, with a good sense of humour.

He was good for the odd comment in the field. He liked the gully position, and from the slips we could hear everything he said. He always went especially hard at Nasser Hussain. As soon as Hussain came in, Waugh would start talking about his dodgy technique and question his place in the side. That always made us laugh. Hussain could get wound up without much of an invitation, and I think we all thought he was a pretty easy target who got too emotional. Mike Atherton also copped a bit from Waugh, who would say things like: 'Do you think you'll manage to get it off the square today?' Atherton was the opposite of Hussain and quite similar to Waugh in that words didn't really bother him. One of Waugh's great strengths in the middle was his concentration. He reached one hundred and fifty against all nine of the other Test countries at some point. Averaging over 50 was important to him as a symbol of being considered a very, very good player.

As said, I was surprised at the reception I received when I put him in the 20s in my *Times* list. He really was a good player, and like other good batsmen he improved as he went on. His position in Australian cricketing history is assured, and his figures are in the book, along with the wins we achieved under his captaincy. All in all, Tugga was a wonderful cricketer, who I think got the best out of himself, and that's all anyone can ask.

STEPHEN RODGER WAUGH

BORN	2 June 1965, Sydney, Australia
TESTS	168
RUNS	10,927 in 260 innings at 51.06 with 32 hundreds/50 fifties
WICKETS	92 at 37.44
ONE-DAY INTERNATIONALS	325
RUNS	7,569 in 288 innings at 32.90 with 3 hundreds/45 fifties
WICKETS	195 at 34.67

27

·······

JASON GILLESPIE

AT ONE POINT IN THE LATE 1990s, I think that Jason Gillespie was the best fast bowler in the world. Yes, even slightly better than Glenn McGrath. To me, he had everything you would want in one of your quicks – basically, he was like McGrath but with an extra yard of pace. He reached 90 mph and could seam and swing it both ways. He was accurate and never got carried away with too many bouncers if the pitch had a bit of green in it. If anything, he was too good, because he had batsmen playing and missing more than almost any other bowler I can think of. Unfortunately for us, he suffered some terrible luck with injuries and dropped down to fast-medium, but he never complained and was always one of the most popular, straightforward guys in our dressing-room. His new-ball partnership with McGrath must go down as one of the most fruitful in the history of the Australia side.

A spell at Headingley in 1997 was among the most devastating I have seen. He had not been in the side for a full year, and he was first change behind McGrath and Paul Reiffel, another bloke who served up nothing to hit. It was an important game because we were 1–1 at the halfway stage – we played six-Test series in those days – but Gillespie just blew away England on the second day after rain on the first. He hit the crease hard and consistently put the ball where he wanted. He took the last five wickets for next to nothing and finished with seven overall. It was typical of his modesty that he said he didn't deserve the Man of the Match award because Matthew Elliott had scored 199. The funny part came during the presentation ceremony when he was asked about his future movements. Not bothering how it might sound, he just said that he would have a lot of beers in a short space of time – classic Dizzy.

He was a big player for Australia, too, when we finally beat India in India, in 2004. By a stroke of luck, the pitch for the decisive game in Nagpur looked tailor-made for our tall, fast bowlers, and Gillespie enjoyed himself most of all. There was a rumour that the groundsman was annoyed with the Indian board and wanted to make a point. Nothing would surprise me in India. McGrath tied them down and went for little more than a run per over, but Gillespie did a lot of damage with five wickets in the first innings and nine in the match. That was the pair of them at their best, working off each other and keeping their feet on the throats of batsmen once they were on top.

When Gillespie first came into the side, there was something of the country boy about him. Even at the end of his career, he could be very set in his ways about cricket, and he wasn't a great one for trying out new ideas. He had his game sussed out and thought that was the way it was – if it worked, then why make changes. An example is the way that he always had to have a square leg when he bowled. I am not saying this to be critical, because that same stubborn streak gave him the mental strength to be able to bowl long spells, work really hard off the field and recover from some nasty injuries. It was all part of his make-up, and if you look at his record, it is pretty clear that he had an excellent international career.

McGrath was his big mate. They were very thick together. We called them Lloyd Christmas and Harry Dunne after the characters in *Dumb and Dumber*. They watched that film over and over again on DVD and used to play out scenes. The two of them were similar characters anyway, but they also had that bond of being bowling partners. Dizzy looked mean with his long hair and assortment of beards – he was very big on his heavy-metal bands – but that gave a false impression; he was always very gentle, kind and loyal. You never had any problems with Gillespie.

Unfortunately, things didn't happen for him in the 2005 Ashes. He was as upset as anybody with his form, the result and the fact that he didn't play in the last two Tests of the series. He realised afterwards that he wasn't at his best. He also found out early in the tour that his wife was pregnant and has said since that he maybe took his foot off the pedal.

But he fought his way back, made the side for one final series against Bangladesh and, in an incredible story, scored two hundred and one not out in his last Test innings having gone out to bat as nightwatchman. He was always perfect for that role, because when he set his mind to it, his defence was very tight. We used to think his bat was stuck to his pad with Velcro – there was just no way through. He said that it felt surreal scoring so many runs and batting for so long. During the innings, Matthew Hayden said that he would run a nude lap of the Chittagong ground if Gillespie made it to the full double-hundred. I am not a great one for authority, but well done the management for knocking that idea on the head.

JASON NEIL GILLESPIE

BORN	19 April 1975, Sydney, Australia
TESTS	71
WICKETS	259 at 26.13
ONE-DAY INTERNATIONALS	97
WICKETS	142 at 25.42

28

· · · · · · ·

SHAUN POLLOCK

SHAUN POLLOCK CAME TO BE THOUGHT of as South Africa's equivalent of Glenn McGrath. For ten or so years, the two of them were in a class of their own as old-fashioned line-and-length bowlers. They seemed to have the ball on a piece of rope and could pitch it exactly where they wanted. In his younger days, Pollock was actually sharp and nasty with a ball in his hand and an excellent bouncer. Off the field, he has always been as gentle as they come. As a bowler, I wouldn't put him quite up there with McGrath, whose extra few inches enabled him to get a bit more bounce. In fact, if Pollock had not been such a good bowler, I am sure he could have made himself into a frontline middle-order batsman and worked harder against the short ball. His genes meant that he was bound to be a cricketer of some sort or other. His father, Peter, was also a new-ball bowler for South Africa, while his uncle, Graeme, is reckoned to be one of their greatest batsmen alongside Barry Richards.

For a while in the late 1990s, his new-ball partnership with Allan Donald was up there with the best in the world. They worked off each other really well, and I think that Pollock gave Donald the impetus he needed. They complemented each other very well. Pollock could be really difficult to hit, at least until his last couple of years when batsmen such as Matthew Hayden began to stand slightly outside the crease to drive, knowing that his speed would no longer force them back. Australia saw the best of him quite early in his Test career, with a heroic performance at Adelaide in 1998 when Donald was injured again, as he frequently was against Australia. It gets really hot down there in January and February, but he bowled more than seventy overs in the game, took seven wickets in the first innings with a mixture of pace and movement off the surface, and nearly bowled them to victory. His control in those conditions was impeccable, and I always thought of him as being top drawer from that point onwards. Even if there wasn't a lot in the conditions, he didn't give away any easy runs, and he always chipped in with wickets when he didn't claim the big hauls. His key was his consistency and patience. His record is very good all over the world. With Jacques Kallis as a batting all-rounder and Mark Boucher chipping in runs at number seven, they had great balance to the side, even before you take into account guys such as Andrew Hall and Lance Klusener, who could be effective on their day. Then there was Brian McMillan, who played with Pollock at the very start of his career. Looking at the South Africa teams on the scorecard, I wonder why they didn't quite make the big breakthrough, but I like to think it is because Australia were simply that bit better and tougher at the key moments and had more variety in the bowling attack. I know that they got annoyed at coming so close in matches – against England as well as us – but not quite managing to finish the job. Perhaps they were too intense. You have to concentrate and want to win, of course, but if you get so hyped up that you cannot play in a relaxed state of mind, it becomes counter-productive and your cricket lacks flair, although Pollock had heaps of flair when he battled.

His bowling in all forms of the game was outstanding, especially in one day cricket, and even in Twenty20 in England in 2008, he still gave nothing to hit. His batting, coming in for the last few overs, is tailor-made for the game. He is the quickest in history to the one-day double of 1,000 runs and 100 wickets.

He took on the captaincy at a troubled time after Hansie Cronje's fall from grace and had the integrity and popularity to see South Africa through. People wanted to play for Pollock because he was such a nice guy. Maybe he was too nice for the job. He was very honest and loyal, but we always thought that his teams were a bit formulaic. Having said that, he was very unlucky when South Africa were knocked out of the 2003 World Cup on a Duckworth–Lewis call at Durban. He couldn't really survive that, although he put the team first in typical fashion and gave Graeme Smith everything in the final years of his career, even when injuries started to push back his pace more and more. He is one of life's nice guys, a true gentleman and now a commentator for Sky Sports. I think South Africa are going to really challenge Australia in 2008–09; it should be a cracking series.

SHAUN MACLEAN POLLOCK

BORN	16 July 1973, Port Elizabeth, Cape Province, Australia
TESTS	108
RUNS	3,781 in 156 innings at 32.3 with 2 hundreds/16 fifties
WICKETS	42 at 23.11
ONE-DAY INTERNATIONALS	303
RUNS	3,519 in 205 innings at 26.45 with 1 hundred/14 fifties
WICKETS	393 at 24.50

29

·······

SAEED ANWAR

ANWAR WAS ONE OF THOSE PLAYERS who could adapt to any condition and any style of bowling – he was equally as good against pace or spin. His record is amazing for its consistency. He averages almost the same in and outside Pakistan, and in the first and second innings. But Anwar is a bloke whose style you remember, not the figures. He had amazing timing and a touch of calmness and grace about him. He became an opener simply because there was no other vacancy in the side at the time. In cricket and in life, you take the hand you are dealt, not the one you want, and because Anwar proved to be successful, he just stayed there. He adapted to his role, and it was important to him. I think the fact that he did struggle in his earliest games was a good thing, as it gave him the mental strength for the main part of his career and made him appreciate that international cricket is tough.

Glenn McGrath used to moan because Anwar's defensive shots could go for four. McGrath hated conceding runs and didn't find this funny at all. Anwar just had such good timing and placement, like all great players. Tendulkar and Lara were the same. Anwar could play what most batsmen would call a bog-standard forward-defensive shot with no follow through and the ball would race past mid-on as if he had given it the full flourish. Having said that, Anwar did go for his shots as well. In the mid-1990s, he was the most dangerous and attacking opening batsman in the world. He liked to play square of the wicket, and like a lot of left-handers, he kept the slips and gully interested. Balls were slanted across him that other players would be happy to let pass, but Anwar had such a good eye that he saw scoring opportunities. He was also an intelligent batsman.

I thought that his footwork against spin was precise and spot on, which it needs to be. Having played a lot of squash as a youngster, he developed strong wrists, which allowed him to put pace on the ball on slow pitches. Quite a few openers at Test level can look ill at ease when the spinners come on, but Anwar had the complete game. I never thought that the Pakistanis in general were as good against slow leg-spin bowling as the Indians, and I've struggled to work out why when they have had guys such as Abdul Qadir and Mushtaq Ahmed in their domestic game. I was surprised when Anwar once told me that he had actually been a spin bowler himself as a kid. Then again, I was a medium-pace bowler, and I know other players who developed in unexpected ways.

The first time I bowled to him in Test cricket was not long after his breakthrough against New Zealand. It was in our terrible game at Karachi in 1994, which I have written about in other pieces. Anwar got a 70-odd and an 80-odd and looked really impressive. In the first innings, he batted at what I think of as his usual pace, crashing the ball around and getting the innings off to a flier. Second time around, he was far more careful and batted, if I remember correctly, for nearly five hours. He was top scorer in both innings. His problem had been that he scored a pair (two ducks) on his debut and was dropped straight away – pretty harshly I'd say, given that the bowlers were Curtly Ambrose and Ian Bishop. Because he then scored runs in one-day cricket, the selectors thought he was a one-day specialist, and it was more than three years before they gave him a chance to prove them wrong.

The funny thing was that his one-day record against Australia was really poor for a bloke of his calibre. He cracked a hundred against us to win a game easily in Rawalpindi, but that was about it. And he only came over once for a Test series, when he was round about his peak in 1999. At least our crowds got to see what all the fuss was about when he scored a hundred at Brisbane.

Looking back, Anwar was one of the first batsmen to bridge the gap between Test and one-day cricket without being a 'slogger'. His spell as captain was not especially successful, and I don't think he enjoyed the responsibility, even though it was a big honour.

Unfortunately, his retirement from Test cricket was also not as clean as it could have been. The selectors said they were giving him a rest and looking at a few young players – which is a reasonable explanation for a month or so but not a full year. He was a hard act to follow, and if you look at his Test averages, they don't tell the true story – one-day stats with 20 hundreds is still pretty special.

SAEED ANWAR

BORN	6 September 1968, Karachi, Pakistan
TESTS	55
RUNS	4,052 in 91 innings at 45.52 with 11 hundreds/25 fifties
ONE-DAY INTERNATIONALS	247
RUNS	8,823 in 244 innings at 39.21 with 20 hundreds/43 fifties

30

·······

ANDREW FLINTOFF

WHENEVER IT RAINED DURING EACH TEST on my four England tours, the television seemed to show highlights of Botham's Ashes. I don't know how many times I've seen the old footage of my mate 'Beefy' scoring his famous 149 at Headingley in 1981. At least our blokes who tour in 2009 will not have to watch that same bit of film. From now on, the default tape will be Freddie's Ashes, featuring clips of his runs and wickets from 2005. I hate making comparisons – the ghost of Botham haunted many a potential England all-rounder from poor old Derek Pringle onwards – but there were definitely similarities in the way that Andrew Flintoff imposed his larger-than-life personality on an amazing series in 2005. For 25 years, England searched in vain for the next Ian Botham. And that was their problem: trying to find another Botham.

I don't mean this in a disrespectful way to Michael Vaughan, Kevin Pietersen, Steve Harmison or any of the other guys who played in that series, but it was Flintoff who carried and motivated England through six or seven weeks when the country became gripped by cricket. Australia, too. None of us had any idea of the impact the series was making back home until we returned. In the month or so afterwards, when our season started to get going, more kids seemed to join clubs and play in the parks. Here is the great irony: in the years ahead, I'm convinced we will see guys play for Australia against England who were inspired to take up the game because of that series. Although we lost, it was a great advertisement for the game and the brand.

Not long after the Ashes, we played against an ICC World XI,

103

including, naturally, the man himself. To promote those games, the ICC distributed Freddie masks in the build-up; wherever you looked, Aussie boys and girls looking like Flintoff stared back.

People were desperate to see him in Australia for the proper business: the Ashes return in 2006–07. We were delighted with the 5–0 result, of course, but I know that Flintoff was really upset that things didn't go well and that our public did not see the best of him. He was under a lot of pressure on that tour as a batsman, bowler and captain, especially later on when he wasn't 100 per cent fit. I said at the time that he was a good appointment to lead the side, and although there was a pretty strong case for Andrew Strauss as well, Fred was the right choice. I know that Flintoff wouldn't have let Strauss down. I described them as Laurel and Hardy, which went down the wrong way in certain quarters but was meant to be a way of saying that they complemented each other really well. I think one of the problems for Flintoff was that he didn't always get the team he wanted. It became pretty obvious some time after the tour that Duncan Fletcher as coach wasn't his biggest fan. Some of the stuff that Fletcher came out with in his book should have stayed in the dressing-room. I don't think he did himself any favours there, because he'd been a big one for keeping confidences when he was coach. Why break his own rules once he stood down? Some things are best left unsaid.

One reason why people love Fred is because he never gives up and plays with passion. I respect that and his commitment to the cause. When you see him outside of cricket he is always at the centre of events – not in a showy way, but because people gravitate to him like a magnet. He is fun to be with. We always liked to have him and the rest of the England players in our dressing-room after a game, whatever the result. He has this trick where he opens a bottle of beer with his teeth that has to be seen to be believed. It makes me wince just thinking about it now. Camaraderie was an outstanding feature of the 2005 series. The image that will stay with me is of Flintoff going down to console Brett Lee after we came so close to winning on the Sunday morning at Edgbaston. Taking those few seconds out when he must have been bursting with the emotion of victory, confirmed that he is a quality individual as well as an outstanding cricketer. That's what captured the public's imagination: the way both teams played.

There are several great Flintoff moments from those games: his attacking innings at Edgbaston when England passed four hundred on the first day; a brilliant over in the same game when he bowled Justin Langer and then had Ricky Ponting caught after two close calls against our captain; his hundred at Trent Bridge; and that lion-hearted spell of fourteen overs either side of lunch at the Oval when we seemed to be on course for a big first-innings lead. Yes, he had the odd stroke of luck as well. At Edgbaston, I remember he nearly clipped a catch to Mike Kasprowicz at mid-off before he was off the mark. But he deserved everything that went his way.

Over the years, I think he has developed from being a batsman who bowled to a genuine all-rounder. Ideally, Fred would bat at seven and bowl. But for balance, England need him to bat at six. True all-rounders' batting averages are higher than their bowling averages. These days, his bowling is his stronger suit.

He has a good attitude against spin. He likes to hit the ball, and I loved his attitude towards Merlyn, the machine used by England to replicate leg-breaks and googlies during the 2005 series. Flintoff reckoned that it wasn't much use because you couldn't read the delivery from the hand as you would a real bowler – it's not the same when a ball comes out of a chute – so he just tried to whack it back as hard as possible and dent the metal. However, in 2005 he could be a bit heavy-handed, firm-footed and didn't always look confident with the forward-press style of play that Fletcher recommended.

How good it was to see Flintoff back against South Africa in 2008. It says a lot for his character that he worked his way to fitness after a fourth operation on his left ankle, and when he did return, you could see that the England attack had missed his pace and bounce – they were even better with his old mate Harmy back in the side. What makes him so awkward is the angle of his delivery, so that when the ball straightens, you can easily get an edge. And he can be devastating against left-handers from around the wicket; just ask Adam Gilchrist. I really hope that he stays clear of injuries now to ignite a couple more Ashes series – though not as successfully as the last one in England, please. I think all international teams would love to have a Freddie in their team.

ANDREW FLINTOFF

BORN	6 December 1977, Preston, Lancashire, England
TESTS	67
RUNS	3,381 in 116 innings at 32.50 with 5 hundreds/24 fifties
WICKETS	197 at 32.02
ONE-DAY INTERNATIONALS	127
RUNS	3,090 in 113 innings at 31.53 with 3 hundreds/17 fifties
WICKETS	146 at 25.10

31

· · · · · · ·

WAQAR YOUNIS

LOOKING DOWN MY RANKINGS, I CAN see why people might think there is an unfair bias against fast bowlers. There are only five in my top twenty. I say this to show that I am not insulting Waqar Younis to rank him where I have. On statistics alone, he would be higher, but, as I've said all along, the numbers are only part of the equation as far as I'm concerned. Making a judgement goes beyond that. In my opinion, Waqar was an amazing bowler with great skill who had incredible days and was a match-winner.

Waqar and Wasim – the partnership has a ring to it. They did not always see eye to eye off the field, but on it they were brilliant in tandem, especially being a left-right combination. They were both genuinely quick and capable of generating orthodox and reverse swing. To me, Wasim got more wickets for Waqar than the other way around. Like Curtly Ambrose and Glenn McGrath, the very top bowlers, Wasim had plenty of tricks. I thought that Waqar was more one-dimensional. If the ball did not happen to swing because of the conditions, he didn't have an obvious Plan B. Wasim could find other ways of moving it away from the right-hander, whereas Waqar sometimes struggled, and pace alone, although uncomfortable to play against, is not always enough to dislodge the very best batsmen.

His big legacy to the game is in releasing some of the mysteries of reverse swing. Bowlers had used it as a weapon before, but thanks partly to Waqar there is a lot more knowledge about it today. I have heard stories that in the old days bowlers noticed that the ball was swinging in the opposite direction to convention but just shrugged their shoulders, thought that it was a bit odd and got on with things. These days the approach is more scientific, and fielding teams go to great lengths to make sure that the ball wears in such a way that reverse swing comes into play. There was a time in the 1990s when it was better to open the batting against the new ball rather than come in against the middle order, where you would face fast, in-swinging yorkers.

Because of the duration of one-day cricket, Waqar was a perfect bowler to have in the final overs. His fast, full balls looping into the right-hander were hard enough to keep out let alone try to score off. His strike rate is exceptional, and it is also very good at Test level overall. That partly reflects the way he was so good at knocking over the tail, who found life really difficult when they first went out to bat. His arm had a low trajectory, leading to a slingy action, and the full length of his deliveries gave the ball every chance to swing late. He did not have the same horrible whippy bouncer as Wasim. Waqar was a 'skiddier' bowler who preferred to aim at the toes rather than the ribs. And I know this from bitter experience, because he broke my left big toe three times.

As you would imagine from the way he bowled, Waqar was a very aggressive player. He often had a word for an opponent – perhaps something nice and pleasant to greet your arrival like: 'I'm going to give it to you today'. Apparently, he picked up this side of his game from Australian bowlers on his first tour in 1989–90. He loved the way that Merv Hughes glared at batsmen and thought it would help his own performance. He suffered from injuries over the years, including quite a nasty back problem, so his speed did come down, though not to the point where you felt confident enough to describe him as a medium-pacer – he just lost that yard.

I remember him giving Steve Waugh some rough times, especially in a game at Rawalpindi. But he was never as effective in Australia as he was elsewhere in the world. We were lucky to have some fantastic, brave batsmen who did not get rattled when life became difficult when they faced him. Waqar averaged something like 40 against us, and his strike rate was getting on for double his overall figure. Our grounds are not as dry and dusty as those in Pakistan, so the ball does not make contact with the abrasive surfaces that lead to reverse swing. In fact, one of the best performances of his I remember was actually at Trent Bridge in a tri-nation one-day series when he knocked back Mark Waugh, Matthew Hayden and Michael Bevan in his first three overs. Overall, Waqar had exceptional skill and was awkward to face. He has a fantastic record in all forms of the game and in tandem with Wasim was part of one of the great opening pairs.

WAQAR YOUNIS MAITLA

BORN	16 November 1969, Vehari, Punjab, India
TESTS	87
WICKETS	373 at 23.56
ONE-DAY INTERNATIONALS	262
WICKETS	416 at 23.84

32

·······

DARREN LEHMANN

AT ANY OTHER TIME IN AUSTRALIA'S cricket history, Boof Lehmann would have been a banker to play a lot of Test cricket. Apart from a few opposition bowlers, I don't think anybody suffered more from the amount of batting talent at our disposal during the 1990s. Lehmann is such a loyal, down-to-earth guy that he's probably happy to have played for his country as often as he did, and at least he became a regular in the one-day side. Down the order, he was a brilliant improviser who made a mockery of field positions by finding gaps in the most unlikely places, and it didn't really matter whether or not you happened to send down a good ball once he was set. He seemed to have two or three options for everything you delivered.

He was a natural batsman who reminded me of Brian Lara in the way he played square of the wicket. I don't think he had much coaching when he was younger. He just found his own way to play and didn't worry too much about changing to suit the textbooks later on. Like most of the players of that generation, he didn't leave school to go straight into cricket, although he actually turned down the chance to go to the Academy at the Institute of Sport. He worked at a car-assembly plant, and with that experience behind him, he was always very level-headed about everything that came along. He is very forthright in his opinions and a straight talker. I just wish there were more people like that involved in the game.

I played alongside him early in my career with Victoria. He had decided to come across from South Australia because he thought he was more likely to get recognised by the selectors. It caused a bit of a stir, because players didn't really move between states in those days. Unfortunately, the switch didn't really work. There were personality issues at the time, none of them involving Lehmann. He struggled to bank the runs that would have given him his break at Test level and in all likelihood set up the career that on sheer talent he deserved. He went back to South Australia but said that he took something positive from his time with the Vics, because he felt that it hardened his approach to the game and opened his eyes to the tough side of playing professional sport.

He finally made his Test debut against India in Bangalore in 1998. There was something a little bit unusual about his introduction. Nine years earlier, he had been 12th man in a game against Pakistan so had received his Baggy Green Cap. Unfortunately, because he hadn't actually played, he was unable to wear it. On the morning of his debut in India, he handed this old but unworn cap to Steve Waugh, whose place he was taking. Waugh then gave it back to him. For the period in between, he had left it in a bag at the back of a cupboard. We all knew Lehmann really well as a one-day player and from the domestic game, so it was a lovely moment for all of us when he finally got to put that cap on his head. He thoroughly deserved it.

By then, he had scored more first-class runs and played more matches than any other Australia player before making his Test debut. That says a lot for his consistency and our depth of talent. Since then, Mike Hussey has taken that record. At least Hussey managed to stay in the side once he got the call – poor old Lehmann soon had another spell out of the team before finally becoming a regular member of the side in his 30s. The timing wasn't quite right for him to be able to play in an Ashes series in England, which was unfortunate because the crowds there loved to watch him bat, and his record for Yorkshire is second to none, even for a county with the likes of Hutton, Sutcliffe and Boycott in their rich history.

On the positive side, he did play against England in Australia. His brother-in-law is Craig White, the Australian who committed himself to England and went on to play against us in the Ashes. Before the Adelaide Test in 2002, White had stayed at Lehmann's house for a few days and then gone back to the team hotel on the eve of the game. A couple of days later, White came out to bat with Lehmann fielding at short leg. Lehmann looked a bit confused for a few minutes, as if something was on his mind. Finally, he twigged. He had shown White some of his new state-of-the-art batting shoes, freshly delivered from a sponsor. Clearly the England player had been impressed, because he'd not only walked off with them, but had decided to wear them in the Test. There wasn't a lot Lehmann could do except keep spluttering. All of the close fielders had a great time with comments like: 'On your feet in close there, Boof.'

He is one of the best guys I have met in cricket and is a close friend. He was a good captain, too. He understood the game and worked well with players; his communication was excellent and players responded to him. His batting when on song was like art; he just smashed every bowler out of the attack.

One of his highlights was hitting the winning runs in the 1999 World Cup final when we thrashed Pakistan. By the next tournament, four years later, he was a fixture in the side, and his slow left-arm – I'd hesitate to describe him as a left-arm spinner – had become an effective weapon. Because pressure was not a problem, he was happy to bowl in the last third of the innings, and batsmen struggled to get under him to hit over the top. He was one of those bowlers opponents sometimes thought they should score more from than they actually did. Lehmann has a great outlook and perspective on life and is someone the game will miss. He really was as good as any batsmen that I have seen.

DARREN SCOTT LEHMANN

BORN	5 February 1970 Galwer, South Australia, Australia
TESTS	27
RUNS	1,798 in 42 innings at 44.95 with 5 hundreds/10 fifties
WICKETS	15 at 27.46
ONE-DAY INTERNATIONALS	117
RUNS	3,078 in 101 innings at 38.96 with 4 hundreds/17 fifties
WICKETS	52 at 27.78

33

·······

KEVIN PIETERSEN

THERE IS NO DOUBT IN MY mind that Kevin Pietersen can become the best batsman in the world. There will be no doubt in his mind, either. He's not far away now! He has bags of confidence, and, let's be honest, he has a lot to be confident about. Not many batsmen can average almost 50 in Test cricket but still look as though they are capable of better. Pietersen is not exactly inexperienced, but he took to international cricket so quickly that it's easily forgotten that he made his Test debut as recently as 2005. People might assume that he started earlier, because most players need at least a year to find their feet. I would say that he is still learning about the game and is yet to reach his peak. As long as he keeps his feet on the ground and remembers all the bits and pieces that go along with playing in a team rather than an individual sport, then there is no limit to what he can achieve. He certainly has the motivation and drive to keep improving. He's hungry and wants to become the best.

As far as Ashes Tests are concerned, he will always be remembered for his 158 at the Oval. I've heard that innings described as the difference between England winning and drawing the series, which would have been enough for Australia to keep the famous urn. There is also a theory that it was the most important innings in the history of England–Australia games. For a first Test hundred, he certainly picked the occasion, but then Pietersen is a bloke for the big stage. There is a bit of the showman in him, and he loves the limelight. With some of his awesome strokes, he is bound to command the spotlight. At the Oval, he decided that defence was getting him nowhere, so he decided to take on Brett Lee with the hook. Most batsmen would have been afraid of how people might react if they got the shot slightly wrong and the ball went to a fielder. But Pietersen has that X-factor, that something to set him apart from the rest. It's annoying how a slice of luck can change things. Gilly dropped him before he got off the mark, and I dropped a chance at slip as well. But he then went on to play a wonderful innings.

Not many players over the past 20 years have been better at tearing an attack apart. Pietersen can destroy you in a session and change the course of a game like Brian Lara or Adam Gilchrist. In fact, he is like Lara in that he strikes boundaries in clusters. The switch-shot against New Zealand in the one-day series in 2008, when he changed his stance to bat left-handed as Scott Styris ran in, underlined what he can do. I predict there is more to come. To pull off a stroke like that is only part of the story. He had to think about it, convince himself he could pull it off, practise and have the courage to play it. As in 2005, he would have looked a bit silly if it had not come off, but the thought of failure does not cross his mind. So there is another vital ingredient: if you decide to do something, make sure you go for it with complete conviction – attack and impose yourself on the game as quickly as you can.

He prepares well for games and is very fit and has a good attitude to batting. However, like all of us, he does get nervous. For a very good player, he can be vulnerable early in his innings. You need to have your wits about you at the non-striker's end when he is trying to push a ball into the field to get off the mark. It was interesting, too, that he did not hold a single catch during the 2005 series. That suggested a bit of anxiety.

I was interested to see how he would get on in Australia in 2006–07 on pitches with more bounce, because bowlers had tried to test him with the short ball. He was still England's best batsman. I don't think he has an obvious flaw in his technique. As a bowler, you just have to concentrate on your own plans knowing that if you do the right things consistently, you have a chance of getting the wicket – it just becomes a question of when.

I was delighted to play with him at Hampshire, and we hit it off straight away. I think that was because I understood the way he wanted to play. I like to think that he enjoyed my style of captaincy, which is to hand responsibility to each player and tell them to back their judgement. He loved the freedom to be able to go out there and express himself. I hope that his game continues to develop and not lose its flair now that he is captain of England. During those early days, a few people asked whether he would hold up at Test level because he likes to get across to the off side and work the ball to leg. But he has great hand-eye coordination, and, crucially, he gets into the right position early to play the shot. He never has to hurry, and he rarely misses them.

There was always plenty of banter when we came up against each other. The media made a big thing of it – understandably, I guess – and things did get genuinely heated from time to time. He wasn't very impressed at Brisbane when he had to sway out of the way when I threw in a ball to Adam Gilchrist. There was nothing nasty intended, and we shared a joke about it afterwards. He understands that cricket is a game best played hard, and he isn't shy of making the odd comment out there himself. As well as being a fine batsman, he is a proper competitor.

I think he is now in his best position: four in Test cricket and three in the one-day side. You want your best batsmen in those important slots, and he has learned the responsibility of playing there. Since his incredible introduction in 2005, he has gone on to score runs in all conditions. If anybody was crazy enough to think that his innings at the Oval was a one-off, Pietersen has proved them completely wrong. The captaincy could be the making of K.P. as he now has to become a giver and try to get the best out of the players and his team. It is a really interesting time, and I will keep a close eye on him from afar. That he is now settled off the field will also help him to progress.

KEVIN PETER PIETERSEN

BORN	27 June 1980, Pietermaritzburg, South Africa
TESTS	43
RUNS	3,890 in 80 innings at 50.51 with 14 hundreds/11 fifties
ONE-DAY INTERNATIONALS	82
RUNS	2,822 in 73 innings at 47.83 with 6 hundreds/19 fifties

34

•••••••

SHOAIB AKHTAR

WHEN HE LOOKS BACK OVER HIS international career, I wonder what Shoaib Akhtar will think deep down. Will he be happy just to recall his great days when everything went right and the crowds cheered and chanted his name? Or will he feel that he should have done more and that too much of his God-given talent went to waste? He probably won't admit it, at least not in public, but I think he will feel a hint of regret. He had his moments, but with a different attitude, he could have been one of the real all-time greats. True fast bowlers such as Shoaib come along once in a blue moon. According to official records, he is the fastest there has ever been, clocking 100 mph. But in the Australia dressing-room, we felt he was only worried about how quickly he was bowling, rather than outthinking the batsmen, and although he had some incredible spells against us, he was also inconsistent. I don't know how a captain could have made plans around him. You wouldn't know what you were getting from one spell to the next, let alone from game to game, but it must have been nice to have him in your team, that's for sure.

For all that, I didn't hesitate to pick him in my top 50. He had that X-factor about him, that something extra that kept crowds interested and could put fear into a batsman. For all of the silly things he has done over his career, he has been great for the game, not just in Pakistan. He has been an entertainer. Everybody with an interest in cricket knows him by his nickname of the 'Rawalpindi Express'. Perhaps I should describe it as his stage name, because I think part of his problem has been the desire to be a showman. He loves the limelight and the celebrity lifestyle. We always felt that he kept his mega-long run-up because he liked the sound of the crowd's applause building up in time with his step. I know that all bowlers are different and that some need a lengthy approach to generate rhythm. But Shoaib practically kicked off from the sightscreen, and if he had conserved some of that energy, he could have bowled longer spells. We knew that he would not be able to bowl more than about five overs at top speed, so when he was bowling well, we could almost tick off the balls one by one in our minds. Although I might sound negative, at times he was exciting to watch and not much fun for the tail to bat against.

Australia saw the best and worst of him as a bowler. He sent down probably the most destructive single over I have ever seen when we played Pakistan at the neutral venue of Colombo in 2002. He was a little bit fortunate when Ricky Ponting tried to cut a wide one and chopped onto his stumps. But next ball he completely beat Mark Waugh with an in-swinger, and two balls later he did Steve Waugh as well, trapped lbw bang in front of the stumps. Not too long afterwards, I became his fifth wicket, all of us bowled or leg-before. That was Shoaib on song, bowling quickly, full and straight. He could be devastating when you first came in, because no matter how well you prepare, his extra pace and late swing takes you by surprise. I remember that he once managed to get Sachin Tendulkar first ball. Even the very best have no answer at that stage of their innings. Shoaib was full of confidence after Colombo and said that he thought he was the inspiration for the rest of the team. He was. I also think he is a little misunderstood. I think he is a genuine person but has just got caught up with the bright lights. He needed Wasim around as his captain for a bit longer so he could have learned more, as he has lacked experienced leadership.

Shoaib was also a great one for taunting batsmen if he went past the edge. He would let you know if he wanted a piece of you. It was funny at times. He and Matty Hayden had some great battles. Perhaps he needed to create those personal rivalries in his own mind to be able to bowl at his most effective. And don't get me wrong: there were times when, again, he bowled really well in that series.

Bob Woolmer, his coach, thought that he was so erratic that he considered finding a psychologist to see if he could get to the bottom of his inconsistency. My advice would have been to 'let them rip, mate' for five overs then have a breather. I really do believe he missed the influence of a senior figure he really respected, such as Wasim Akram, who used to field at mid-on or mid-off and help him through. In 2007, he missed the World Twenty20 after a fight with one of his teammates, Mohammad Asif. He didn't always sound happy with life, and his career seemed to be at a crossroads more often than he would have liked. Shoaib was brilliant, but erratic – maybe that's why we like him.

SHOAIB AKHTAR

BORN	13 August 1975, Rawalpindi, Pakistan
TESTS	46
WICKETS	178 at 25.69
ONE-DAY INTERNATIONALS	138
WICKETS	219 at 23.20

35

• • • • • • •

VIRENDER SEHWAG

VIRENDER SEHWAG IS ONE OF MY favourite batsmen in world cricket today and one of my favourite personalities. This is a guy I would pay to watch. Alright, he could get caught at third man to a big slash or a top edge in the first or second over, but he could just as easily bat for an hour in a way unmatched by anybody else in the world. You take pot luck with Sehwag, although the fact that he averages more than 50 in Test cricket shows that his style pays off for him more often than it does for most other batsmen with the same approach. Only Don Bradman and Brian Lara can match his achievement of scoring two triple-centuries in Test cricket, and the second of Sehwag's, against South Africa, came at better than a run a ball. When he is on song, he can take pace bowlers and spinners apart, and the great thing for a captain about scoring runs so quickly is that it creates more time to bowl out the opposition twice.

Basically, when our pace men bowled to Sehwag they tried to take his head off and to give him no width. That was the plan. As a rule, the Indian batsmen are not great against the short stuff. Pitches over there offer precious little bounce, so they are not used to ducking and weaving or hooking if they try to take it on. The increase in the number of games played nowadays has given their players greater exposure to different conditions, and they cope far better away from home.

The trick with Sehwag was not just to bowl a bouncer or two, but maybe to put in a third as well when it really wouldn't be expected. It became a game of bluff and double-bluff, with the batsman starting to think he was being pegged back so that he would be slightly hesitant in coming forward and nick behind when the ball was pitched up. But those bouncers had to be effective. We looked to bowl straight and shoulder height to Sehwag. Eventually, of course, he would get the one that nipped in, aiming for a bowled or lbw. Sometimes it worked; sometimes it didn't. The great thing is that it only has to go right once to get the wicket, although his average against us is slightly better than it is overall.

If I was his captain, I would look to pump him up at every opportunity, reminding him that he is a match-winner. In the Indian side, you have Rahul Dravid to stick it out – he is a great player to have at the other end. If Sehwag came back into the dressing-room after what looked like a soft dismissal, my attitude would be 'bad luck, you'll get it right next time'. It is worth paying the price for the little mistakes for the times when he absolutely destroys the opposition and wins you a game.

He does not just settle for hundreds, but goes on from there to make really big scores. One innings when he hit 155 at Chennai in 2004 sticks in my mind – roughly two-thirds of his side's runs were made while he batted. His form had been a bit patchy up to that point, but it underlines what I say about sticking with him. He played some amazing shots through mid-wicket against the spin. Afterwards, somebody asked him why he didn't try to pad me away defensively like a lot of other batsmen. 'My pad has no role,' he said.

Comparisons with Sachin Tendulkar are unfair, although you can see why people look at the pair of them together. Physically, they are similar, and Sehwag has obviously learned from his mate. I just think it is unfair to bracket anybody with Tendulkar because he is such a fantastic player who has been at the top of the world game now for almost 20 years. Take him for what he is. Take Sehwag for what he is as well, and sit back and fasten your seat belt when they are going at it together. Their opening partnership in one-day cricket was usually worth the admission fee alone, especially during the power plays with only two fielders outside the ring.

Sehwag's style makes him perfect for the shortened form of the game. If I was picking my world one-day side, he is the first opener I would put on my list. And I wouldn't underestimate his little off-spinners, either. He has a knack of getting a wicket, and on slow pitches he can keep the rate down for a few overs. Tendulkar is the same, and both are very handy back-up, especially on the subcontinent. Over the years, Sehwag has dismissed some of our best one-day batsmen, including Adam Gilchrist and Michael Bevan.

Off the field, I find him to be a really funny guy. He loves to have a laugh. Jeremy Snape told me a great story about him while we were working together in the Indian Premier League. Sehwag and Snape were batting for Leicestershire against Middlesex when Abdul Razzaq started reverse swinging the ball in the way that the Pakistan bowlers do. Sehwag came up to Snape and said: 'We must lose this ball. I have a plan.' Next over, he whacked that ball clean out of the ground, forcing the umpires to pick another from the box that would obviously not reverse straight away. To which Sehwag said: 'We are alright for one hour.' Smart, I say.

VIRENDER SEHWAG

BORN	20 October 1978, Delhi, India
TESTS	57
RUNS	4,813 in 102 innings at 51.75 with 14 hundreds/14 fifties
WICKETS	24 at 36.29
ONE-DAY INTERNATIONALS	191
RUNS	5,810 in 186 innings at 32.45 with 9 hundreds/29 fifties
WICKETS	80 at 41.41

36

·······

ALLAN DONALD

WHEN CONDITIONS WERE IN HIS FAVOUR, Allan Donald was the quickest and possibly the best out-and-out fast bowler in the world, very similar to Australia's Craig McDermott. He could be hostile and menacing, and he loved to dictate terms out in the middle. But there were other times when, for a bloke who was capable of making you hop around desperately, he did not seem to relish putting in the hard yards. In the Australia dressing-room, we recognised all of his qualities but also thought that his morale suffered a little bit too easily if you got on top of him early, dictated terms and imposed yourself on his bowling. He was the opposite of Merv Hughes, who seemed to thrive more when the challenge grew tougher. In those situations, Donald did not always impose himself on batsmen or give the impression that he really believed he would strike at any moment. Maybe he was more insecure than people imagined. There is no better example of the way that pressure can affect people than the terrible run-out between Donald and Lance Klusener in the 1999 World Cup semi-final when they needed one more run to win, and I reckon his head dropped too quickly when he was struggling.

When South Africa came to Australia and we played in Melbourne he took nine in the game and became their leading all-time wicket taker in Tests. There is no doubt that he could bowl and had amazing skill, and his duel with Mike Atherton in the Trent Bridge Test in 1998 is one of the best contests between a batsman and a bowler I can remember. We were all talking about that in Australia, because it was the kind of full-on cricket that we really appreciate. On that occasion, Donald went at it full pelt, and his glares in between balls looked fierce and genuine. Generally, though, we were not convinced by the fist-pumping and badge-kissing. Sometimes it looked as though he was trying a little bit too hard to put across his message; it wasn't natural. It was like he was putting it on. I think people saw through that.

Our approach was to go after him as early as we could. Sometimes that was not possible, because a new ball attack of Donald and Pollock could be very dangerous. But if the chance was there, we looked to dictate terms and hit him off his length to see if he could respond. The plan was to get on top in the hope that he would give us more bad balls. It also seemed as if he would drop back to second gear and just coast waiting for a breakthrough when a partnership had formed.

As a bowler, Donald had a very good action. It would be impossible to generate his sort of pace without that. He also had a good brain, and his experience of playing in England with Warwickshire meant that he had a lot of cricket behind him by the time he became a regular in the Test team. He liked to bowl the bouncer, and I can recall him doing Steve Waugh in Sydney with the old trick: a succession of short ones followed by a ball pitched further up. It bowled Waugh while he was still on the crease waiting to rock back once again. Since retiring, Donald has become a bowling coach, and I can see him doing very well in that job. He is great with people: a straight, quite softly spoken guy who is extremely respectful and humble. He played with a lot of dignity at an important time in South Africa's history and helped to make them one of the best sides in the world.

ALLAN ANTHONY DONALD

BORN	20 October 1966, Bloemfontein, South Africa
TESTS	72
WICKETS	330 at 22.25
ONE-DAY INTERNATIONALS	164
WICKETS	272 at 21.78

37

·······

BRUCE REID

BRUCE REID WAS ONE OF THE best bowlers I played with or against. Unfortunately, we were not in the same Australia side as often as either of us would have wished. His reputation today would be even greater but for the injuries that unfortunately ended his career prematurely and held him back all too often throughout it. That was a real shame, and people tend to think of Reid with a sense of regret at what might have been. I can see where they are coming from, but I hope they also remember what he achieved on the occasions when he did play for Australia at a time when we were starting to claw our way back up from the lows of the mid-1980s.

Being a left-arm bowler gave him something different and added variety to the attack. In that category, only Wasim Akram would rank above him during the past 20 or so years. He had good basic speed, with clever changes of pace, and great control. Playing at Perth where the pitch always had pace and bounce, especially back then, meant that he was even more effective on home soil. But his biggest asset – his height – also turned out to be his weakness. Unlike the cases of, say, Joel Garner and Curtly Ambrose, his frame was not strong enough to support him being 6 ft 8 in. tall.

He tried to put on weight, he did all the exercises and strength and conditioning work that was laid down, and he didn't very often say no to a beer. But his shape just stayed the same. He had a very good action, which helped him to swing the ball back in to the right-hander, but fast bowling is a hard job, and the pressure he put on his body was too much for him to be able to play for month after month after month. Whenever he did get injured, he worked really hard to come back. With all of the programmes and knowledge of biomechanics and advances in sports science these days, I wonder how he would have got on in the present era. As a bowler, he would have dominated, that's for sure.

When I said at the start that I'd like to have played alongside him more often, I wasn't kidding. My Australia debut was the one and only time we played together. And even then we weren't on the field together for long because he broke down with a strained side muscle after bowling four overs. It took us more than 160 overs in all to get through India in their first innings, so we could have done with Reid being out there, not least because he had a big psychological and technical grip on the Indians after taking 12 wickets in the game before at Melbourne when I was in the crowd as a spectator. There's a good chance that he wouldn't have known who I was at that point, but I certainly knew him, as he stood among our most valuable players.

That period tends to get overlooked nowadays in the light of what we went on to achieve as a team towards the end of the decade and beyond. I think the biggest tribute to Reid is that while his twenty-seven games were spread over nearly seven years, he was always a first-choice pick, without hesitation, when he was available. He took more than 100 wickets and 13 in a game against England at Melbourne in 1990, so that alone should be enough to keep him in our record books.

Over the past few years, he has become one of the leading bowling coaches in the world. He worked with Paul Terry and me at Hampshire for a while, and all of the guys were able to relate to the way he put over his message. He is not one of those coaches who feels that he needs to tinker with an action to justify his position. He talks common sense and uses it. The best way to describe his character is laid-back and precise. He has also worked with India, and it is probably not a coincidence that they have more than your average number of left-arm bowlers fighting for Test places, including Zaheer Khan and Irfan Pathan. Our own Nathan Bracken is another left-armer who swears by him. Reid has helped Bracken to become one of the leading one-day bowlers in the world, which has allowed Ricky Ponting to have extra variety in his attack.

'Chook', as we called him, was just rhythm and so lovely to watch. He had pace, bounce and was very, very competitive. His angle of delivery combined with his height caused all sorts of problems. But one of the impressive things about Reid was his record outside Australia. He was very effective on the flatter pitches of Pakistan, where swing is a vital weapon and the new ball is important.

BRUCE ANTHONY REID

BORN	14 March 1963, Perth, Australia
TESTS	27
WICKETS	113 at 24.63
ONE-DAY INTERNATIONALS	61
WICKETS	63 at 34.96

38

·······

MICHAEL CLARKE

VERY FEW CRICKETERS HAVE GIVEN ME as much pleasure as Michael Clarke. As well as being a really good batsman with talent and potential to burn, he is one of my closest friends. He kept me going through some difficult times in England in 2005 while I was away from my family. We poured our hearts out a few times on that tour, but he is a great guy to confide in because he has an easy, optimistic outlook on life. Anything is possible with 'Pup', which is one reason why I think he will go on to be a really good Australia captain when Ricky Ponting steps down. The selectors have done the right thing by appointing him as Ponting's deputy now. He has a good cricket brain and a great personality. He will be the right age, probably somewhere around the 30 mark, with plenty of experience behind him by the time he takes on the job. Without putting too much pressure on his shoulders, I would expect Australia to continue to play a good, attacking brand of cricket under his leadership. That is the way he goes about his own game.

When I retired from the one-day side, I handed down to him my number-23 shirt. In Australia, we have a good sense of where we come from in cricket terms and huge respect for the players who have preceded us. I would say as players that we're more aware of our cricket past than those from any other country, and the respect works both ways. There are very few ex-players who make a habit of bagging the next generation. When a player retires, they hand their number down to the player they believe epitomises the way they played the game. I thought that Pup most reflected my approach to cricket. Defensively, he is tighter now than when he first came into the side, but he is still a wonderful stroke-maker who can take sides apart once he is set. Like Ponting, he is very light on his feet. He is similar, too, in that he made a really good start to his Test career, found himself left out for a while and then came back stronger. I think Pup has matured very quickly as a player and as a person.

Being dropped in 2005 gave him a chance to get out of the limelight and look at his game away from the heat of the Test cauldron. I know that it felt like a big setback at the time, but it was made pretty clear to him that his technique was generally sound and that he didn't need to get too low on himself. Basically, he was a big part of the future, and he would be back. And since he has come back, he has been in awesome form, and in the coming years I believe he will be the number-one batsman in the world. He has the temperament and attitude, and is extremely hungry.

It was great to have him around for the 2006–07 Ashes series against England when he scored two magnificent hundreds. The one in Adelaide was outstanding and showed his class and the trait that sets apart good from great: the ability to get a hundred when the team needs it the most. When he gets going, he has so much style. He is very 'wristy' for an Australian batsman – it was just a delight to watch him bat in Adelaide.

Maybe he suffered from people expecting too much too soon. He scored 151 on his Test debut in Bangalore in 2004, but it was the manner of the innings as much as the number of runs that led people to believe he could conquer the world and captured everyone's attention. He rattled along at about five an over with Adam Gilchrist, and bear in mind that our batsmen have not always had the greatest success in India. He started a bit nervously, but once he realised he could cope, he drove the ball beautifully. I remember a shot against Anil Kumble where he danced down the pitch and clouted it over mid-wicket for six that just oozed special talent. It got quite emotional when he neared his hundred. He swapped his helmet for the Baggy Green Cap and kissed the badge to a standing ovation all round when he completed the landmark. I think it was more than ten years since one of our players had scored a hundred on his Test debut.

By then he was already a regular in the one-day side. He likes the format because there is a bit more licence to go out and play shots, especially with our depth of batting. He has scored runs in practically every position, including the opening spot. We are still looking for a new opening pair after the retirement of Adam Gilchrist, but to me his best spots are at number four in Test and one-day cricket, and opener in Twenty20 games. You want an adaptable guy there, and Clarke is very good at reading the game and understanding the match situation. He has good game awareness, and he can adjust his style depending how many overs are left when he comes out. He is also a really athletic fielder, and his left-arm spin gives a captain a good option.

Overall, I think Pup has the capabilities and the attitude to become the number-one batsman in the world and graduate from vice-captain to the captaincy. He is well respected by the team and has all the ingredients to be very successful. He is currently the best player of spin in the Australian side and his game is going from strength to strength. Another strong point about Pup is that he is a very good listener and cares about people. This will hold him in good stead in the future!

MICHAEL JOHN CLARKE

BORN	2 April 1981, Liverpool, New South Wales, Australia
TESTS	35
RUNS	2,212 in 54 innings at 47.06 with 7 hundreds/8 fifties
ONE-DAY INTERNATIONALS	137
RUNS	4,037 in 121 innings at 43.40 with 3 hundreds/30 fifties

39

· · · · · · ·

MICHAEL SLATER

MICHAEL SLATER WAS AN AMAZING PLAYER, and the rate he scored his runs at Test cricket often helped us have more overs to bowl a side out. He was awesome at the top. Slater didn't play like your traditional opening batsman of the time. He looked to take on the new ball with his big backswing and nimble feet, and when it came off in the first innings, it could demoralise the other side for the rest of the game. He imposed himself and stamped his authority early. His Test career started and finished in England, which is a pretty good way to come and go to my mind, and there were some incredible innings in between, such as his 123 from 184 balls against the Poms at Sydney in 1999. The next highest score was 24, and none of the rest of us reached double figures. That was Slater all over: a genuine match-winning player.

Crowds warmed to him. His celebration when he scored his maiden Test hundred at Lord's in 1993 showed just what it meant to him to play for Australia and be successful. At Sydney six years later, we thought he was going to run all the way to the dressing-room when he got to three figures, waving his bat above his head before kissing the coat of arms on his helmet. He set the ground alight with that innings, but all of his centuries were prime-time viewing. Then there was the incredible start he gave to our innings at Lord's in 2001 when he crashed 18 off Darren Gough's first over. England thought they had taken the initiative after one of those frustrating last-wicket stands where nothing goes to hand and all the edges fly to the boundary, but in the space of a few minutes, Slater had pulled things back.

I can remember something similar at Cape Town in 1994. We had struggled to chase small fourth-innings totals to win, but this time, with only 91 needed, we decided in a little pep-talk that the best way to get the runs was quickly. At which point all heads turned towards Slater, the perfect man for the job. We won by nine wickets. The key for bowlers playing against him was to stick to the basics and try to tie him up. If he was offered anything wide or off-length, he would go for it straight away, and with attacking fields in place, there were always plenty of gaps in those early overs. He was dynamite on anything short. He was a really good junior hockey player before he started to concentrate on cricket, and one thing he always had was amazing hand-eye coordination.

Openers work as pairs, and it was interesting to see that after Slater was dropped in 1996, the form of Mark Taylor began to drop off, too. They were both from the same town of Wagga Wagga and got on really well off the field as well. I think that Taylor thought he needed to take more responsibility for scoring quickly and moved outside his own game with Slater no longer performing that role. In fact, by messing up the bowlers' lines with his blazing approach, Slater probably made scoring easier for Taylor when they were together. They also made a left-right combination, which presents issues for bowlers straight away.

When Slater came back, he scored more than 1,000 runs in his first full year, so maybe dropping him was the wake-up call that he needed. He was just fun Slats, whether on the field or in the dressing-room. He was one of the good guys and a great team player.

Away from the game, we have a few similarities. Both of us are into our cars. But I don't have his confidence as a singer. The sight of Slater on stage with a microphone, gyrating his hips and booming out the vocals, is something to behold. He has done a few guest spots with Brett Lee's band Six and Out. It can be harder to get him off the stage than to bring him onto it. He was a real bubbly asset to have in our dressing-room, although he could become a different creature after a few drinks in the evening. We nicknamed him 'Sybil' after the film about the girl who developed split personalities. I think deep down he would love to be Jon Bon Jovi, his favourite person and band; having said that, wouldn't we all.

Unfortunately, he suffered a few personal issues a few years ago, and I know that things got pretty emotional for him at the back end of our Ashes tour in 2001. He was left out for the final game at the Oval on probably the best batting track of the summer, and once Justin Langer took his place, there was just no way back. Langer's style made it look as though he hadn't a worry in the world, but Slats was a bit of a worrier. Slats was fun to play with, and we all miss his batting and flamboyant approach. When he burst onto the scene, every young player wanted to bat like Slats.

MICHAEL JONATHON SLATER

BORN	21 February 1970, Wagga Wagga, New South Wales, Australia
TESTS	74
RUNS	5,312 in 131 innings at 42.83 with 14 hundreds/21 fifties
ONE-DAY INTERNATIONALS	42
RUNS	987 in 42 innings at 24.07 with 9 fifties

40

·······

STEPHEN FLEMING

STEPHEN FLEMING TOOK OVER THE CAPTAINCY of New Zealand as their youngest-ever skipper and finally stood down as their best. I think of him as an all-rounder rather than a batsman, because his leadership was worth so much to the team. How many times were his side described as playing above themselves? A lot of that 'extra' came from the captain communicating with the other ten guys so that they knew their roles and felt inspired to give their absolute best. Some of the toughest games of my career were against the Kiwis. They were very competitive but very fair. In that, they mirrored the character of their captain.

Because he was such a calm-looking guy and an elegant, stylish batsman, his sheer will to win was sometimes hard to spot from the other side of the boundary. I've heard that David Gower, another sublimely attractive left-hander, was the same. Unfortunately, our paths didn't quite cross at international level. I did, though, get to know Fleming's game inside out, and we have become great mates off the field. He is a very caring and loyal guy. On the golf course, as on the cricket field, he doesn't mind having a go.

Down the years, we had some really interesting chats about captaincy. Stephen Fleming was one of those cricketers who was true to himself and was comfortable with who he was. He had an inner confidence. You do not have to make a song and dance about everything or shout your head off to let everybody know that you are the man in charge. Mind you, it does help sometimes when you have wandering players in the field. Players ought to be self-sufficient and get the most out of preparation time if they work out what they need to do themselves, rather than having a bloke tell them what to do. He gave his players responsibility, and they seemed to thrive in that atmosphere. It was also Fleming's way of saying that he had confidence in his players.

Taking on the captaincy so young can be a daunting proposition. Graeme Smith is another who was thrust in charge a few years earlier than he might have wanted because of circumstances. When that happens, it is usually because something has gone pretty badly wrong. Fleming was only 23 and had a new regime behind him. However, his ability with the bat made it easier for him at the start. Unlike his predecessor, Lee Germon, his place in the team was never in doubt. Everybody knew that he needed time to get things right, and he repaid that faith to become the best captain I played against at any level, without a doubt.

I was amazed when the ICC left him out of their World XI for the one-off Super Series matches against Australia in 2005. To me, he was a natural choice to lead both the Test and one-day sides. They went for Smith instead, but he did not have the experience or, I think, the same respect at that stage among players around the world. Whoever picked that team should have named the best captain and then picked the other ten players. Those games were quietly shelved after the first year, so Fleming was never able to take up his due role.

His public image is second to none. He always speaks articulately but without the bluster you sometimes hear from captains when things are going wrong. Fleming told it as it was but in a considered way, and he did not spare himself from blame if he thought that he had made an error. He was the same on the field when he gave out instructions: very clear and with a natural air of authority. None of the decisions he ever made reeked of panic, even when there were times when our batsmen were well on top of their bowlers. It is important for players to be able to see a captain who looks as though he is in control. Maybe there were times when he was at his wits' end and had run out of ideas, but if that was ever the case, he hid it well.

He believes that conditions in New Zealand, with let's just say a challenging climate, make it difficult for batsmen to come through. The standard of pitches can be variable out there, but Fleming is a real stroke-maker with impeccable timing. You can see that coordination as well in his catching at slip. He could make tough chances look easy. He had tremendous hands, and I thought he was up there with Mark Taylor and Mark Waugh as a slip fieldsman.

Back in 2001, he almost pulled off what would have been a big upset! New Zealand held us to a 0–0 draw over three Tests and came pretty close to beating us in a classic decider at Perth. We needed four hundred and forty to win and finished on three hundred and eighty-one for seven. It is a game I remember well, because Dan Vettori got me out for ninety-nine in the first innings. Fleming had played for Middlesex earlier in the year and took a big interest in the Ashes in England. Player for player, he knew we had the edge, but he came up with plans for each batsman, which were spot on and well executed. They should have won in Brisbane as well, except Glenn McGrath bowled a great second-last over. I thought that series showed one of cricket's best brains at work. See you on the golf course with that dodgy handicap of yours!

STEPHEN PAUL FLEMING

BORN	I April 1973, Christchurch, New Zealand
TESTS	III
RUNS	7,172 in 189 innings at 40.06 with 9 hundreds/46 fifties
ONE-DAY INTERNATIONALS	280
RUNS	8,037 in 269 innings at 32.40 with 8 hundreds/49 fifties

41

· · · · · · ·

SANATH JAYASURIYA

SRI LANKA DID NOT WIN THE World Cup in 1996 purely because of Sanath Jayasuriya, but I don't know if they could have lifted the trophy without him. Everybody with an interest in cricket remembers the tournament for the way Sri Lanka's batsmen attacked the new ball, and Jayasuriya was their main man at the top of the order. He won the Player of the Tournament award and he was devastating at the top of the order. His wily left-arm did a job, and he played his role to a tee. He is one of the great limited-overs cricketers – he also took more than 300 wickets – and he averaged more than 40 in Test cricket before he retired from that form of the game. He will go down as one of the most important players during my time in the game. Since 1996, the only teams not to include a Jayasuriya-type opener in one-day cricket are those who haven't been able to find one.

There is an idea that he came from nowhere and was unknown before that tournament, but we knew all about him in Australia. A month before the World Cup got underway, he scored his maiden Test hundred against us in Adelaide. Alright, that was Test cricket, but the way he went about his innings gave a pretty good clue about his approach: he was always looking to attack. During that innings, he played one of the best shots I have ever seen. He hit McGrath for six over the Victor Richardson gates at cover – it went miles.

Jayasuriya is a small bloke with a gentle side who looks as though he wouldn't harm a fly. But he has the strength of a six-foot hulk, competes fiercely and doesn't mind piping up with the odd word to try to unsettle you at the crease. I don't know how many hours he spends in the gym, but his handshake could crunch a walnut. The

136

big thing, though, is his courage to go for shots. He executes his plan to the letter and doesn't bail out if he feels he isn't quite there. His reflexes are very quick, and he has a good eye, but he isn't a slogger. You can't slog and get away with it for all those years.

Eight years after his great World Cup, Jayasuriya blasted another hundred against us in Test cricket – this time even quicker – at Kandy, in a remarkable game that we managed to win despite being bowled out for 120 first time. He was under a bit of pressure for his place at the time, and I had to laugh when I saw him quoted the next day saying that his plan was to occupy the crease. To read that you'd have thought it was Geoff Boycott out there.

Adam Gilchrist and Jayasuriya are the reference points used to describe the sort of one-day opener that everyone wants – they have the capability to get the team off to a flyer. Jayasuriya wasn't the first to play in that style – I can think of Mark Greatbatch and even Ian Botham having a go earlier in the 1990s – but he was the first to really capture the public's imagination. I guess that was because people didn't expect Sri Lanka to be successful. Also, he had a partner in Romesh Kaluwitharana who went about the job in the same way. Sri Lanka just took the idea to its limits. It was Twenty20 cricket played in the 50-over game. They were just as likely to get caught at third man as anywhere else; in fact, that spot became an attacking position when they were going after the new ball.

His weaknesses were also his strengths. If you stuck to what you knew was a good plan, there was always a good chance of getting his wicket, even if it cost two or three boundaries along the way. Our seam bowlers tried to exploit his desire to score quickly from the word go. If you tied him down even for a few balls, he would almost certainly take on the short one, so deep square leg was a good spot for a fielder. And he would look to slash anything wide – again, hard and with complete commitment, but you might get a catch on the boundary. From my point of view, I knew that if he was still at the crease by the time I joined the attack in a one-day game, it was going to be fun. I would put the seatbelt on and try and knock him over.

His slow left-arm was very underrated. To hear him described as a part-time bowler always left me shaking my head. He was really effective and a great foil for Muttiah Muralitharan, because he darted the ball in on leg stump from a low trajectory and had a knack of finding yorker length. This is a great tactic in the final third of an innings when batsmen try to get under the ball to lever it over the top. As with his batting, he was at his most effective on the low, slow pitches on the subcontinent. Put all this together, and it was easy to see why he fetched nearly $1 million in the Indian Premier League auction – even at the age of 37.

SANATH TERAN JAYASURIYA

BORN	30 June 1969, Matara, Sri Lanka
TESTS	110
RUNS	6,973 in 188 innings at 40.07 with 14 hundreds/31 fifties
WICKETS	98 at 34.34
ONE-DAY INTERNATIONALS	410
RUNS	12,688 in 407 innings at 32.87 with 27 hundreds/65 fifties
WICKETS	310 at 36.36

42

•••••••

STUART MACGILL

STUART MACGILL HAD WHAT I CALLED rage on the ball when he bowled. He had a massive leg-break and a huge bag of tricks. He was an excellent bowler and took his chances when he was selected. He claimed over 200 wickets for Australia, which is a great achievement. I was hoping when I retired that Stuart would play for a few years until we unearthed another young spinner, but unfortunately injuries took their toll, and Stuey decided other things were more important. There is a really big opportunity now for a young spin-bowler to come forward and play for Australia.

As a pair, we used to get lumped together as leg-spinners, as though we were two of a kind. Broadly speaking, we were, I suppose, but whenever anyone took the trouble to look a little deeper, it was clear that our styles were quite different. I thought we could have played in the same side more often than we did. When we did get together, it tended to be in Sydney or Adelaide, where the pitches help spin. Otherwise, the selectors were reluctant to leave out a seamer. I can understand that, because when MacGill was really challenging, we had three top pace bowlers in Glenn McGrath, Jason Gillespie and Brett Lee. Until Andrew Symonds cemented his place in the side, we didn't have an all-rounder to give us the extra option that would have brought MacGill into play more often. Shane Watson was not selected either, which was strange at times. Even then, you wouldn't really think of Symonds as a third seamer in all conditions.

MacGill looked to get big turn on his leg-break as his stock delivery. But he used his googly for variety, and it was probably a more effective ball for him than it ever was for me. He saw himself purely as a wicket-taker, so the statistic he looked for was not the usual average of runs per wicket, but the number of balls it took to get a dismissal. MacGill just concentrated on turning the ball as far as he could. He has an excellent strike rate in Test cricket. Because one of my own strengths was control, a few people criticised MacGill if he conceded a couple of boundaries. The fact is that he wouldn't have been as effective a wicket-taker if his first thought had been line and length.

In the years ahead, I hope people remember him in his own right and not just as a guy who stood in for me, although it is probably inevitable that the pair of us will always be compared. In the 1998–99 Ashes series, he was the most successful bowler on either side, with twenty-seven wickets in four matches – he was left out at Perth – and I know that helping us to beat England ranks among the proudest achievements of his career. In fact, when I did come back into the side for the final game at Sydney, he bowled exceptionally well and took 12 wickets to win the Man of the Match award. We also bowled together in the ICC Super Series game versus the World XI in 2005, which was an important contest for us as a team, because it was our first after the Ashes defeat. We wanted to reassert ourselves, especially at home. We showed then that we could bowl in harness and that batsmen didn't get comfortable when facing wrist-spin from both ends. Again, though, it was easy for people to say 'Oh well, it's just Sydney'.

Sometimes MacGill struggled to control his temper. But to me that was his release from the pressure and frustrations he was feeling. In a Shield game in Australia, he got frustrated at an umpire who turned down a couple of what he thought were decent appeals. When the umpire tried to break the ice, MacGill said something like, 'Your job is to count to six and hold my hat.' And you know what? He's right. MacGill is an interesting character and a bright bloke who likes reading and has developed a serious interest in wine and cooking. He refused to go to Zimbabwe on a matter of principle. Whatever he does for the rest of his life, it will never be dull. A lot of people said we didn't get along. To begin with, our relationship was a bit testy, but I think towards the end we became friends and enjoyed each other's company, which showed in our results. I wish Mac good luck and happiness in the future.

STUART CHARLES GLYNDWR MACGILL

BORN	25 February 1971, Perth, Australia
TESTS	44
WICKETS	208 at 29.02
ONE-DAY INTERNATIONALS	3
WICKETS	6 at 17.50

43

·······

KAPIL DEV

THERE IS A THEORY IN INDIA that each decade should be linked with a player. So the 1970s belonged to Sunil Gavaskar and the 1990s to Sachin Tendulkar. Nobody would argue with either of those two, or with a similar connection between Kapil Dev and the 1980s. As a kid growing up, I got really into the rivalry between the four great all-rounders of the time: Ian Botham, Imran Khan, Richard Hadlee and Kapil. I always wondered why Australia couldn't produce that kind of player. Of the four, Kapil was the only one I managed to sneak in early enough to play against. In fact, he was the first bowler I ever faced in Test cricket.

Kapil was an exceptional player. Even then, in his 14th year as a Test cricketer, he was a massive presence in the India team. His performance in the fourth Test at Adelaide, my second, summed up his career with a brisk half-century in India's first innings and a monumental spell of bowling in our second – it wasn't just that he took five wickets but that he bowled fifty-one overs in all. His stamina was incredible. He never flagged or lost heart as we tried to grind them down. His big asset was his away swing, and he claimed three wickets in the first innings. I don't know what the Indians received for a match fee in those days, but Kapil would have been good value to them at double the price for those five days' work.

Twenty years earlier, it would have been laughable to imagine that an Indian pace bowler would hold the world record for Test dismissals. Pitches were slow, and the baking heat didn't encourage anybody to sprint 25 or 30 yards over and over again in long spells.

But Kapil managed to go past Hadlee's record of 431 wickets, finishing with three more. I reckon you can see his legacy in India now. He inspired kids to want to bowl fast, and nowadays there is no shortage of quicks. If anything, they have gone too far the other way. In the land of Bedi, Chandrasekhar and Anil Kumble, they are starting to wonder where the next bunch of spinners will come from.

The turning point was the 1983 World Cup final. I remember watching at home as India produced the biggest shock in the history of the game up to that point, when Kapil inspired them to beat the mighty West Indies. There was a big function to launch the silver jubilee of that victory not long after I got back to Australia from the Indian Premier League. Kapil has been involved with the so-called 'rebel' Indian Cricket League (ICL) and has copped a bit of flak from officials, but it was a real shame that the Indian board left the celebrations to other people to organise. My own take on the ICL is that it promotes the game, and I don't see why guys taking part should be banned from playing anywhere. In fact, I seriously thought about joining the ICL myself before I joined the official Indian Premier League.

Kapil could be pretty strong-minded, but I remember him as a gentleman. I once heard a funny story about a conversation he had with Dennis Lillee at a function. He asked our great fast bowler why he swore at batsmen when he bowled. Lillee said that he wanted to get the batsman out with every ball. This baffled Kapil, who said that he wanted to do the same. 'Yeah,' Lillee said, 'but you're not express pace like I am.' A few days later, India came to Australia for the Melbourne Test, and Kapil took five wickets – including Lillee's – to bowl us out for eighty-three in the second innings. As Dennis tells it, the pitch was pretty uneven by that stage.

It is always great to bump into Kapil around the circuit. It is a pretty small world. He is a cricket bloke through and through who will always be involved in the game. His appearance hasn't changed. He still has that jet black hair and moustache. And he is still surrounded by people wherever he goes. In 2002, there was a big event to find India's 'Cricketer of the Century' – why they hadn't got round to doing it a couple of years earlier, I don't know. Kapil managed to pip Gavaskar and Tendulkar to win it and almost broke down when he heard the result. He described it as his finest hour and very generously said that he hoped Tendulkar would go on to break all records.

What I liked most about Kapil was his style. I loved the way that he batted at a time when scoring rates in Test cricket were much lower and a side scoring 300 runs in a day was reckoned to be taking crazy risks. Kapil had a different attitude. Maybe he wanted to save his energy for bowling and didn't think he could afford to spend a long time out there in the middle to score his runs. The best example was when he blasted Eddie Hemmings for four straight sixes in a row to avoid the follow-on in a Test match at Lord's. You need skill and confidence to do that. Kapil had a lot to be confident about.

KAPILDEV RAMLAL NIKHANJ

BORN	6 January 1959, Chandigarh, India
TESTS	131
RUNS	5,248 in 184 innings at 31.05 with 8 hundreds/27 fifties
WICKETS	434 at 29.64
ONE-DAY INTERNATIONALS	225
RUNS	3,783 in 198 innings at 23.79 with 1 hundred/14 fifties
WICKETS	253 at 27.45

44

. . . .

GRAEME SMITH

YOU CAN KNOW AN OPPONENT AS a cricketer but you only start to
know him as a bloke when you play in the same side. As it turned
out, the Graeme Smith I played alongside for the Rajasthan Royals
in 2008 was different to the Graeme Smith I faced in the Test
arena. That was the great thing about the Indian Premier League.
It brought together players from all countries to share ideas, swap
experiences and take the game forward worldwide. We had a
laugh and a joke about the things we had said in the past. They
sounded quite funny looking back. I know he has a few regrets,
but, all credit to him, he sees the funny side.

Any flies on the wall when we shook hands for the first time
in Jaipur would have been disappointed. A few of the media had
stirred things up, speculating whether we would be able to work
together – as if teams are always made up of your 11 best mates.
Well, it was easy. I just said: 'G'day, Graeme, how are you?' And he
said: 'Great.' That was the reply I wanted to hear. We started talking
about cricket, life, India in general and how the Royals could go
on to win the tournament. We did just that, and although Smith
was unfortunately injured for the final, he had a big impact on and
off the field to help us get there. His experience at the top of the
order was crucial, and his leadership was always spot on as well.
He played a big part.

He is one of those blokes who must have seemed mature when
he came out of the womb. With his size and strong voice, he is a
physically imposing guy, and the fact that he has been the captain of
South Africa for five years now makes people think he is older than

he really is. Taking on that job at 22 would have been a challenge for anybody, and I'm not surprised that he took some time to get it right. He thought that big, bold pronouncements were the way to look tough, but you have to be able to back them up with action. He put pressure on his team rather than taking it off them. Not only did South Africa lose the series in Australia in 2005–06, but Smith's own runs dried up. It was a harsh lesson for him, and one he admits to. We talked a lot about that in the IPL, and our conversations always ended up in a lot of laughter.

I think it took him some time to work out how he wanted to be portrayed as a captain and what sort of team he wanted to lead. That kind of thing can only come with experience. In Australia a few years ago, he came across as being quite uptight, but I thought that he seemed a lot mellower throughout the IPL. I don't think that was simply down to missing the pressures of captaincy. A lot of it was simply growing up. In India, he was always chilled out away from the game and laughing at things he might have taken seriously in the past. Being able to relax on the field is a great advantage.

There was never any doubt about his ability. He is a very solid opening batsman who is excellent through the on side, with an appetite for big runs. He will cream away anything on his legs, and he copes as well as anybody with the short ball. There are some good comparisons to be made with our own Matthew Hayden, another towering left-hander at the top of the order. Smith has the extra demands of captaincy to think about, but his record suggests that he can compartmentalise the two aspects. It is not easy for a captain to just switch off from the thought processes of being in the field and then switch on to the demands of facing the new ball ten minutes later. Michael Vaughan, for example, dropped to number three to give himself more time.

Smith has become very mentally strong and has that competitive streak. He wants to make himself the best player he can be, and I was impressed by his work ethic in India. In some of our games, he destroyed the bowling and clubbed the ball around to all parts. But he could also judge an innings really well and never lost his head if he didn't score for a couple of balls. He was a big steadying influence on our young Indian opener, Swapnil Asnodkar.

GRAEME SMITH

At Test level, I reckon Smith could now be on the verge of something pretty special. South Africa have the makings of a side that can really start to challenge Australia, with a mix of experience and promise in the batting and real penetration in their pace bowlers. I am still not convinced by their spin options, but Dale Steyn has had a lot of success over the past 12 months, and Morne Morkel is genuinely brisk and is going to be a handful in Australia. That pair have the potential to lead the attack for some time, and as Smith really starts to blossom as captain, his job will be easier with two genuine wicket-takers in his armoury. Overall, I really enjoyed Graeme's company, and it was nice to clear the air. As far as talent with the bat is concerned, he's got lots. I am looking forward to the South Africa tour to Australia in 2008–09; it's going to be a great contest.

GRAEME CRAIG SMITH

BORN	1 February 1981, Johannesburg, South Africa
TESTS	66
RUNS	5,392 in 124 innings at 48.57 with 14 hundreds/22 fifties
ONE-DAY INTERNATIONALS	133
RUNS	5,016 in 132 innings at 41.11 with 7 hundreds/36 fifties

45

·······

RAVI SHASTRI

THE GAP BETWEEN OUR DOMESTIC GAME and the next level up is said to be smaller than in any other part of the world, and I think that has proved to be the case over time. However, the distance seemed to be broader than the width of the Grand Canyon when I stepped to the plate after four Shield games for Victoria and bowled to the Indians in the 1991–92 summer. Test cricket just seemed to be impossible, and my figures of 45-7-150-1 reflect this. Even the wicket tells a story: Shastri caught at deep cover trying to whack my 244th ball over the boundary. As he had scored 206 by that stage, it is fair to say that he had the better of our meeting.

Afterwards, Ian Healy told me that he rated Shastri as one of the best players of spin he had seen. That at least made me feel a little bit better. Shastri was a slow left-armer himself – he actually started as a bowler before moving towards all-rounder status and finally playing as an opening batsman who offered a few overs to support the rest of the bowling attack. He would have known, then, how I felt at Sydney in 1992 when he became the first Indian player to score a double-hundred on our soil. Spin bowling can be a lonely job, but in the merciless world of Test cricket there is no room for sentiment and support – that comes after the close of play.

It was quite a deflating experience after the incredible high of looking up at the electronic scoreboard to see the words 'Congratulations, Shane Warne, you are Australia's 350th Test player'. That is one of my proudest moments, and it had been at the forefront of my mind ahead of Shastri's innings – even if the selectors had decided to put me back into Shield cricket, never to return. Since retiring, Shastri has been involved in television work all over the world, so we have bumped into each other at regular intervals. It isn't too long before Ravi mentions that innings. As an old song goes, I can smile about it now, but at the time it was terrible. It didn't do me any harm in the long run, because I realised early that I needed to think hard and work on my game to make a success of it.

Shastri's overall record in Australia was particularly good. He averaged more than 70 in Tests over here. Some of the players from the subcontinent struggle on quicker pitches and don't like the extra bounce. Shastri, at well over six feet, did not have the same problems, because he could get over the ball and guide it around. His figures also confirm his bravery. He was a stroke-maker, and I remember him hitting me inside out through the off side on a number of occasions.

He always said that he was not especially talented but played alongside some top players, learned quickly and found a way that was good enough to cope. There might have been a bit of modesty in his self-assessment, because he was only the second player in history to hit six sixes in an over. He did it in a domestic game, and from that point on he was a hero in India. He says that he is better known for that feat than anything he achieved in the international arena. Me? I'm quite happy for people to forget his double-hundred and to remember those sixes instead. As if to show how volatile crowds can be in his own country, he told me that only a week before he went ballistic he had been pelted with fruit by the crowd in Calcutta for taking seven hours over a hundred in a Test match against England.

Actually, his double-hundred didn't get the credit it deserved. In the opening position, he averaged almost 45, a very good figure. People have very short memories. It was interesting that a year or so ago when Shastri was the India manager and Tendulkar was under scrutiny, the 'Little Master' received huge public backing from his former teammate.

As an all-rounder, Shastri was a very effective one-day player, where he was more likely to find the extra gear than when it came to the five-day game. His spin could be more defensive than the traditional 'flighted' Indian way. Because he started playing for India in his teens and seemed to have been around for a long time, people thought he was older than he really was. When he retired less than a year after Sydney, he was still only 30. I don't envy his knee trouble, but it was nice not to have to face him in another series.

RAVISHANKAR JAYADRITHA SHASTRI

BORN	27 May 1962, Mumbai, India
TESTS	80
RUNS	3,839 in 121 innings at 35.79 with 11 hundreds/12 fifties
WICKETS	151 at 40.96
ONE-DAY INTERNATIONALS	150
RUNS	3,108 in 128 innings at 29.04 with 4 hundreds/18 fifties
WICKETS	129 at 36.04

46

· · · · · · ·

JUSTIN LANGER

NOBODY CAN HAVE ENJOYED A BETTER Test career after having been written off so often than Justin Langer. If you listened to the wrong people, he always seemed to be the bloke who was about to make way in the side. I came across plenty of more talented batsmen in my time, but very few with the same dedication and hunger as Langer, and none who squeezed as much from their natural ability. He worked so hard on his game, his fitness and his mental approach that he deserved everything that came his way. Finally, 14 years after his Test debut, he was recognised universally for being the batsman he was and the embodiment of everything we expect of an Australian cricketer, or, as Justin would call it, the 'Fabric'. There were a few tears shed by Justin when he played his final Test; it meant everything to him. He wasn't himself on the first day because the emotion simply got to him. As always, he wore his heart on his sleeve as conspicuously as the Baggy Green Cap on his head.

By the end of his career, he had played more than 100 Tests and scored 23 Test hundreds. Whatever the opinion outside the dressing-room, he was highly valued inside it. And his statistics are even more impressive when you think that he had to play with constant speculation about his future, at least for the first half of his career. He actually had two golden runs: first at number three around the turn of the decade, and then after being dropped at the start of the 2001 Ashes when he forged his long-standing partnership with Matthew Hayden. He must have been one of our most courageous and resilient openers, with exactly the qualities required for the position he eventually made his own.

In other circumstances, that great pairing might never have come to fruition. Towards the end of the 2001 series, the decision was taken to leave out Michael Slater at the Oval. However, Langer wasn't really thought of as an opener. Had Slater played in that game, he would have either scored runs and retained his position for our own summer or the selectors would have gone for a specialist opener instead. Langer, being Langer, never looked back. A few weeks earlier, Steve Waugh had told him to score hundreds, and that is what he did at the Oval. Then, in the next two Tests he scored hundreds again – this time he really was on his way and nobody would stop him until he decided to quit on his own terms. He and Matty Hayden formed a great partnership, and I reckon Hayden's attacking mindset rubbed off on Justin.

He must have copped more blows than a lot of batsmen put together, even those who played in the famous Bodyline series. Ian Bishop hit him on the helmet on his debut, and, as if to book-end his career, he was walloped on his farewell appearance by a ball from Steve Harmison. Even his 100th appearance, in Johannesburg, left an unfortunate mark when he has hit so badly by Makhaya Ntini that Langer thought about his future in the game. Had the next opponents been anybody other than England, he might have finished there and then. His next Test was actually the first of the 2006–07 Ashes, and, to the surprise of none of us, he marked it with a hundred. In fact, that comeback innings at the Oval I mentioned in the previous paragraph was brought to a sudden end when Andrew Caddick forced him to retire hurt after misjudging a hook. It sounds like he was no good against the short ball, but he was an excellent puller and hooker.

Like Hayden and Damien Martyn, Langer had to wait a while for opportunities in the side after being called in at a young age. They all needed strength of character to fight back, but it took a couple of years in English county cricket before Langer seriously began to unleash his talent. Until that point, in the late-1990s, he was a defensive batsman who needed time to grind out his runs. County cricket proved to be a liberating experience for him. He enjoyed playing day-in, day-out and developed confidence to try a few more strokes. I think he was a more versatile batsman when he came back into the Australia side. He could still scrap – and that is first and foremost the way he will be remembered – but he was also quick to spot scoring opportunities. In 2000, he scored a hundred at almost a run a ball against New Zealand in Hamilton.

He is a very solid, genuine and caring bloke. Because of his own ups and downs, he understood what players were going through during their difficult times, and a lot of us sought him out for a chat at one point or another. He helped Mark Taylor a lot during his struggles in 1997. And the one thing you knew about Langer was that he put the needs of the team first. He worked hard to get the Baggy Green Cap, and although it is battered and smelly, I'm sure it now takes pride of place in his home. Even now I can imagine a tear dripping from his eye when he looks at it and remembers the bumps and bruises he took in the name of what it represents. He is one of the good guys to have played with.

JUSTIN LEE LANGER

BORN	21 November 1970, Perth, Australia
TESTS	105
RUNS	7,696 in 182 innings at 45.27 with 23 hundreds/30 fifties
ONE-DAY INTERNATIONALS	8
RUNS	160 in 7 innings at 32

47
·······

ROBIN SMITH

TRYING TO RANK THE CRICKETERS I played with and against has been a near-impossible task, but choosing the nicest guy would be easy. No praise is too high for Robin Smith the bloke. He is warm, selfless, full of integrity and sheer good fun. Throughout the game, he was known as 'Judge' because his hair resembled a judge's wig, but he always saw the best in everybody and would never have had the heart to deliver a guilty verdict. One of the main reasons I came to Hampshire in 2000 was to play with him. I had fancied a dart at county cricket for several years and might have arrived sooner in different circumstances. But I knew that under Smith's leadership I would be involved in some great games. Unfortunately, he didn't get to lift the trophy he so desperately wanted for his county, but that was not for a lack of thought and effort on his own part.

England had few more destructive batsmen during my time. Everybody in England knew about his signature shot: the square cut. His power came from strong forearms, and with good timing the ball would spring away as though it had been fired from a catapult. I do not think they always treated Smith as well as they should have, using him in so many different positions. Basically, wherever England were struggling, Judge would bat there.

Going to England that summer was a real eye-opener for me. The ECB's policy selection was just baffling at times. Selectors can never get everybody to agree on everything, but Australia teams have always been chosen pretty consistently. We usually knew exactly where we stood and who was next in line, but trying to work out the England side between Tests could be a matter of guesswork before the

154

announcements were made. Instead of putting their best batsmen, such as Gooch and Smith, in their best positions, they asked them to fill the areas of weakness that were causing concern. Surely you should play around your strengths, not compromise them.

However badly the selectors treated him at times, Smith himself always put the interests of England before his own preferences. He would have had no qualms about opening if he thought that was required. They were happy to juggle him around the middle order, but despite this uncertainty, he still managed to average in the mid-40s during a tough period for batsmen in the international game. His Test career could easily have gone on for longer. Strangely, for such a good player, he lacked confidence and was a worrier. The uncertainty around England rubbed off on him. But he was wonderful to watch when he was on song, and he was also a fast scorer of runs.

As I expected, playing at Hampshire was a fantastic experience. Smith was the most sociable animal in the game, and it was impossible to get the first round in at the bar if he was around to ask, in his clipped South African accent: 'What are you having, China?' We managed to reach the quarter-final of one competition and the semi-final in another during that 2000 season. Unfortunately, we didn't make a Lord's final and, even worse, suffered relegation in the championship. Smith was in despair for a time and thought the failure was down to his captaincy, but nothing could have been further from the truth. He even wondered whether he should go back to playing purely as a batsman and hand over the captaincy to someone else. The fact was that everybody wanted to play under him because of his 100 per cent commitment to the county.

At that time, Hampshire were going through a transitional phase, with a different management structure off the field and a move from the atmospheric but decaying Northlands Road ground to the spanking new Rose Bowl. Robin was one of the constant factors, a player and person to provide that feeling of stability while things were changing. The club owes him a great debt for his years of service, and he will be one of the proudest blokes in the stadium when it hosts its first Test match in 2011. The Judge really is a true character of the game and a very good friend. He is the nicest guy I have ever met, and is a wonderfully loyal person. I'm sure England would love to have him playing now.

ROBIN ARNOLD SMITH

BORN	13 September 1963, Durban, South Africa
TESTS	62
RUNS	4,236 in 112 innings at 43.67 with 9 hundreds/28 fifties
ONE-DAY INTERNATIONALS	71
RUNS	2,419 in 70 innings at 39.01 with 4 hundreds/15 fifties

48

·······

DEAN JONES

DEAN JONES WAS A CLASSY BATSMAN in all forms of the game, but he probably makes my top 50 more for what he did in one-day rather than Test cricket. The bloke was simply ahead of his time. He played in the second half of the 1980s and the first few years of the '90s – but looked every bit a batsman of the present day. When he took on the fast bowlers or sneaked what looked like impossible singles, some people sneered and thought he was heading for a fall. He was actually heading towards recognition as a bloke, like Sanath Jayasuriya a few years later, who changed the way that one-day cricket could be played. He also realised the importance of fielding and had a brilliant arm himself. All of his success stemmed from great self-confidence, a very strong competitive streak and an intelligence that often took him 'outside the box' in his thinking.

Getting on for a couple of years ago, there was a poll of every living Australia one-day player to choose our all-time XI for an imaginary 50-over match. There were just over 160 of us at that point, and roughly 130 voted. The numbers are important, because such a comprehensive survey gave a lot of weight to the eventual result. We finished with a mix of the old (such as Dennis Lillee) and the new (Andrew Symonds and Brett Lee), and Dean Jones was in there at number four – one of the key spots in the batting line-up – ahead of Greg Chappell, who was down as 12th man. That demonstrated how highly Jones was regarded by his peers.

Jones was always watching the best players for ways to improve his own game. He took some of his style from Viv Richards, and liked the way that Javed Miandad worked the ball into gaps and set off for a run like a hare. Jones was dynamite between the wickets – one of the best I ever saw. However, he had an unfortunate knack of rubbing up the opposition the wrong way. I remember a game when he asked Curtly Ambrose to take off his white sweatbands because he was losing sight of the ball from the hand. From the dressing-room, we could see Ambrose starting to huff as Jones pressed his case. I don't know if the television cameras caught us shaking our heads on the balcony, because that summed up what the rest of us were thinking. Jones had broken the golden rule: don't wind up Curtly. Lo and behold, the big man slipped up about ten gears, went on the rampage and knocked us all over. So, thanks for that one, Deano. And yet, for all that, he was a bloke you would rather play with than against.

For all his one-day brilliance, he is probably best known for his 210 against India in the tied Test at Chennai in 1986. That innings has gone down in legend to the point that Jones could probably live off it if he did not have so much energy to put into other areas of his life. Mention India and Australia, and that knock will be one of the first associations people make, along with V.V.S. Laxman's double-hundred in Calcutta. At the time, Jones was a young player trying to make his way in an emerging side. The heat and humidity was so bad that he ended up in hospital on a drip. He reckons that as he lay in the bed with all these tubes wrapped around him, he couldn't remember a thing about the second half of his innings, though it is fair to say that he has picked up the details since. You don't have to be a big cricket fan to know the story about Allan Border out in the middle telling Jones that if he was too weak to carry on batting, he would find somebody else who was tough enough to play for Australia.

At international level, our Test careers had only a slight overlap. We played together for much longer with Victoria. I knew him as a guy who liked to attack all bowling and used his feet against spin. He wanted to be involved in every aspect of the game, and he understood what was going on. He put the needs of the team ahead of his own. He was only 31 when he played his final Test, and he wasn't too happy, as he'd top-scored in both innings in his penultimate match, in Sri Lanka. Afterwards, whenever we played at his home ground of the MCG (Melbourne Cricket Ground), you could count on a few supporters draping banners saying 'Bring Back Deano'. He probably was unlucky, but with Steve Waugh and Damien Martyn coming into the side, the selectors wanted to look to the future. Jones continued to be a great player for Victoria and is still the leading run-scorer in our history.

Overall – and while I didn't agree with him on everything all the time – he was great fun to have in the team. He had a real passion for cricket and made things happen on the field. Even in a tight situation against the best bowlers in the world, he played with a smile. He relished the big stage. With his strong opinions, he is probably tailor-made for his job as a commentator, but don't be surprised if he makes a career switch over the next couple of years. He is a really good golfer and has his eyes on a place on the senior tour. Anything is possible where Dean Jones is concerned.

DEAN JONES

BORN	24 March 1961, Melbourne, Australia
TESTS	52
RUNS	3,631 in 89 innings at 46.55 with 11 hundreds/14 fifties
ONE-DAY INTERNATIONALS	164
RUNS	6,068 in 161 innings at 44.61 with 7 hundreds/46 fifties

49

DILIP VENGSARKAR

THE ENGLISH WEATHER BEING WHAT IT is, we always had plenty of hours to kill around the grounds on our Ashes tours. At Lord's, one way to fill in the time as the rain lashed down was to look at all the names on the famous honours boards in the dressing-room. Everybody who scores a hundred or takes five wickets in an innings against England in a Test match at the ground has his name inscribed – it is up there for ever as an inspiration to the players and teams who follow. Whenever one of our guys joined the exclusive band, we would write his name on a bit of tape and stick it up there until the engraver came in to do it properly in the evening. One of my few little regrets is that I never managed to join those names on the boards.

All of this brings me round to Dilip Vengsarkar. He is up there three times, and almost every time I sat in the dressing-room, either at an international or county match, somebody would point it out and say: 'Jeez, he must have been a player.' By the time we got to 2005, the last of my four Ashes tours, I felt a bit embarrassed to say that I was actually old enough to have played against him.

But I can't be that old, because my memory is good enough to recall bowling to him at Sydney in 1992. That was my debut, and I've written a fair bit about it in my piece about Ravi Shastri. Vengsarkar made a fifty batting at number four and took his time about it. I have a very vivid recollection of his sheer presence. He was tall, quite thin and his moustache gave him a military bearing. They called him 'The Colonel', which I thought was pretty appropriate. He did not dominate or make a huge score like Shastri, but I have picked

The Top Ten

#1 Every aspect of Sachin Tendulkar's batting
is top drawer – he has been a great ambassador for
the game for nearly 20 years.
(© Getty Images)

#2 At his best, Brian Lara was the most destructive batsman I
ever faced, and with his strut and swagger, he
always commanded attention. (© Getty Images)

#3 If you were stupid enough to rouse Curtly Ambrose, he could be devastating – as tight as Glenn McGrath but with an extra yard of deadly pace.
(© Getty Images)

#4 Allan Border was a rock-solid batsman, bloke and a great Australian who gave me the confidence to believe I belonged in Test cricket.
(© Getty Images)

#5 Glenn McGrath never forgot that cricket is a game best
kept simple, and he became our leading pace bowler over
more than a decade of playing at Test level.
(© Getty Images)

#6 Wasim Akram delivered the fastest spell of bowling I ever saw, and his quick, whippy bouncer was the most effective in the game. (© Getty Images)

#7 Whatever anybody thinks about Muttiah Muralitharan's action, he has been great for Sri Lanka and could possibly finish with 1,000 Test wickets. (© Getty Images)

#8 Even as a scrawny 16 year old, Ricky Ponting had that touch of class, and he has more than fulfilled his potential as a batsman and Test captain.
(© Getty Images)

#9 Mark Waugh was a good buddy and a gifted batsman
and fielder who also opened the bowling in an
Ashes Test match.
(© Getty Images)

#10 Quick hands and deft footwork were central to Ian Healy's brilliant wicket-keeping, and he also chipped in with vital runs when we needed them.

(© Getty Images)

him for this book on his overall record, his reputation and from the opinions of people I respect. When I played against him, I thought he had something about him.

Nobody should underestimate the difficulties in batting at Lord's, with its eight-foot slope from one side of the field to the other. It is very easy for players to lose their balance in their stance or misjudge the extra movement taking the ball down the angle. It really tests your judgement, and I guess it must be even harder for an Indian, because balls do not swing or seam anywhere near as much as in the conditions they are used to at home. Vengsarkar was the first from overseas to score three Test hundreds against England at Lord's, an achievement which strikes me as being truly awesome. His long reach would have helped him, and I know from my brief experience that he looked to play the ball late.

India rated him as the best number three in their history until Rahul Dravid came along. He played for the same club in Mumbai as Sunil Gavaskar but did not come from a traditional cricket-playing family. It amazes me the number of players on the subcontinent who simply learn their game on the streets or in parks. Indian cities have these enormous expanses of grass called *maidans*, where you see sometimes dozens of informal games of cricket going on at the same time. I remember spending an hour or so at one of them in Mumbai, where Vengsarkar would almost certainly have played at some point. Boundaries overlap between the games, so it is impossible to work out how the fielders are set for your particular match.

I asked Allan Border about Vengsarkar, as their careers ran roughly parallel. He thought a lot of him and told me about a really good hundred Vengsarkar scored in Bangalore when they were both quite young. Slow pitches make life hard for bowlers – as a spinner, I like a bit of pace so the ball fizzes off the surface as well as turns – but they also make it difficult for batsmen to be able to play their shots. Vengsarkar had good concentration and would wait patiently for a bit of width so he could give the bat a full swing and get some power on it. The bats were not as good in those days, and you could not edge a ball to the boundary as happens today – just one more example of the way the game has become harder for bowlers!

Sachin Tendulkar is another mate of mine who I have a lot of time for. He once told me the story about how he came to make his debut for Mumbai at the age of 15. Sachin was not much more than 5 ft tall and had been invited to net practice. Vengsarkar was the India and Mumbai captain at the time. He asked Kapil Dev to bowl a few balls to Tendulkar, but Kapil was so concerned about this frail-looking boy that he wouldn't run in off more than a few paces. Vengsarkar had never seen him bat before but was so impressed that he made sure Sachin went into the first team. I know how much of a thrill it was to Tendulkar to play alongside Vengsarkar at that level.

Recently, Vengsarkar has served as the chairman of India's selectors. Not an easy job, that one! I have come across him a few times down the years. As he showed when he spotted Tendulkar at such an early age, he is a good judge of a player. I must admit I don't envy him trying to pick an India side, with so many demands from the numerous state sides to look at their own players. You need the diplomacy of Henry Kissinger for that job, but, then, as I briefly discovered all those years ago, Vengsarkar is a very patient man.

DILIP BALWANT VENGSARKAR

BORN	6 April 1956, Rajapur, Maharashtra, India
TESTS	116
RUNS	6,868 in 185 innings at 42.13 with 17 hundreds/35 fifties
ONE-DAY INTERNATIONALS	129
RUNS	3,508 in 120 innings at 34.73 with 1 hundred/23 fifties

50

· · · · · · ·

STEVE HARMISON

I THINK THERE WILL BE QUITE a lot of regret in England if Steve Harmison is not involved in the 2009 Ashes. There are plenty of very good fast-medium bowlers around the country in England, but none of them with the same pace and awkward steepling bounce that Harmison at his best can generate, and he adds variety to the England attack.

Briefly, Harmison stood at number one in the world rankings. He ought to remember that, because he strikes me as a guy who lacks a bit of confidence. On his day, he can be devastating; some of his figures prove it. When he gets everything right, when his long arms and legs are working in straight lines, he is awesome to watch. He played a massive part in the 2005 Ashes win. I thought he was brilliant and raised the bar at the start of the innings. Even though we won the first Test at Lord's, he set the tone for the series in his first spell, hitting Justin Langer on the elbow second ball and then Ricky Ponting on the head. We knew straight away that this was a different England side from those we had trounced on previous tours.

I've never understood why he doesn't always take the new ball. It must come down to confidence. It is as though he realises the importance of those first dozen overs and gets a bit worried that he might waste the benefits. Michael Vaughan knows what makes him tick and was happy to use him as the kingpin in 2005. He built up Harmison and told him to go at us hard and cause some damage. He was at his best when his mind was uncluttered by coaches telling him this, that and the other. Perhaps that is what started to happen when his success dried up. The last thing you need to do with Harmison is to start getting technical. Just tell him to bowl as fast as he can.

As a bloke, he is very straight, funny, loyal and down to earth. I can see why he gets on so well with Freddie Flintoff. They are both good fun to be around. There are stories about Harmison developing homesickness and not enjoying life on tour. It can be challenging for all of us at times; we all miss our kids, and the routine of nets-game-travel can take its toll. I don't know too much about the mental side of Harmison, but in Australia I guess we would think of him as being a kid from the bush who is very laid-back, doesn't enjoy city life, likes his routine and his regular pub, and doesn't bother too much about the material things.

As far as bowling goes, he is very clever and has nice subtle changes of pace. He came up with a great slower ball at Edgbaston in 2005 to get rid of Michael Clarke at a crucial stage on the Saturday evening. That was an excellent piece of thinking, and he also had the skill to execute the plan. Then, the next morning, it was Harmison's short ball to Mike Kasprowicz that gave England the win by two runs. Anything of that length will unsettle a lower-order player, and poor Kasprowicz was devastated after gloving a catch as he tried to take evasive action.

England were fortunate that summer to have a proper group of match-winners in the bowling attack plus Kevin Pietersen and Michael Vaughan among the batsmen. In the past, we knew that if we could get through, say, Darren Gough and Andrew Caddick, life would be easier against the support seamers. It wasn't like that this time: you battled through against Harmison only to find Flintoff or Simon Jones steaming in. With Harmison, you get the bad with the good, and the depth of the attack meant that Vaughan, a decisive captain, used him well, bringing him on for short, sharp spells to keep him fresh.

Things didn't quite work out the same way in 2006–07. The first ball by Harmison to open the series at Brisbane, veering away to second slip like a car being driven by a drunken motorist, has come to symbolise those games. A few people have said since that it finished him for the series. We did not see it like that in our dressing-room. It took us by surprise, but most of us just laughed and assumed he would get over his nerves as the game went on. Maybe he was just making sure Freddie, his mate and captain, was concentrating. There had been an incredible build-up to the series, and it was just one of those things.

The selectors will face a difficult task in 2009, because the likes of Ryan Sidebottom, Jimmy Anderson and Stuart Broad have worked well together, and Flintoff will be essential to give the side balance. The pressure will be on, and those guys who won in 2005 have the experience behind them of knowing what it takes to beat Australia. In my opinion, if England want to win the Ashes, they need Harmison, and it's great to see him firing on all cylinders once again.

STEPHEN JAMES HARMISON

BORN	23 October 1978, Ashington, Northumberland, England
TESTS	57
WICKETS	212 at 31.39
ONE-DAY INTERNATIONALS	46
WICKETS	67 at 30.70

51

· · · · · · ·

CHRIS CAIRNS

CHRIS WAS ONE OF THE BEST entertainers of my time in international cricket, and with better luck on the injury front, he could have gone down as one of the all-time great all-rounders, up there with Beefy Botham, Keith Miller, Kapil Dev, etc. Like Beefy and later Freddie Flintoff, he was a larger-than-life character who dragged the rest along.

When he gave up Test cricket, he had hit more sixes than anybody else at Test level, and when you realise that number two in the list was no less a batsman than Viv Richards, it puts that achievement into context. Adam Gilchrist and Brian Lara have since overtaken him, but Cairns has a better ratio than either of them – 87 in 62 matches. And batting was only half of his game. He was a clever bowler who could swing the ball around at a good pace. He played for New Zealand for 15 years, but after all the ups and downs, he still managed to finish with a batting average greater than his bowling figure, the best indication, in my opinion, of a true all-rounder.

With some batsmen, you remember innings, but in the case of Cairns it is shots that spring to mind – and not many of the forward-defensive variety. The most incredible of them came in a Test match in Hamilton. He put his front leg into the rough outside leg stump, swivelled around so that he faced square leg and whacked the ball as it turned in on the angle. It soared over the square-leg boundary. There aren't many situations that leave me lost for words, but this shot had to be admired. Basically, it was a straight drive out of the rough over square leg. Amazing. That shot was probably the best stroke anyone played off my bowling.

Physically, he was very strong. Again, there is a good comparison with Flintoff. Coming from a cricketing family, he was identified as a talent at an early age, and he could be a formidable competitor. It is no coincidence that when New Zealand took the ICC Champions Trophy in Nairobi in 2000, it came on the back of a Cairns hundred in the final against India. He had also been their most economical bowler. I know that Stephen Fleming always wanted him in the side. Chris had the ability to inspire the rest of the guys with his presence and example.

In his early days, he was a bit of a rebel, and I'm not sure he always knew the cause. I'm not sure, either, that he was handled particularly well by some of the New Zealand bosses, who didn't realise that he needed a bit of leeway and space. But later in his career, he helped to end a players' strike; I guess that is all part of growing up. It was a great shame that he decided to end his one-day career a year or so before the 2007 World Cup, because he desperately wanted to play. Chris was an amazing and awesome cricketer, who entertained when he played, and any New Zealand team with Chris Cairns in it was a strong one. Early on, Chris and I had some run-ins, but as time went on and we got to know each other, we developed a good friendship. I admired the way he played the game. He was a real competitor and fun to play against, and I also enjoyed the way he went about getting his runs.

CHRIS LANCE CAIRNS

BORN	13 June 1970, Picton, Marlborough, New Zealand
TESTS	62
RUNS	3,320 in 104 innings at 33.53 with 5 hundreds/22 fifties
WICKETS	218 at 29.40
ONE-DAY INTERNATIONALS	215
RUNS	4,950 in 193 innings at 29.46 with 4 hundreds/26 fifties
WICKETS	201 at 32.80

52

·······

BRIAN MCMILLAN

THERE IS STRONG, THERE IS ROCK hard and then there is Brian McMillan. However, the more we played against Brian, the more I realised that, although it was well hidden, he did have a soft side and that like most of the best competitors he was ready to forget allegiances and share a couple of beers in the dressing-room whatever the result. He was probably the best all-rounder in the world when I started my Test career, and he finished a few years later with his batting average still higher than his bowling figure. He lost maybe four or five years at that level because of the ban on South Africa. Otherwise, he would have played a lot more international cricket and left an even bigger mark.

He was not always comfortable against spin bowling and preferred pace. However much he was struggling, though, he never tried to slog his way out of trouble, even though he liked to score at a good pace and could be a destructive one-day player. He liked to play on his intimidating presence. He was tall, broad-shouldered and liked to get in your face. We called him 'Depardieu' after the French actor with the big nose. McMillan didn't like that one. He threatened to make me disappear when we went back for a return series in South Africa. I laughed it off, but one lunch time at Johannesburg, he stormed into the players' dining area waving a gun and screaming: 'I've had enough of you guys.'

It seriously seemed as though he had flipped and had lost the plot; we all shit ourselves. This went on for a few seconds as his face went redder and redder. And then he burst out laughing. 'Only joking, boys, only joking,' he said. I wonder whether a firearm would transgress the

ICC Code of Conduct. Probably not – they're more worried about the serious stuff, such as the size of advertising logos on bats.

For a big guy, he was an incredible slip fielder. He did have enormous hands, but how he managed to get down to some of the low catches, I don't know. I would rank him right up there with Mark Taylor, Mark Waugh and Stephen Fleming. He also used his position close to the wicket to offer advice about your batting, or in other words sledge you!

The funny thing is that McMillan never hit the ball as hard as you would expect a big man to. He preferred to caress the ball rather than whack it. And when he bowled, he always tested out the bounce in the wicket and got his quota of short balls in. Big Mac was really important to the South Africa team because of the balance he offered, and he could probably have played as a batsman in his own right.

He never scored a hundred against Australia, but he was a good player off his legs against the quicks, and I remember an innings at Cape Town in 1994 when he batted more than four hours to score seventy-four to slow us down when we were on a bit of a roll. That was an example of the way he could dig in when he clearly wasn't finding batting very easy. South Africa had a pretty negative mindset at the time and did not always kick on from decent positions. For all that, they were very hard to beat, and McMillan was one of the toughest obstacles they placed in our way. To me, Mac was a good guy who loved the challenges that were presented to him, meeting them head on.

BRIAN MERVIN MCMILLAN

BORN	22 December 1963, Welkon, South Africa
TESTS	38
RUNS	1,968 in 62 innings at 39.36 with 3 hundreds/13 fifties
WICKETS	75 at 33.82
ONE-DAY INTERNATIONALS	78
RUNS	841 in 52 innings at 23.36 with 1 hundred
WICKETS	70 at 36.98

53

• • • • • • •

MOHAMMAD YOUSUF

IT TOOK MOHAMMAD YOUSUF A FEW years to step up from being a good player to a world class one. He's a bit like Shivnarine Chanderpaul that way, although their styles are as different as chalk and cheese. While I thought that Yousuf had some talent, I wasn't so sure that he would end up hitting the heights of the past four to five years. His improvement has been incredible. He developed so much that in 2006 he scored more runs than any player ever before in a calendar year. Viv Richards held the previous record, to put Yousuf's achievement into context. True, there is more international cricket than ever these days, but during 2006 Yousuf did not play against Zimbabwe or Bangladesh and hit nine hundreds in all. Two of them were in England, including a double at Lord's, so he starred in different conditions. In fact, the more you analyse those performances, the more impressive the feat becomes. Pakistan have produced some great and natural batsmen down the years, but Yousuf has to rank up there with them, and he certainly sits in the best half-dozen or so in the world today.

When somebody kicks on from performing at a lower level, you are bound to look for a turning point. My old mate Bob Woolmer, now sadly no longer with us, thought that it came when Yousuf converted to Islam in 2005. Woolmer was the Pakistan coach at the time, and he said that the player's approach to batting changed. He became calmer, more relaxed and clearer in the way he thought. I had a lot of respect for Bob – and so did everyone in the game – so there is probably something in what he said. Personally, I am just not qualified to comment on that area. Maybe Yousuf felt more comfortable in the dressing-room after he took that decision, but it was probably a case of a combination of things coming together over a period of months. I can certainly remember an innings against Australia at Melbourne in the Boxing Day Test in 2004 that a few guys at the time thought could mark an important turning point in Yousuf's career.

I might not be an authority on religions of the world, but I do know that he batted really well on that occasion and belted me for three straight sixes. He clearly wanted to lead by example as a stand-in captain. He played beautifully with Younus Khan, another guy with a bit of style and quality about his play. The crowd gave him a great ovation when he got to his hundred. Can one innings turn a career? I think it can. Does Andrew Symonds in the World Cup in 2003 ring any bells? Yousuf didn't need runs to save his place, but it might have given him confidence to be able to play in that free, expressive way against the best sides. Up to then, there was a feeling that he only really imposed himself against weaker attacks and didn't feel he was able to do the same against the ones with bigger reputations.

If anybody had thought he was soft, he lost that tag in Melbourne. I've noticed since that he's played some of his biggest innings when the chips are down – in England during his golden year, for example, when I kept a good track of the series when I was playing with Hampshire. At Lord's and Headingley, he dragged Pakistan out of serious trouble. He is a very strong off-side batsman and looks to play late, a good method in England if the ball is moving. He has very deft hands that allow him to be able to place the ball between fielders. And he always looks like a gentle batsman. He does not appear to really whack the ball, but his timing is so good that he can stroke it sweetly enough to get to the boundary.

Woolmer told me that Yousuf is really big on practice. He said that Yousuf worked out daily by getting somebody to bounce the ball off a special marble-topped slab to generate the steepling angle and pace of a tall fast bowler. That definitely sounds like one of Bob's innovations, but it hasn't done Yousuf any harm. He has also worked on his fielding to become competent, because a weak throw can be a liability. As he doesn't bowl, either – not even a bit of spin, like many Asian batsmen – it is probably just as well that he is so strong at his main job.

Even before his emergence over the past four or five years, his story was inspirational. His family were so poor that he couldn't afford a bat, and he learned the game playing with planks of wood in the streets. At one point later on, he pretty much had to give up for a year to earn some money. The system in Pakistan looks amazing to outsiders, but I wonder how much talent never sees the light of day. Even so, they always find enough players to stay competitive and on their day beat anyone if everything fires at the same time. The selectors are happy to pick guys young and see if they sink or swim. I must admit that I wondered which group Yousuf would join when I first saw him in about 1998. He came over to Australia a year later and looked far more convincing, with a couple of good innings in Brisbane on a very good pitch. Looking back now, I wonder how there could have been any doubt. He is a very good all-round player.

MOHAMMAD YOUSUF

BORN	27 August 1974, Lahore, Pakistan
TESTS	79
RUNS	6,770 in 134 innings at 55.49 with 23 hundreds/28 fifties
ONE-DAY INTERNATIONALS	269
RUNS	9,242 in 254 innings at 43.18 with 15 hundreds/62 fifties

54

·······

MICHAEL VAUGHAN

MICHAEL VAUGHAN COULD HAVE RETIRED AFTER the 2005 Ashes. It must have been a tempting thought, and I reckon there would have been times during the next 18 months when he seriously thought about packing it in after going through rehabilitation following a third knee operation only to find that surgery hadn't done the trick. It says a lot for his mental strength and quiet determination that he knuckled down through yet another long recovery to start the campaign to get the Ashes back in 2006–07, but as a player not the captain.

The 2005 summer was fantastic for cricket because crowds went up, young kids were drawn to the game and people who didn't follow cricket became absorbed by the contest. I'd be taking the point a bit too far if I described the loss as being good for Australia, but it certainly made us look at our own game a bit more closely than might have been the case if we had drawn or won. England, on the other hand, rested on their laurels and went about business as though they had achieved everything they wanted instead of recognising victory as the starting point. That was the way we looked at things after beating the West Indies in 1995.

I do not know how much of 2005 was down to Vaughan as captain, but I would say he played a huge part. I also don't know whether the result in the 2006–07 series would have been anything other than a 5–0 whitewash had he been fit enough to take charge. I doubt it, because we were up for it with bat and ball and took our chances ruthlessly when they came along. Nobody should underestimate how much we wanted to win that series. Injuries are part and parcel of sport – England had the luck on that front in

2005 when they got through the first four Tests unchanged, whereas we suffered from the freak accident when Glenn McGrath hurt his ankle before the toss at Edgbaston.

There I go. I hadn't planned to ramble on about 2005, but once I start, I keep thinking back to moments here and there. It was a great series. Vaughan has described it as the best in the history of the game and was very kind about my own role in it when he asked how I could have been on the losing side with 40 wickets and nearly 250 runs. Both teams played fiercely out in the middle but mixed afterwards and enjoyed each other's company in the dressing-rooms. I would love that to be the norm rather than the exception.

Vaughan will now go down as the most succesful England captain, but I think he deserves to be remembered for more than those few weeks. He is a very tough competitor behind that calm exterior and a very rational, unemotional bloke when it comes to making decisions. He decided that the best way to beat us was to take us on, starting with the Twenty20 at the Rose Bowl and then throughout the one-day series. I sensed quite early on that the batsmen wanted to be more positive against me than England players had been in the past. Vaughan's view was that if I beat him with a leg-break, then so what? He wasn't going to get into a defensive mindset as a result. They were also pretty good at rotating the strike, so I didn't get long periods of trying to wear down the same guy.

There are similarities between Nasser Hussain handing over to Vaughan and the way that Allan Border passed our captaincy to Mark Taylor, having dragged us from the depths. They did the right thing in going for young players who had not been scarred by losing previous Ashes campaigns.

But when I think of Vaughan, I look beyond captaincy. In 2002–03 in Australia, he batted as well as any opponent over the course of several games with the exceptions of Sachin Tendulkar and Brian Lara. He is a lovely looking batsman, very upright and stylish, especially when he drives. And he always looks like he has a plan. There is a theory in England that batsmen from the north have softer hands because they grow up on damper pitches. There could easily be something in that, because Vaughan at his best has impeccable timing, playing the ball late and stroking rather than forcing it away. His hundred at Sydney in the 'dead' fifth Test was immaculate.

As a man, I have found him to be a very straight talker and easy company, whether he is chatting about cricket or life in general. He is a genuinely good bloke. He does not worry too much about his game, which is a sign that he has confidence in his technique to get him through any trouble he might be having. His resigning as captain of England came as a shock to a lot of us, but he has the ability to bounce back and still be a significant player for England. I also remember a really nice gesture when I took my 600th Test wicket at Old Trafford in 2005. He was at the non-striker's end to Marcus Trescothick, and he made a point of coming down the pitch as we were celebrating to shake my hand. That was typical of the sportsmanship that summer, and of his class.

MICHAEL PAUL VAUGHAN

BORN	29 October 1974, Manchester, England
TESTS	79
RUNS	5,679 in 147 innings at 42.69 with 18 hundreds/18 fifties
WICKETS	6 at 93.50
ONE-DAY INTERNATIONALS	86
RUNS	1,982 in 83 innings at 27.15 with 16 fifties
WICKETS	16 at 40.56

55

·······

MOHAMMAD AZHARUDDIN

IT WASN'T EXACTLY A PLEASURE TO be smacked around the park by Mohammad Azharuddin, but if I had to pick a single batsman to hit the ball about with, he would be up there with the best of them. He was such an elegant player, the sort who could probably only have come from India, with his great 'wristiness'. When V.V.S. Laxman started to make an impact, the comparisons were inevitable, although Azharuddin played for longer and also had the extra responsibility of captaincy. Unlike Laxman, he did not score as freely against Australia as other countries for the most part, but when he batted for any length of time, you could be sure his performance would stick in the memory. I have ranked him above batsmen with better figures because he was an entertainer, the sort of player who would encourage kids to go to their nearest sports shop, buy a bat and get playing – even though they used to say that Azharuddin used a wand rather than a piece of willow.

He had a reputation of playing spin well, as I discovered very early in my career. Having been taught a few lessons by Ravi Shastri and Sachin Tendulkar on my debut, I then suffered at the hands of Azharuddin in my second game at Adelaide – at which point the selectors thought it was time for me to take a breather. Out of curiosity, I looked up his innings on the Internet while I was writing this piece, just to see how quickly he reached his hundred. It came in 144 balls, which might not sound special these days but at the time was considered electric. I remember the shots better than the figures – the cuts, pulls and drives. We had opened up a big lead in the third innings, and Azharuddin decided to go for his strokes with nothing to lose. He kept on going, and India almost reached their target.

The feeling was that he struggled against very quick bowling, especially the short ball. He began his Test career with hundreds in three successive matches, but they were all on home soil with low, slow bounce. Expectations were high, but he found things more difficult in different conditions, and the great West Indian quicks at the time caused him problems with the bouncer. I've always thought that a good, well-directed bouncer will trouble anyone – it isn't a nice ball to receive – but Azharuddin never managed to entirely shrug off the reputation. That did not stop him from hooking, and we used to feel we had a chance of getting the wicket if we put two men out on the boundary. He didn't mind hitting the ball in the air in any case, and he was not always in control when he shaped to play the stroke.

The plan was less effective in India. We didn't win a series over there until Azharuddin's career was over. His record at Eden Gardens is amazing. He scored a lot of runs there over the course of his career, and on one occasion in 1998 he took three fours and a six from a single over of mine on his way to another hundred. Thanks, Azza.

If you bowled straight and full, he would whip you through midwicket as though you had strayed onto leg. He could stroke the ball without looking as though he was really hitting it with any force. The key was fantastic reflexes and a terrific eye for the ball, which also enabled him to be a brilliant catcher at slip. People in England rated him especially highly because he reserved some of his best innings for their bowlers. He was also a really good one-day player. When he stopped playing, he had more runs in the shorter form of the game than any other batsman, and he was also the first player to notch 300 appearances. It was a very different game when he stopped than when he started, but his own princely ability made him a serious player from first to last.

As a Muslim, it was a big thing for him when he became captain of the national side. He was the most successful Indian skipper until Sourav Ganguly broke his record. Azharuddin took a while to realise that he needed to be firmer in charge and had to be slightly aloof from the rest. Sometimes that was perhaps misinterpreted. There was a lot of responsibility on his shoulders and nothing that a humble background would have prepared him for. I always liked him as a bloke, as did the rest of us in the Australia dressing-room. He was a shy, modest guy who spoke softly but took great pride in his appearance and turned himself out immaculately on and off the field.

MOHAMMAD AZHARUDDIN

BORN	8 February 1963, Hyderabad, Andra Pradesh, India
TESTS	99
RUNS	6,215 in 147 innings at 45.03 with 22 hundreds/21 fifties
ONE-DAY INTERNATIONALS	334
RUNS	9,378 in 308 innings at 36.92 with 7 hundreds/58 fifties

56

· · · · · · ·

DAMIEN MARTYN

DAMIEN MARTYN TOOK US ALL BY surprise when he announced his retirement from cricket during the 2006–07 Ashes series and promptly left the country. He decided to step down his way. That was Martyn to a tee. He wasn't too bothered about conventions or formalities. Marto and I started first-class cricket at around the same time. We were at the Academy together and our international careers started at roughly the same time. We were the two young guys in the team in the early 1990s and hung out together a lot. Marto and I were pretty tight as mates, and he was one of the most talented players I saw. Personally, I've never seen him in anything other than a good light, going right back to the days when we were breaking into the Test side as the first graduates of the Academy in Adelaide.

At his best, there were few more attractive players in the world, let alone Australia. He was a beautiful timer of the ball, a real stroke-maker in the middle order. In the early days, a lot was expected of him, and he made an impact in the Test side at a young age. Unfortunately, it seemed he took the rap for a poor all-round batting display against South Africa at Sydney in 1994 when he went into his shell a little bit as we chased a small target. We fell just short, and people started to question whether he had the temperament to succeed at that level after all. To me, he was the scapegoat, and it wasn't fair. He was only twenty-two at the time, didn't quite know how to handle it and had to wait another six years for a second chance. He didn't know himself or his game at that stage.

When he returned, he admitted it had been a long, hard slog, but he did enough to keep his place and really took off in England in 2001 with hundreds at Edgbaston and Headingley. The amazing thing is that he scored his maiden hundred in his 12th Test, more than eight years after his debut. It is an old cliché, I know, but the game really was the winner, because it would have been a travesty if cricket lovers outside Australia had not seen him in full flow. For the first Test in England that summer, the selectors had a tough call to make between Martyn and Justin Langer, two guys from Western Australia who were often confused because of their similar looks. In the end, they went for Martyn at number six, with Ricky Ponting moving up to three. He repaid that faith, and the comfortable win in the series was the best justification of all. Martyn had worked hard to get back into the side – not that Langer ever lacked anything in the hard work department – and he was perfect for number six, because he had the shots to be able to punish any attack.

He would generally keep the gully fielders interested, but he was also capable of making some of the hardest shots in the book look easy with his great timing. He scored runs all over the world and was one of our leading stars in India in 2004 when we finally broke our bogey. I remember him hitting Anil Kumble out of the attack on the way to a hundred at Nagpur, but an innings in the previous game at Chennai was just as important, because it helped us to save a Test from a difficult position. You would not imagine it was possible to be so elegant in defence. There were some fantastic players on both sides over those few weeks, but Martyn stood comparison with any of them. He sometimes lacked a bit of confidence in his own ability, which struck me as strange. He had an amazing talent and that X-factor. He was a very dangerous player.

In one-day cricket, he became a very effective number four, a buffer between the explosive openers and Ricky Ponting and the second wave of big-hitters and finishers to come afterwards. He was one of the best in the world at working the ball into spaces and rotating strike, an ideal partner for a guy such as Andrew Symonds, who could bash it over the ropes. A good example of him at his best was the 2003 World Cup final when he batted with Ponting through the second half of the innings. His contribution to that stand was easy to overlook.

DAMIEN MARTYN

Away from the game, he grew up quickly in his 20s, so by the time he came back into the side, he had matured. Around the turn of the decade, as part of the team-bonding process, we would take it in turns to talk to the rest of the squad about a subject of interest. Martyn spoke about how he survived Cyclone Tracy in Darwin on Christmas Eve, 1974. He was only three years old and got through the ordeal with the rest of his family by sheltering under a dining-room table before being evacuated to Perth in a military plane. We were all gripped by the story. The other thing about Marto was that he was a very funny man and always great company. He was a good team man and could adapt to any situation.

DAMIEN RICHARD MARTYN

BORN	21 October 1971, Darwin, Australia
TESTS	67
RUNS	4,406 in 109 innings at 46.37 with 13 hundreds/23 fifties
ONE-DAY INTERNATIONALS	208
RUNS	5,346 in 182 innings at 40.80 with 5 hundreds/37 fifties

57

•••••••

TIM MAY

OF ALL THE SPINNERS I PLAYED with, my favourite to bowl with in tandem was Tim May. That might be partly because he was at the other end on my first Ashes tour in 1993 when we struck up a really good partnership. I have very fond memories of that trip. There is a good balance between a leggie at one end and an off-spinner at the other, because the ball turns different ways and asks different questions of the batsmen. If the selectors pick two spinners, in a perfect world you would have an offie and a leggie, although I reckon things worked pretty effectively with me and Stuart MacGill as well. There is no doubt in my mind that May's input into that victory in 1993 has always been overlooked. The media focused on the new kid on the block, and I guess I must have seemed a little bit different in those days, especially in England, where leg-spin had all but died out. Within the squad, though, May was certainly recognised as one of our major players.

It was a terrible summer for England on all sorts of levels. I remember in particular how they got themselves into an incredible mess at Edgbaston even before the game began. They picked four seamers and sent out instructions for the groundsman to prepare a helpful green track. When they arrived, it was white and bare. The day before, they had to call up John Emburey, who by the way was England's best spinner at the time, along with Shaun Udal. May's first ball spun big. I remember he caused Matthew Maynard all sorts of trouble on his first Test for five years and Maynard, as anybody from Glamorgan will know, was quite a good player of spin at first-class level. We took five wickets each in the second innings and bowled nearly one hundred overs between us. God, we were knackered at the end of it. But what a great example of spinners working as a pair.

He was not one of those 'offies' who speared the ball into the legs to keep an end tight. He gave it a genuine rip from an attacking line outside of off stump, encouraging the drive, and his spinning finger – unusually the middle one in his case – was often gashed after a long bowl. He had the perfect side-on action, which meant that very little could go wrong with it. Even when the wickets did not come, he was able to maintain his accuracy, so it was very rare for him to get collared. You could pick him in a one-day match, knowing that he would give you control. But he hated fielding. It wasn't that he was too bad at it; he just didn't like the ball coming to him. At Lord's in 1993, he was at fine leg when Graham Gooch hooked one high into the air. The ball stayed up for ages, and May got himself into such an anxious state that by the time he held the catch he'd forgotten who he had helped to dismiss.

On that tour, the squad split into teams of 'Nerds' and 'Julios' for things such as warm-up battles and the little contests that go on off the field to keep things running smoothly, such as tenpin bowling, fancy-dress events or golf days. The 'Julios' were named after Julio Iglesias. They – I should say we – were the ones who tried to look good and took care of their appearances. The 'Nerds' didn't bother too much about how they looked, and Messrs Taylor, (Steve) Waugh and May were the senior Nerds. For a while, May was the 'King Nerd'.

He almost turned the game the first time we played together, against the West Indies at Adelaide in 1993. They beat us by one run when we needed one hundred and eighty-six to win. We were eight down for one hundred and two. May and Craig McDermott shared a good partnership, only for McDermott to glove a short one through to the keeper. The tension in our dressing-room was incredible – probably on a par with the Edgbaston match in 2005. That was a great introduction for me to the bravery of Tim May, because he stayed out there with an injured hand. He had also taken five for nine in their second innings. I think he was batting on air displacement at one stage.

He is very bright, the sort of partner you want when you are playing Trivial Pursuit. These days, he does some really good work for the cricketers' associations. His diplomacy helped to avoid a strike in 1997–98 when the Australia players were in dispute with our board over the way that money coming into the game was split. I imagine that he can be a tough negotiator, but he is always very fair, and he has the interests of the cricketers and the game overall at heart. On that occasion, it was not just a case of Test players trying to get an increase in pay. We wanted to put a system in place that was good for all of Australian cricket, and Shield players also felt the benefits.

His quick brain made him a good source of sledging on the field. There was a game against New Zealand in Hobart when we were being held up by Ken Rutherford, who was playing the odd shot, and Blair Pocock, a stubborn opening batsman who was really struggling. When they somehow managed to get their stand up to 50, the man on the public-address system offered his congratulations and the details of the partnership. As May passed Pocock, he said: 'It had nothing to do with you.' It must have roused Pocock, because next ball he ran down the pitch to try to hit me over the top – and gave Ian Healy a stumping instead. 'Doink', or 'Maysie' as we liked to call him, was a great guy to have around the dressing-room. He was a funny and positive person, and his off-spin was good as it gets.

TIMOTHY BRIAN ALEXANDER MAY

BORN	26 January 1962, Adelaide, Australia
TESTS	24
WICKETS	75 at 34.74
ONE-DAY INTERNATIONALS	47
WICKETS	39 at 45.43

58

• • • • • • •

ANDREW SYMONDS

IT IS AMAZING TO THINK THAT as recently as a few years ago Andrew Symonds was in and out of the Australia one-day side, with pundits questioning whether he had what it took to hold his own at that level. Look at him today: a middle-order blaster who has destroyed the best attacks in the world, an outstanding fielder and a bowler who can switch from seam to spin depending on the needs of the occasion. He is arguably the best all-round one-day player in the world. The Hyderabad franchise certainly thought so when it came to the eagerly anticipated auction for the Indian Premier League. Every franchise seemed to fancy Symonds, and the bidding went up, up and away until finally stopping at a cool $1.35 million. Back home, Symonds shrugged his shoulders and got on with life.

His big breakthrough came at the 2003 World Cup in South Africa when he cracked a hundred at better than a run a ball in Australia's first game against Pakistan. He came in at a difficult period and stuck it out against a good, experienced bowling attack before starting to really fire in the closing stages. He had batted like that before but not for so long and not in such an important game. Over the next three years, he established himself so firmly that he became one of the first names on the team sheet. In fact, it was only when he injured tendons in his arm and had to sit out a few games that people started to appreciate just how important he had become. With his clean hitting, especially straight, he would be worth a place as a batsman alone, but his versatility gives the side so many options.

I know that people in England expected him to make an impact earlier in his career. He took a lot of criticism in the mid-1990s for his decision to commit to Australia, having played county cricket and being qualified to play for England. But after chatting to people during my own years on the circuit, I know that the Gloucestershire crew remember him very fondly – not just because of his big hitting, which once included sixteen sixes in a single innings – but for his attitude towards practice and his strong work ethic. He rubbed off well on the other players around the club at the time. In part, he is one of those on a long list who was denied a place in the Australia side because of the depth of talent around. Perhaps the way we were configured for so long with six batsmen and four bowlers also counted against him. He was judged as a pure batsman, not a batting all-rounder, which would be the best description of him in the five-day game.

His Test career has been a bit like his progress at one-day level. Again, he found it a struggle at first. He came into the side in Sri Lanka, which can be a tricky place even for experienced players, with Muttiah Muralitharan turning the ball big distances both ways. But, again, he eventually chose a good time to lay down a marker with a hundred against England at Melbourne in 2006. We had already taken a 3–0 lead in the series, but our eyes were on a whitewash, and we were struggling in what looked like being a low-scoring contest when he came out. He grew in confidence gradually, and it was fitting that his great fishing buddy from Queensland, Matthew Hayden, was there with him when he reached his maiden hundred. Somehow Hayden managed to lift Symonds off the ground, which tells you a lot about the strength of our great opening batsman.

Symonds is a seriously tough man. You wouldn't mess with him. What you see is what you get, and off the field he is as uncomplicated as he is at the crease. I think he's a pretty impressive individual. When he was done after his famous late night in Cardiff in 2005, he fronted up straight away rather than pretending that nothing had happened. He learned from that experience. And he was never one for John Buchanan's motivational books or left-field ideas as coach, just sticking to the principle that cricket is a game best kept simple. He wants to give the ball a whack, but as the years have gone on, he's become better at judging those to hit and the ones to treat with a bit more care. There is also more thought in his bowling, with a good mix of deliveries. He has a terrific eye, and there are not many fielders who hit the stumps as regularly.

ANDREW SYMONDS

The humour in him probably doesn't come across. He helps the dressing-room to tick over, and his impression of Geoff Boycott is uncanny. I don't know where he picked that up from – probably his time in England, where he is always in demand as an overseas player. Although he is heading towards his mid-30s, I think he has another World Cup in him and will keep on getting better at Test level. His knowledge of English conditions will be important in 2009. Up to now, he has been competing with Shane Watson for the all-rounder's slot; indeed, if Watson had not been injured at key moments, Symonds might not have had his opportunity in the side. I don't know whether it is realistically possible, but if the two of them play in the same side, it will open up all sorts of possibilities for the selectors.

ANDREW SYMONDS

BORN	9 June 1975, Birmingham, England
TESTS	22
RUNS	1,295 in 34 innings at 44.65 with 2 hundreds/9 fifties
WICKETS	23 at 36.47
ONE-DAY INTERNATIONALS	193
RUNS	5,006 in 157 innings at 40.37 with 6 hundreds/29 fifties
WICKETS	129 at 37.68

59

·······

CRAIG MCDERMOTT

CRAIG MCDERMOTT WAS ONE OF THE new-ball bowlers when I came into the side. He seemed to have been around for a few years, but he was still only in his mid-20s – they called him 'Billy the Kid' when he first played for Queensland at 17. By that stage, he knew his game inside out, and when conditions were in his favour, he could be devastating. A really good side-on action helped him to swing the ball away, and he had good pace as well – any bowler who can do those things consistently has a great chance of making an impact. However, if things did not suit him, he lost a bit of his effectiveness. He was not like Merv Hughes, for example, who could almost get you a wicket through sheer willpower and determination alone.

The 1994–95 Ashes will have to go down as his best series; he bowled beautifully. McDermott took 32 wickets and won the Man of the Series award. He had been desperate to do well in England in 1993, because he was on the tour eight years earlier when we lost and then missed out in 1989. Unfortunately, he picked up a terrible injury in 1993. We were sitting in the Lord's dressing-room when we suddenly heard these groans. It sounded like the noise you hear in old haunted-house films, and I wondered if the ghost of W.G. Grace had come back with a message. But it was really serious. McDermott was gasping for air and hardly able to move because he was in so much agony. The problem turned out to be a twisted bowel – thankfully not an injury you hear about every day – and it was pretty obvious that he wouldn't be playing any more that summer. Anyway, by the time we got to Brisbane for the first Test in 1994, McDermott was like a greyhound after a rabbit, wanting to chase the Poms out of town.

England had a crazy idea that series of trying to take us on with pace. To pick Devon Malcolm was fair enough, but they also went for Martin McCague, who was raised in Australia and known to most of us from his days of state cricket.

McDermott was brilliant all the way through that series. I don't think I had ever seen him bowl with the same fire and aggression before. What made it more impressive was the fact that he had three different new-ball partners in Damien Fleming, Glenn McGrath when he was new to Test cricket and not yet the force he would become, and Jo Angel, who was on the fringes for a couple of years or so. McDermott just puffed out his chest as if to say 'I'm in charge here'. I remember the final Test at Perth when we wanted to wrap up the series in style. At one point, he bowled with seven catchers around the bat, and he ended the game by knocking Devon Malcolm's middle stump clean out of the ground. You don't get much more emphatic than that, and McDermott gave the Poms a real touch and showed his class.

He was also the victim of one of the best pranks I've seen pulled on a cricket field, at Bristol during the 1993 tour. 'Billy' had made a pretty average start to the trip, and it looked as though a lack of wickets might be getting him down. He used to take a lot of friendly ribbing about the size of his ears, so somebody thought it would ease a bit of his tension if we set him up for a trick. We found a joke shop and bought ten sets of big clown's ears, then took them out into the middle in our pockets until the appropriate moment. The cue came as he was walking back to his mark. As he turned, set in concentration, he looked up to see all of the fielders wearing these huge ears that made our faces resemble the FA Cup. It took a few minutes before the laughter died down and he could bowl again.

Away from Australia, he did struggle at times. He suffered a bit from homesickness. People saw this big, strapping bloke, a fast bowler with red hair who appeared to have everything in his favour, but they didn't appreciate the uncertainties he felt behind his confident appearance. A combination of his raw talent and the guts of Merv Hughes would have given you a 500-wicket Test bowler.

Having said that, I really believe that you have to take people for what they are and appreciate their strengths.

He still has one of the best records for an Australian fast bowler. By the time he retired, only Dennis Lillee had taken more Test wickets. McDermott came into the side at a time when Allan Border was beginning to turn things around but results were still not great, and that can be pretty dispiriting for a young guy starting out, especially when he is built up as the next big thing. He was a really important player for Australia because of his role in helping us climb back up the ladder. His record deserves every respect.

CRAIG JOHN MCDERMOTT

BORN	14 April 1965, Ipswich, Queensland, Australia
TESTS	71
WICKETS	291 at 28.63
ONE-DAY INTERNATIONALS	138
WICKETS	203 at 24.71

60

·······

MIKE HUSSEY

NOBODY DESERVES HIS SUCCESS IN THE Australia side more than Mike Hussey. The guy is absolutely committed to the game. He had to wait so long for his opportunity, but when it came, he cemented his place within a matter of months and grabbed his chance with both hands. The biggest tribute to him, which went unseen by the public, came in a quiet moment in the dressing-room after the final Ashes Test at Sydney in 2007 when Justin Langer handed down to Hussey the job of leading our victory song, 'Under the Southern Cross I Stand'. If there was any doubt in his mind – and there shouldn't have been – this honour meant that he was accepted as a regular member of the side and a top-class bloke who was trusted to follow in the steps of some of the best and toughest Australia players.

People in England were surprised that Hussey took so long to break into the side. He must have wondered himself whether he would take the next step, but he never, ever stopped working to give himself the best possible chance of success. By the time he made his debut for Australia, he had been playing for 11 years and had 15,000 first-class runs in the bank. During the past 20 years, we've been blessed with batsmen, and I've no doubt that in a different era he would have come in far earlier. The Victorian Brad Hodge was a very similar case. But the fact that he had to wait meant that he knew his game inside out by the time he was chosen. He also had the benefit of playing for eighteen months or so in the one-day side, so he wasn't going to be fazed by the big occasion. Within six months of his first innings, he had passed one thousand runs in Test cricket. I think he appreciates everything that has happened over the past three years, because his chance was so long in coming.

The nickname 'Mr Cricket', which was given to him by Andrew Symonds, is spot on. All the statistics, all the records and all the players: Hussey seems to know every one. And even now, as an established player, he trains as hard as anyone. He chose a great role model in Allan Border. As a kid, he switched from batting right to left-handed because he wanted to be like Border. There is another great story from his days as a club player in Perth when he asked Border for some advice. Tongue in cheek, Border suggested he should spend six hours in the nets to replicate batting for a whole day. Hussey did exactly that – even breaking for forty minutes at lunch and twenty minutes at tea. And I don't have first-hand experience of this, but his roommates have said that he talks in his sleep as though he is batting at the crease and calling his partner for a run.

As well as his dedication, versatility is another big asset. He spent most of his career as an opener but has become a top-class middle-order player for Australia. That was the spot that became available, and he wasn't going to turn it down. I believe, though, that Australia are best balanced when Hussey is opening, which means that Shane Watson can play in the side. He can also switch easily between Test and one-day cricket. In 50-over matches he soon became our finisher, another Michael Bevan, timing his innings to perfection. His scoring rate is up there with the best, and he is a very unselfish player. And he showed in the IPL that he can go quicker again in Twenty20, blasting a hundred from 50 balls against an attack that included Brett Lee – and he played some great shots.

One of his innings I remember best came when we beat South Africa by two wickets in Johannesburg in 2006. The second innings was a nail-biting run chase, even though it was a 'dead' game in the series. Hussey, who was opening the batting, played a very clever, 'wristy' knock supporting Damien Martyn, two guys who came through the same club side in Perth and knew each other's games inside out. Hussey showed all of his strength through the leg side. The pitch was playing lots of tricks, but he showed real guts in the early stages, and when he said afterwards that he needed a bit of luck, I thought he was being modest.

His big ambition was always to score a hundred in the Boxing Day Test at the MCG, one of the great annual sporting occasions in Australia. He did it in stunning fashion against South Africa, with most of his runs coming after the fall of the ninth wicket – and this with Glenn McGrath as the last man. Looking to keep McGrath off the strike, he managed to go from 27 to 122 before being bowled by Makhaya Ntini, and he didn't just slog. His placement was excellent, and he drove a couple of sixes against Andre Nel, which left the bowler steaming. His adaptability is his real strength.

MICHAEL EDWARD KILLEEN HUSSEY

BORN	27 May 1975, Morley, Western Australia, Australia
TESTS	25
RUNS	2,325 in 42 innings at 68.38 with 8 hundreds/9 fifties
ONE-DAY INTERNATIONALS	90
RUNS	2,307 in 68 innings at 54.92 with 2 hundreds/14 fifties

61

· · · · · · ·

DESMOND HAYNES

YOU WOULDN'T IMMEDIATELY THINK OF BRACKETING Muttiah Muralitharan with Dessie Haynes, but in both cases I have the same picture in my mind: two men with big, sunny smiles. And why wouldn't you be happy playing cricket for a living in Barbados? Haynes is a bloke who just loves the game. He'd been on the international circuit for about 15 years by the time I came up against him at Test level, and he knew all the tricks of the trade. He was the rock in a team bubbling over with style but always put his dismissal behind him as soon as he unstrapped his pads. He didn't seem to have the mental hang-ups that can destroy players if they get too deep. As a kid, I remember watching him play with Gordon Greenidge, and it's easy to think of them together even now. They will go down as one of the greatest opening partnerships in the game and Haynes as one of the most popular of the many cricketers to come from his island. He had all the shots and was an attacking player always looking to score!

He was the link between eras from the West Indies side around the time that Kerry Packer's World Series came into being to the team in the mid-1990s when Brian Lara was top dog. Their line-up around 1983–84 is reckoned to be one of the best of all time, and a lot of people would put them right at the top. Haynes was never the most glamorous of the batsmen, but he gave them perfect balance, with Greenidge and Viv Richards batting around him. The fact that he was an automatic selection throughout that time is a tribute to his ability, technique, resolve and sheer stubbornness. It is interesting that he forged a friendship with Geoff Boycott during his career, a bloke who was brought up to give nothing to bowlers.

In the field, he was different to a lot of the West Indians who would try to get at you with long, hard stares. I imagine making eye contact with Richards would have been a really scary experience for a young kid trying to make his way in Test cricket. I didn't play against Richards – and I would have loved to bowl to him – but Haynes took a different approach to get an advantage. His trick was to wind up Courtney Walsh or Curtly Ambrose by pretending that one of us had delivered an insult. You know, something like: 'That Warnie, he's just said you're not as quick as usual this morning.' As if I was likely to say any such thing within earshot!

A background of playing against West Indian fast bowlers in the Caribbean was bound to sort out the tough from the weak, so once Haynes came through that into the Test team, there couldn't be many questions about his bravery. I saw an example at Perth in 1993 when Jo Angel struck him on the grille of the helmet, which was forced back onto his cheek. Blood seeped out, and as Haynes had not been in great form through the series, it was an opportunity for him to go off and take stock while he cleared his mind. Our skipper, Allan Border, suggested he take a break, but when Haynes finally decided to go, it was only reluctantly. I found out afterwards that he had never retired hurt before in more than a hundred Tests – and needless to say he was back at the crease the next day.

He had the respect of all his bowlers because he never gave away his wicket, even when he was out of touch. He did not come out of that 1992–93 series with a great average, and he stopped playing a year or so later, but I remember Mikey Holding saying that Haynes was a really versatile batsman. He would drop anchor in the five-day game but then throw the kitchen sink at it in the fifty-over matches. That tells you he was a team player, a bloke who does what is needed in the situation. Of course, if the ball was there to be hit in the first over of a Test match, he would crash it as hard as any of them. He is deeply proud of his roots and has since helped with the enormous challenge of trying to lift the West Indies back towards the standing in the world game that he remembers.

I have got a lot of sympathy for the guys who have had to follow Haynes and Greenidge in the opening slots. Even if their cricket had not dropped off – and I don't know if that is as a result of new attractions such as soccer and basketball – they would have struggled to replace either of those two. A solid opening pair is so valuable to a team, because they help everything else slot into place. You don't want your stroke-makers in the middle order having to come up against the new ball, and that is why the Haynes defence was so important and never overlooked within his own side. Chris Gayle is more in what you think of as the Caribbean tradition – a bit more like Greenidge, I guess. They would love to have another Haynes up there alongside him today.

DESMOND LEO HAYNES

BORN	15 February 1956, Holders Hill, Barbados
TESTS	116
RUNS	7,487 in 202 innings at 42.29 with 18 hundreds/39 fifties
ONE-DAY INTERNATIONALS	238
RUNS	8,648 in 237 innings at 41.37 with 17 hundreds/57 fifties

62

·······

MIKE ATHERTON

IN A DIFFERENT ERA, MIKE ATHERTON might have been a completely different batsman. He had plenty of strokes in his armoury, but England seemed to require him to be their rock. I don't know if he ever thinks about the batsman he could have become in a successful, stable England side – a stylish number three, I believe. He was not one to worry about the ifs, buts and maybes in cricket.

He is a very intelligent guy, with some interesting ideas about the game. I can see why so many people thought he was destined to be a captain. Unfortunately, the state of the England side meant that the opportunity came a couple of years too early, before he was really ready, and his leadership was probably not as successful as the selectors or he had hoped. I do know that he had the respect of all the regulars in his side, who saw the great example he set as a batsman. On that score, he had the respect of everybody in our own dressing-room, too.

Athers was one of those batsmen you knew you had to get out. That might sound obvious, but what I mean is that he very rarely played a loose shot to give you an easy wicket. You had to earn his wicket. Even though Glenn McGrath had the wood on him throughout his career, the wickets fell as the result of good balls and not, as a rule, through a careless drive or pull. McGrath's length, just short of being full, left Atherton unsure whether to go forward or back, and he gave away a lot of little nicks behind, but as an opener you're going to be dismissed by the opening bowler more often than by a spinner, say. For sheer concentration, I would put him up there with guys such as Allan Border and David Boon.

197

The funny thing is that I actually enjoyed watching him bat. His style of batting has started to go out of fashion in Test cricket. But I think that every side needs an Atherton-type player. This is how you build a side, and you could never get at him with a chirp when he was batting. He seemed to be deaf to everything, although I reckon at times he had a little chuckle. He wasn't shy to make the odd comment himself when England were in the field, usually a word to a teammate within deliberate earshot of an opponent.

He took over the England captaincy at Edgbaston in 1993 and actually led his side to victory in the dead game at the Oval. There were no central contracts in those days, and the selectors used to chop and change the side as if they were pulling names from a hat. It must have been hard to captain England at that time. We used to wonder who they would come up with next. That made it very hard for Atherton to achieve any continuity. He must have despaired at times, and I'm sure it must have worn him down.

I was playing in the infamous game at Sydney in 1995 when Athers declared with Graeme Hick on 98 not out. Out in the field, we could not believe that he had called him in. I am a big believer in putting the needs of the team before any individual, but in this case it just looked as though something had gone wrong – a breakdown in communication perhaps. Hick didn't react as though he expected the declaration, because he was very upset, and I think the experience knocked him back when he was beginning to make the impact that everybody anticipated. I suppose there was a plan, and it showed that Athers was not afraid to make a tough decision for the team.

To me, Atherton was one of those really determined cricketers who loved to think of ways to improve the game. I think he has an excellent cricket brain, but don't be fooled: he is a very competitive guy and had a lot of strokes as a batsman. It was always a challenge to bowl to him.

Athers would be fantastic as England captain now, with the players they have. I always felt he was working towards a plan, whether I was watching at slip or bowling to him. With nearly 8,000 runs in Test cricket, he really did perform well at international level. I also think he enjoyed the battle of facing spinners, as it was a test of patience, wits and trying to read the ball. He is a good guy to have a beer with and has a very good sense of humour, which might surprise a few people.

MICHAEL ANDREW ATHERTON

BORN	23 March 1968, Manchester, England
TESTS	115
RUNS	7,728 in 212 innings at 37.69 with 16 hundreds/46 fifties
ONE-DAY INTERNATIONALS	54
RUNS	1,791 in 54 innings at 35.11 with 2 hundreds/12 fifties

63

·······

DANIEL VETTORI

THERE IS NO WAY I COULD fail to put in a few good words for Daniel Vettori. He ripped me out more times than any other bowler in Test cricket – nine times in all in fourteen matches. And there's no doubt in my mind what the worst of them was. I was on ninety-nine in Perth in 2001, but instead of doing the sensible thing and pushing the ball for an easy single to make sure I raised my bat, I went for glory and tried to whack it over mid-wicket for six. The ball sailed to the safe hands of Mark Richardson and that Test hundred never came. I was left asking myself why I'd gone for the bold approach.

Dan's strength as a bowler is his subtle change of pace. That's his big asset. His approach to the game mirrors his student-like appearance. We have had some good chats down the years, and even when he first started, with his long hair and teenage spots, his intelligence as a cricketer shone through. New Zealand didn't see any risk in picking him as an 18 year old or appointing him to succeed Stephen Fleming as captain. Vettori was lucky to have Flem as his skipper to guide him and show him the ropes, but he was also a really tough act to follow, especially with a number of other senior players going out at around about the same time. However, Vettori has stamped his own authority on the team without making a big song and dance about anything, and I expect him to be in charge for a long time as the cornerstone of a changing side.

You can see that he has learned from Fleming, especially in his calmness in the middle. I guess that comes down to character, but there are also times when you have to hold back your natural feelings, because your teammates do not want a leader who is not in control of his emotions. Having said that, it is harder to remain calm as a bowler, I think, because you feel personally the edges that drop short, the leg-before appeals that don't quite go your way and the strokes that go for runs without coming off the middle of the bat. Vettori also knows to let other players take responsibility for themselves. I noticed that Fleming always gave Vettori licence with his own field placings, and Vettori appreciated that trust.

The fact that he is a decent batsman – probably the best number eight in the world today – means that he also understands the way that his direct opponent is reading a game. When he bats, he does not think like a tail-ender, looking to either smash a few quick runs or hang in to provide a supporting role. He could easily move up a place in the New Zealand order, but it makes sense to have an experienced guy there as back-up while younger players bed in above him. The point is that because he thinks like a proper batsman, Vettori always has a shrewd idea when he bowls about the thought processes of the bloke at the other end.

Vettori always had potential as a player and a leader because of his maturity. He has developed into an all-rounder. I just like the way he goes about his game, thoughtful and attacking. He once took 12 wickets against us in a game at Auckland when he was only 21.

As a bowler, I am really pleased that he has started to get the credit he deserves in world terms over the past few years. I see him as a traditional left-arm spinner. He does not turn the ball as much as some of the other spinners in this book, but he creates problems with changes of angle, pace and flight, and his arm ball is second to none. He has not worried about the doosra, a ball that is phenomenally difficult to bowl without straightening the arm. These days, most batting sides are happy to play him out of the attack in one-day cricket, because there is a better chance of more adventurous shots coming off at the other end. At Test level, only Richard Hadlee has taken more wickets for New Zealand, so he sits in very good company.

There are times when he has had to be the strike and stock man in one. I was fortunate to play almost all of my Test career in the same side as Glenn McGrath, and it is a great shame – for world cricket, not just Vettori – that Shane Bond did not feature more often for New Zealand because of injuries. But Vettori is still not 30 – maybe he looks more like a mature student than an undergraduate these days – and has every chance of overtaking Hadlee's total of 431 wickets if his body holds up to all of the pressures. He has a great understanding of the game and a wonderful awareness of the way it is headed. I think he will be a very succesful captain for his country.

DANIEL LUCA VETTORI

BORN	27 January 1979, Auckland, New Zealand
TESTS	83
RUNS	2,745 in 123 innings at 26.65 with 2 hundreds/16 fifties
WICKETS	257 at 34.43
ONE-DAY INTERNATIONALS	219
RUNS	1,406 in 136 innings at 14.95 with 3 fifties
WICKETS	225 at 32.18

64

· · · · · · ·

SHIVNARINE CHANDERPAUL

UNTIL THE LAST COUPLE OF YEARS, Shivnarine Chanderpaul ranked as one of the most underrated batsmen in the world. Perhaps because he never took attacks apart or looked elegant when he scored his runs, he slipped under the radar, but he was always a bloke you needed to crowbar away from the crease. Now he is getting the credit he deserves after an unbelievable run of scores based on watertight defence. Three times in Test cricket, he has gone for more than 1,000 minutes without being dismissed. That takes exceptional concentration and patience, and the West Indies would have been in a real state without him to hold innings together since the retirement of Brian Lara. I'd guess that his temperament comes from his background. He was destined to play cricket from an early age and spent hours and hours as a kid batting in his little village in Guyana. Sounds like paradise.

He does look pretty unusual at the crease. His crab-like stance can really put you off as a bowler, because you feel you ought to bowl slightly differently to compensate. The key is to stick to your own methods. At the time the ball is released, Chanderpaul gets himself into a more orthodox position – and obviously there's nothing wrong with the shots themselves. A stance is like a signature, an individual thing, and I wonder how many of the great batsmen down the years have done everything to the letter of the MCC coaching manual. Not many, I'd suggest. Kim Barnett, who played for a few English counties, took little steps from outside leg stump as the bowler approached – he was like a fielder walking in. It was a trick to make you bowl the line he wanted; by the time he hit the ball he was pretty much on middle anyway and had a clear hit. Other guys have looked as though they were playing French cricket, facing you straight on.

We always thought of Chanderpaul as a very brave player. He looks younger than his age and is not a physically imposing man, but he hits the ball extremely hard. Away from the game, he is very humble and shy, but we found there were players in their side who had more of a strut but less of a backbone. The West Indies thought he was mentally strong enough to play as a teenager, and this at a time when their resources were deeper than they have been of late – although I think, happily, there are signs that they may be on the way back from rock bottom. He would not hurt you quickly, with the exception of a 69-ball hundred at his home ground in Georgetown during my enforced break, but if the ball was right in the slot, he would cut and pull, favourite shots of most short batsmen. We looked to bowl a bit fuller and wider to him to try to get him to play through the covers or try to shape the ball in for an lbw if it was swinging.

Not too many players can say they got absolutely everything out of their ability, but Chanderpaul belongs in that group. It is a tribute to the way that he keeps working on his game and his sheer enthusiasm for cricket and batting in particular. Captaincy was not really for him. He likes to concentrate on his own game – not in a selfish way, but to leave his mind uncluttered by the day-to-day things that crop up around the team. The only criticism to make is that I'd rather see him spend more time in the field. After a long innings, he generally finds a reason to get a substitute on in his place and takes the easy option to rest. It has happened too many times now for him to say that he needs treatment for a niggle.

In the early days, he had a very poor conversion rate, but he has recently started turning more of his fifties into hundreds. Although it took him a long time to make his first century, he was fairly consistent right from the start. Now he is still consistent but at a much more productive level. Another impressive factor to remember is that he has scored runs in all conditions. Some of the pitches in the West Indies can be dubious at the start of a match, so it needs decent technique to play well innings after innings out there. He has also scored hundreds in England and India, so his all-round game must be in pretty steady order. His record in Australia is not quite so good, but he has done as well as most against us in the Caribbean. Wrist spinners such as Anil Kumble and Danish Kaneria have had some success against him. He is a very experienced cricketer and knows his own game inside out.

SHIVNARINE CHANDERPAUL

BORN	16 August 1974, Unity Village, Demerara, Guyana
TESTS	112
RUNS	8,001 in 193 innings at 49.08 with 19 hundreds/49 fifties
ONE-DAY INTERNATIONALS	235
RUNS	7,573 in 221 innings at 40.49 with 8 hundreds/52 fifties

65

·······

CARL HOOPER

I DON'T LIKE USING THE WORD 'enigma' or writing that a cricketer has underachieved. It sounds too much like an insult. A lot of time and effort usually goes into making the game as far as your national side and as much again to stay there. Opponents get wise quickly, spot any sign of weakness and give no quarter on the field. But in the case of Carl Hooper, I think there he had much left to offer. He played more than 100 Tests for the West Indies, so nobody can say that he didn't have a career. With his raw talent, though, he could have become one of the great players who spread fear through a bowling attack when he walked out to bat. At times, the game just looked too easy for him.

He was so talented that unless he felt he was being properly challenged, he seemed to get bored at the crease. One of our tactics was to bring on a little medium-pacer such as Damien Martyn or one of the Waugh boys, hoping that he would lose concentration and relax. Steve Waugh actually got him out six times in Test matches, more than any other bowler except Merv Hughes. You'd have thought that Hooper might have got wise to that trick after the first couple of times, but he kept getting sucked into the trap instead. It was pretty weird to watch, and there were jokes about him being Waugh's bunny.

He played spinners better than any of the West Indies batsmen I came across, with the exception of Brian Lara. It would be a difficult call to separate them. A lot of the West Indians got themselves into either hitting or blocking mode. If they patted back a couple, there was a fair chance they would look to attack regardless of where the next ball landed. Hooper liked to attack as much as any of his colleagues, but he was also content to take the ones and twos in between. By picking the length early, he gave himself options, and he had enough shots to be able to find most of the gaps. He could sweep, drive inside out to open up areas in the off side with the spin or hit over the top if the field was up – even in some cases when it was right back. In the first Test in Barbados in 1995, he hit my first three balls to the boundary, even though the West Indies were three down for not very many.

One of the tricks for a spinner is to get into the mind of the batsman and work out when he is looking to dance down the pitch and aim for the big hit. I found Hooper the hardest of all to read. During the 1995 series, this really nagged away at me, because I couldn't spot any of the usual clues even though I knew there had to be a sign that would give him away. On a number of occasions, I stopped at the point of delivery to see if he was giving anything away with his footwork. Most batsmen would be looking to get out of their ground at that point, whereas Hooper just stayed set. In the end, after watching him closely time after time, I managed to crack it. When he wanted to hit over the top, he just looked at me instead of tapping his crease as usual and looking down. Of course, my knowing what he was going to do did not always stop him from doing it.

There was a touch of Mark Waugh about his style. He was a very elegant player. Unusually, he never wore a thigh pad. The first time I noticed, I just thought that he'd forgotten what for most of us is an essential part of protection. Not the case. He took the view that the ball would hurt if he was hit in that region, so by refusing to wear a thigh pad, he concentrated harder on getting the bat in position first. It was like a red rag to our fast bowlers, but Hooper was good enough to avoid the danger – he saw the ball early enough to be able to cope.

At one-day level, he was a genuine all-rounder. He could give you the full ten overs of off-spin, and his quicker ball would hit 80 mph. We used to say in the dressing-room that he was up there on the speedometer with Glenn McGrath – a sure-fire way of winding up McGrath. But Hooper could be effective at the end of an innings, and, of course, his batting was ideally suited to the shorter game.

As if all this wasn't enough talent to give to one man, he was also a brilliant slip fielder. When kids look through the records in 50 years' time and see Hooper's Test average in the mid-30s, they will have no idea of the supreme gifts of this guy.

I remember doing an advert for Pepsi with Carl and Sachin Tendulkar at around about the time of the 2003 World Cup – it was a really weird little story that involved Sachin being buried underneath hundreds of falling cans in a supermarket and being whisked out of the shop in a trolley onto an aeroplane destined for Honolulu. It was designed for an Indian audience, so maybe the tale loses something in translation. But we had great fun making the commercial, and in between talked a lot about the game. Hooper really understood cricket and loved it but he was also a very determined player as well.

CARL LLEWELLYN HOOPER

BORN	15 December 1966, Georgetown, Guyana
TESTS	102
RUNS	5,762 in 173 innings at 36.46 with 13 hundreds/27 fifties
WICKETS	114 at 49.42
ONE-DAY INTERNATIONALS	227
RUNS	5,761 in 206 innings at 35.34 with 7 hundreds/29 fifties
WICKETS	193 at 36.05

66

·······

HANSIE CRONJE

I CAN SEE WHY THIS CHOICE will be controversial. Hansie Cronje is better known today for his part in the match-fixing business, which is a shame for all concerned. It threatened to blow our game apart, so his runs for South Africa and the occasions when he led them to success as a strong-minded captain can be overlooked. Hansie was a very good batsman, especially against spin, and his captaincy was very thoughtful and impressive. There are lessons for everyone in his demise, and his shocking death in a plane crash at the age of 32 is a tragedy by any definition. Whatever you think of Cronje's legacy to cricket, he was a wonderful player.

As a batsman, I would say that he played me better than any other South African. There is not a great deal of spin in the country, so maybe it was inevitable that some of them would struggle as a result of their inexperience. Cronje, though, seemed to have a plan. He would look to play his shots and wasn't afraid to use his feet to come out to drive down the ground. In fact, he was one of the best cover drivers against me from any country. Not many batsmen looked to play through that area because of the line of the ball, but Cronje would hit inside out, late and along the ground. With the timing required, that could be quite a difficult shot. He also had control when he slog-swept on length, and in other situations, when he dropped anchor, he could be almost impossible to prise away. I remember a Test match in Sydney in 1998 when South Africa scored less than 200 on the first day.

We had some great games with South Africa down the years, and for a time in the 1990s they ran us close for the number-one spot.

The 1993–94 series was especially tight, but we won the final Test in Adelaide to level 1–1. Cronje stood in as captain for the last two games, but they were just as tough as they had been under Kepler Wessels – and Wessels, as a former boxer, was very tough. We then went to South Africa for the rematch, which we won 1–0, another of the hardest-fought series I was involved in during my 15 years. And then, of course, there were the two sensational games in the 1999 World Cup. The tie at Edgbaston was the greatest one-day game of my career. By rights we ought to have lost, and I remember Cronje had a face like thunder after the famous mix-up between Allan Donald and Lance Klusener. South Africa had a reputation for choking under pressure, and this was more ammunition against them. Afterwards, I went to Cronje to say 'bad luck', but he just couldn't reply. He was simply shell-shocked by the turnaround.

Little images like his reaction that day added to the surprise I felt as the whole match-fixing business started to unravel. On the field, Cronje was always a really intense competitor. I remember another occasion at Adelaide when he became so angry at a decision and a dropped catch that he speared a stump through the door of the umpires' changing-room. He hated losing. Like everybody else who was involved in cricket at the time, I have tried to think back to situations where something not quite right might have happened. All I can think of is this guy leading from the front and giving us nothing. I will admit that I struggled to believe the allegations straight away. You can only take people as you find them, and the truth is that I liked Cronje as a bloke. I enjoyed his company away from the game and respected him as a cricketer. I just think that he got caught up in things, got in too deep and could not find a way out. We all make mistakes.

A few days after his first confession, Australia had to go to South Africa for three one-day games. Shaun Pollock stepped up as captain, and I wondered how the crowds would react, because they can be pretty volatile. There was a morale issue, and the South Africa players seemed to be as shocked as anybody. But the grounds were full, and it seemed obvious that the country wanted to rally round the rest of the side and try to move on. These days, it seems that most South Africans, from players all the way down to the general public, think of Cronje as a victim rather than a crook, and I agree.

It feels wrong to condemn him now that he's gone. Fundamentally, I think he was a good guy who just got in too deeply with the wrong people. He could not find a way out of a horribly difficult situation. There is a warning for everybody in the way he dragged himself deeper and deeper into trouble with the bookmakers. It is a big lesson that somebody so senior and highly respected in the game could be brought down to earth by something that must have seemed trivial to begin with – everybody needs to be vigilant. Nowadays, young players are a lot wiser about the pitfalls surrounding the game. As a sport, we went through a couple of difficult years when we knew that every ball we bowled and every stroke we played would be scrutinised. I am certain that the integrity of the game has been restored.

WESSEL JOHANNES CRONJE

BORN	25 September 1969, Bloemfontein, South Africa
TESTS	68
RUNS	3,714 in 111 innings at 36.41 with 6 hundreds/23 fifties
WICKETS	43 at 29.95
ONE-DAY INTERNATIONALS	188
RUNS	5,565 in 175 innings at 38.64 with 2 hundreds/39 fifties
WICKETS	114 at 34.78

67

·······

HARBHAJAN SINGH

HARBHAJAN SINGH IS A GUY WITH exceptional talent and a great spin bowler for India, because his style is so well suited to their pitches. It took me a couple of tours to work out how to bowl there, but once I sussed things out, I could see why Harbhajan was so effective. It comes down to the pace of the different surfaces. On slow pitches in Australia, you have to try to push the ball through a bit quicker. In India, those balls can sit up to be cut or pulled. You need to try to slow things down, try to put overspin on the ball and tempt batsmen to drive. Those conditions are perfect for Harbhajan's top-spinner, probably the best ball he has in his bag. He has taken around two-thirds of his wickets in India at a good rate, but his average in Australia is more than 70. I am sure that when he comes over next he will be more effective for having gone through those difficult experiences in the past.

He bowled brilliantly against us in the famous 2001 series. V.V.S. Laxman got a lot of credit for his brilliant 281 in Calcutta, and rightly so, but Harbhajan bowled fantastically during the second and third Tests, which they won. He was Man of the Series, and although I don't like regurgitating figures, I want to do so in this case just to show how much he influenced things: seven for one hundred and twenty-three and six for seventy-three in Calcutta followed by seven for one hundred and thirty-three and to crown it all eight for eighty-four in Chennai. Unfortunately, in the first game I became the third man in a hat-trick, following Ricky Ponting and Adam Gilchrist back to the hutch. Eden Gardens is a frenzied place anyway, but the crowd just went crazy with excitement – it was almost worth the dismissal to experience it.

I think this was the series when he picked up the nickname 'The Turbanator' by the press. It took us a while to work out that we could not really play him from the crease because of the bounce. He managed to turn his basic off–break sharply, and he also had an arm ball. The variety made him particularly awkward to face early on. Things became easier after the first 15 minutes or so of batting against him, and batsmen who got in looked to be more aggressive. In a great finish, we nearly managed to defend a small target to win the series, but we ended up losing by two wickets to go down 2–1. Harbhajan had not been shy with the verbals when we were struggling at the crease, but by the end there wasn't really much we could say back except 'well bowled'. He backed up everything he said, and I think his attitude was good for their dressing-room and in the field.

Without Anil Kumble to lead the spin attack, Harbhajan was pretty much in charge of that department during the series, but I think India in general are best with the two of them together. They are a good team, with Harbhajan spinning the ball a bit more and Kumble making very subtle variations and bowling at a good pace. They are a pair of real fighters. Another thing that impresses me about Harbhajan is his determination. It is one thing to keep going when wickets are tumbling but another when batsmen are on top and conditions are unhelpful. Harbhajan has never struck me as a shirker, and although he hasn't been too successful in Australia, he has always sent down a good share of the overs.

At times, he has been a bit hot-headed, and from what I understand he is no stranger to the match referee's room. I'm all for being competitive and having a bit of an edge as long as it is channelled in constructive ways for the good of the team. Smacking one of his teammates, which he did in the Indian Premier League, was taking things a little bit too far. He was banned for 11 matches, which gave him plenty of time to work out that he needs to tone down his act to continue to make the best use of his talent. However, if you sucked the passion from him, you would lose something of Harbhajan as a bowler.

With spinners tending to mature relatively late, he should still have plenty of years ahead of him. He will be an important figure when Kumble eventually stands down. He has recently had some

333333333333333333

333

experience of captaincy, which will also help him to understand the wider aspects of the game. Having the eyes of your teammates on you and taking their cue from you is a great way of learning that you have to stay calm outwardly even if you are boiling inside. All being well, he will settle down in a way that is good for himself, the India team and for cricket in general. He may not have a great fan club in Australia after recent incidents with Andrew Symonds, but he is still the kind of exciting player spectators want to watch. I thought he handled the situation in Australia last year pretty badly and should have been punished more than he was.

HARBHAJAN SINGH

BORN	3 July 1980, Jalandhar, Punjab, India
TESTS	66
WICKETS	275 at 31.03
ONE-DAY INTERNATIONALS	171
WICKETS	189 at 33.51

68

·······

JONTY RHODES

YOU WOULD BE FORGIVEN FOR THINKING that I wouldn't get on with Jonty Rhodes. He is a clean-living guy and a devoted Christian, whereas I'm usually up for a beer and a hand or two of poker. They say that opposites attract, and Rhodes and I hit it off straight away. He loved cricket, but more important than that was his great enthusiasm for everything he did on and off the field. Some of the South Africans could be fairly dour and serious, but Jonty liked to laugh and could see the funny side of most situations. His attitude to the game was fantastic. And that's why people loved him all over the world. This rubber-man with the Colgate-white smile showed kids that fielding wasn't just something to do in the gap between getting a bat and a bowl. He made it cool to dive around and have some fun.

The usual statistics are almost worthless where he is concerned. How many runs did he save in the field throughout his Test career? None of those great stops go measured in the figures. Nor do the singles that batsmen probably could have taken but opted not to because they remembered that it was Rhodes at backward point. He was lightning fast at retrieving the ball and then getting into a balanced position to throw. You had to be crazy or super-confident to take him on, and often the split-second it took to make the calculation instead of running by instinct swung the balance against setting off.

When he toured Australia, it was inevitable that he would face a lot of scrutiny from our media, who all wanted to know his story. He passed that test impeccably, never letting the publicity get to his head or affect his game.

I remember a one-day game on that tour in Melbourne when he ran out David Boon and Steve Waugh with direct hits. He did Boon with an incredible throw from point while he still seemed to be tumbling forward, hitting the stumps from side on. The technical skill required for that was amazing. Boon was possibly our best batsman at that time, and we had made a really good start to the game but ended up losing by seven wickets. It was the fielding of Rhodes that gave them the initiative. He is the best backward-point fieldsman I have seen, although Ricky Ponting and Michael Clarke would give him a run for his money!

However, quite a lot of his work really did go unseen in the stands. He was always the bloke who would run to the bowler to collect a sweater or cap and hand it on to the umpire or make the effort to give the same guy a pat on the back at the end of each over, even if it meant running 50 or 60 yards. He always led the encouragement during the long, tough sessions. As players, you notice those things and appreciate them. Every team needs a bloke like that to keep up the energy levels.

He was also a good batsman in his own right. An innings at Sydney in 1994 sticks in my mind. South Africa were still behind with five wickets down in the second innings when he put together a long partnership with Dave Richardson, who is now a bigwig at the ICC. They managed to set us a target of one hundred and seventeen and won by five runs. Rhodes was prepared to take on Craig McDermott with the hook and swept me against the spin. We were going for the jugular and set attacking fields, but he managed to find gaps, and, of course, he was so quick between the wickets. That is what helped to make him such a good one-day batsman in the middle order. When a guy completes a single which really shouldn't be there, or turns a one into a two, it is really annoying for the bowler. I bet Rhodes didn't play out too many maidens during his career.

Against spin, he could be pretty unorthodox. I always fancied myself against South Africa, because I thought they got themselves into too much of a one-method attack: just sweep. Jonty was good at that, and when he used to come to the crease, I would say: 'Got the broom out again today?' He would just laugh and say: 'Yes.' Rhodes found his own way and was brave enough to back his judgement, even if it didn't always look pretty. At least in the early days, he could not read my flipper, so he went all the way back and tried to play it off the pitch, occasionally in front of him. His reflexes were so good that he was one of the few batsmen who could get away with doing that.

The South Africa players had a big responsibility after being re-admitted into the international game, and Rhodes soon became a role model. I remember going with him into one of the townships to promote a development and coaching programme, and the young kids just worshipped him, irrespective of the colour difference. There couldn't have been a better ambassador. He was genuinely interested in them, where they came from and what they wanted to do. And most of the kids, naturally, just wanted to be another Jonty Rhodes. And why not? He was a lovely man, with a beautiful family, and a very competitive person.

JONTY NEIL RHODES

BORN	27 July 1969, Pietermaritzburg, South Africa
TESTS	52
RUNS	2,532 in 80 innings at 35.66 with 3 hundreds/17 fifties
ONE-DAY INTERNATIONALS	245
RUNS	5,935 in 220 innings at 35.11 with 2 hundreds/33 fifties

69

·······

ALEC STEWART

ANYBODY WHO COULD SCORE TWO HUNDREDS in a Test match against the West Indies when they were still a force must have had plenty of guts and determination, not to mention plenty of skills as a batsman. With Alec, you could see the pride he took from playing for his country, and he made sure that his preparation for games was absolutely spot-on. That is why he managed to keep going, like his great mentor Graham Gooch, until beyond his 40th birthday. Given the fitness and concentration required to be a wicket-keeper, that is an incredible achievement.

If he had been able to play as a specialist opening batsman throughout his career, his record against everybody, Australia included, would have been better. I think that was his best position, because he was a solid player who was not scared of the new ball or the bruises that came with it. He was such a sweet timer of the ball and had a range of strokes. With Mike Atherton, he formed a pretty decent opening partnership. Although the pair of them were chalk and cheese as characters, they had a big appreciation of each other's ability. Stewart was a more adventurous batsman, and the attacking fields in the early overs left plenty of gaps for him to find.

Unfortunately, he kept switching from opener to number three and then further down the order, sometimes playing as a specialist batsman and sometimes as a batsman/keeper. Because of his versatility, he was underestimated as a gloveman. People maybe thought of him as no more than a stopgap in his early days. By the end of his career, he was plenty good enough to do the job, especially standing back to the quick bowlers. He was a genuine all-rounder because he could perform both tasks, and that helped to balance the side, although it was asking a huge amount of him to keep wicket for long periods and then go straight into opening the batting.

Alec was another England player like Robin Smith that wherever England were struggling they would try and put Alec there to shore up that particular problem. To me, he was an attacking player who had a touch of class about him and was never bogged down. He was always looking to score or get on top of the bowling, which meant that he would occasionally play a loose shot, but he had such a wide range of strokes and played the pull shot with lots of power. One of my best flippers was to Alec. It was always a tough challenge to bowl to him, so I was proud to knock him over a few times. I think he preferred pace rather than spin.

Off the field, I think Stewart is much maligned. People seem to think of him as this very strait-laced bloke without a blemish on his character who never says a word out of place. That might be true, but I have always got on very well with him and enjoy his sense of humour. To me, Alec played in the right spirit and always attacked. He is also good company away from the game.

ALEC JAMES STEWART

BORN	8 April 1963, Merton, Surrey, England
TESTS	133
RUNS	8,463 in 235 innings at 39.54 with 15 hundreds/45 fifties
DISMISSALS	263 catches and 14 stumpings
ONE-DAY INTERNATIONALS	170
RUNS	4,677 in 162 innings at 31.60 with 4 hundreds/28 fifties
DISMISSALS	159 catches and 15 stumpings

70

·······

RICHIE RICHARDSON

RICHIE RICHARDSON WAS ONE OF THE last batsmen I remember coming out without a helmet as a matter of course. He seemed to be a throwback to a different age when he took on the short ball without any protection. The story went that he hadn't come across a helmet until he made it into the West Indies side, then tried one on and found it so uncomfortable that he kept going the way he knew. It was only late in his career, at a memorable game in Kingston, that he bowed to what I suppose was inevitable and swapped his maroon sunhat for something a bit stronger. Mind you, he was having to open the batting so perhaps did not feel so confident about his eyes and reflexes. That was a difficult, energy-sapping time to be the West Indies captain, and I prefer to think of him as a dashing player, one of the best Caribbean batsmen I came across and a bloke I used to watch on TV years before the dream of playing for Australia became a reality.

The game in Kingston I mentioned was a turning point for both countries. I think it was the moment we swapped positions as best and second best in the world. And I think that the pressure of knowing that must have got to Richardson when he said afterwards that we were the worst Australia side he had faced. It didn't say much for his team. I think he was just embarrassed and had a bruised ego after losing. There wasn't any need for a remark such as that, and it was totally out of character coming from a bloke who was liked and respected in our dressing-room. He was a really sporting player. You have to understand his disappointment at the time – to Richardson, it was probably the equivalent of our losing the 2005 Ashes. He copped a lot of flak for his comments in our papers back home, but not as much as came his way from the Caribbean people who were used to winning and wanted to know why things had gone wrong.

I actually don't believe they had played badly. In fact, it took a great effort on our part, some of the best batting I saw from Steve and Mark Waugh and wholehearted bowling from Glen McGrath. The power of our teamwork shone through. There were rumours of rifts in the West Indies side, and when Richardson eventually stepped down, he said that he'd known teams in the past with far greater respect between players. When a team is winning, those things are never discussed or don't seep into the public domain. People do not look beyond results as long as they are good. There lies a strong reason why West Indies cricket declined steeply. Administrators expected them to be successful, because that is all they had known. They thought the glory days would continue inevitably. The lesson for all of us is to keep an eye on the future.

Richardson did everything he could to keep the West Indies going. Even in that Kingston game, he scored a hundred. He liked to play in the traditional Caribbean way, hitting the ball on the up. The more pace in the pitch for him, the better, so he could slash hard and square. He knew that spectators wanted to watch stroke-makers, not pushers and prodders, and he loved the buzz that went around those grounds, all of them full of character, when a batsman started to take on the bowling. By 1995, he had reined in some of his instincts; he had to at Kingston, with wickets falling around him. He batted for nearly six hours in all, and if it hadn't been for the Waugh boys putting together a great stand, it might have gone down as a grafting, match-winning innings.

I had actually played against him in our previous series in 1992–93, and his dismissal at Melbourne is still one of the favourites of my career. To do a player of Richardson's calibre with a flipper felt really good, and his reaction when he stared wide-eyed at the wicket with his off stump out made it even better. His reaction confirmed to me that I'd managed to outsmart one of the best batsmen in the world. It gave me confidence.

He was always thought of as the heir to Viv Richards, an even greater Antiguan who wouldn't think of wearing a helmet except as a show of weakness to the bowlers. Guys such as Allan Border remembered them playing in the same side, with Richardson taking on his mentor's favourite spot at number three. He had an amazing record against Australia, with nine hundreds in all, home and away. Our plan was to try to keep him quiet and hope he would take a risk. If there was any movement, he might hit through the line and nick one. Personally, I found him quite a careful player against spin compared to some of the other West Indian batsmen.

He is still around the game these days when he isn't playing guitar with one of his great mates, Curtly Ambrose. Allen Stanford has signed him up as a director of his tournament, and Richardson is trying to encourage kids to take up the game in the region. He believes that youth cricket is the way forward and knows – probably from his own experience – that a few good results here and there do not mean that the job is complete. It never is.

RICHARD BENJAMIN RICHARDSON

BORN	12 January 1962, Five Islands Village, Antigua
TESTS	86
RUNS	5,949 in 146 innings at 44.39 with 16 hundreds/27 fifties
ONE-DAY INTERNATIONALS	224
RUNS	6,248 in 217 innings at 33.41 with 5 hundreds/44 fifties

71

·······

DARREN GOUGH

OCCASIONALLY YOU SEE OR HEAR SOMETHING that makes you realise that we live in a strange, unpredictable world. That is how I felt when I discovered that Darren Gough had entered a television ballroom-dancing competition. He never struck me as being another Billy Elliot. What didn't surprise me, though, was hearing a few weeks later that he had actually gone and won it. That is Gough all over. Whatever he does, he sticks out his chest and expects to be successful. I bet if he'd not come out top he would have cursed the shine on the dance floor or shaken his head at the judging. But let's go back to cricket. Of all the England players I faced in eight Ashes series, none of them had a bigger heart than Gough. I thought he was the closest to playing like an Aussie.

We always thought of him as being one of our own. His enthusiasm struck us straight away. I'm sure there was some Australian blood in there somewhere, though you wouldn't have known from his strong Yorkshire accent. He had none of the traditional English reserve. He was as proud to play for his country as we were to represent ours, and he let everybody know it. A bowler like that is a dream for a captain, because you can throw him the ball at any time, knowing he will give you every ounce of effort. He thought that anything was possible, and the way he fought back from a serious knee injury to become a regular player again in England's one-day side, even the Test team briefly, should be an inspiration to anybody who ever suffers that kind of setback. I hit it off with him from the start.

Gough liked playing at Sydney and actually took a superb hat-trick on that pitch. I was at the non-striker's end as he had Ian Healy caught behind, bowled Stuart MacGill with an in-swinger and then clipped Colin Miller's off stump with one going the other way. After the first and second wickets, Dominic Cork came out with a drink to offer a bit of advice. Whether Gough took it on or not, I don't know, but I shook his hand straight away and said: 'Well done.' By coincidence, he was the middle wicket in my own Ashes hat-trick at Melbourne in 1994. That was the day he said that he finally realised the huge size of the MCG as he sloped off from a first-baller with the sound of a duck going 'quack, quack' from the big screen and the crowd pumping up the volume.

Our attitudes have always been very similar. It was probably more apparent in the way we batted rather than our bowling. Both of us wanted to go out and hit the ball and not worry too much about defending for long periods. He likes to lead from the front, but he's also got some good ideas, and I know it was a big thing for him to be able to go back to Yorkshire to lead his county.

Stories about Gough are legendary. The time he was asked to explain his nickname 'Rhino' is one of the funniest. 'Because I'm as strong as an ox,' he said straight away. Sometimes we used to watch him as he walked back to his mark after one of his quicker balls. He couldn't help looking at the speedometer to see what he'd managed to register. If he didn't like the figure, you could see him pull a face or shake his head in bemusement. To be fair, he could be genuinely sharp. He wasn't particularly tall, but the ball would skid on rapidly when he bent his back. He could swing it, and his control of length and changes of pace made him very effective at the end of one-day matches.

He probably started to produce his best bowling consistently when Nasser Hussain became England captain. His new-ball partnership with Andrew Caddick was highly effective. You could easily wind up Gough by suggesting that Caddick was the quicker of the two. Hussain really believed in Gough. He was a big fan of his character, and although I didn't particularly like the way Hussain spoke to some of his players, he was prepared to give them all the backing they needed. Gough was also one of those who immediately benefited when England introduced central contracts to manage

his workload. In return, he helped to lift them up from being rock
bottom in the world game.

DARREN GOUGH

BORN	18 September 1970, Barnsley, England
TESTS	58
WICKETS	229 at 28.39
ONE-DAY INTERNATIONALS	159
WICKETS	235 at 26.42

72

· · · · · · ·

JOHN WRIGHT

LIKE A FEW OTHER GUYS IN the book such as Kapil Dev and Ian
Bishop, John Wright caught me just at the start of my Test career.
Although we only played against each other in a single series, in
1993, our paths have crossed many times in the years afterwards.
Younger cricket fans will know him as a successful coach who
was the organiser and quiet influence behind Sourav Ganguly and
India. I think of Wright as being an old-fashioned type of cricketer.
He used to love the chats in the dressing-room or the bar over a
beer at the end of play. Like me, he swears by that interaction as
being part of the game's finishing school and thinks it is a real pity
that this culture is not always as strong as it was in the past.

He told me that he learned so much in the early 1980s from
listening to Dennis Lillee chat about the ways he tried to bowl to
opening batsmen. Wright was an opener himself, for New Zealand,
so the information he picked up was invaluable. He reasoned that
he might well wake up with a hangover the next morning, but there
was always a chance that he would be clear-headed enough to recall
something useful as well. It must seem incredible now to think of an
opponent giving away his secrets.

I remember Wright coming into the Australia dressing-room after
his final Test match in Auckland. New Zealand had won the game
to level the series. Wright was quite an unorthodox player, and
Mark Taylor did a hilarious impression of his stance and some funny
movements he made before the ball was delivered. I don't know of
any other batsman who held up play as often to make a little change
in the position of the sightscreen or a person in the stands, but he

was very apologetic. Usually, he would ask for whatever it was that was distracting him to be moved by no more than a few centimetres. It must have been a nervous thing rather than a change to improve his line of sight. But Taylor had us all in stitches, and Wright was laughing louder than anybody. As a batsman, Wright had all of our respect. He was rock solid and had a good technique.

Wrighty thought deeply about the game, which is one reason why he has become such a good coach. For instance, at one point he was struggling with his top-hand grip, so he superglued a glove onto his bat handle to make sure that it was in the best position. The great thing about Wright is that he can laugh at himself, but behind all the jokes and the comments, I admired him for being a batsman who valued his wicket. There is nothing worse for a bowler who has run in for a day and a half on a flat pitch than to see your own batsmen then get out cheaply. He was also the first player to be given out by the third umpire – not something he'll want to remember!

During the 1980s, while I was a kid watching games on television and taking more and more of an interest in cricket, he was part of perhaps the best-ever New Zealand side. When they beat us home and away, Richard Hadlee and Martin Crowe were the stars, but they couldn't have done it without rock-solid professionals such as Wright giving them outstanding back-up. He took a lot of responsibility for his game and played at a time of fast and crafty opening bowlers such as Lillee, Ian Botham, Bob Willis and Imran Khan even before you think of the West Indians. He believed that the worst time to face the likes of Mikey Holding and Andy Roberts was in bed the night before a game, stewing at the prospect ahead. Once you were out there, he said, there was no time to worry. You just got on with it.

His diligence shines through in his coaching and preparation. Before he went for his interview for the India job, he bought a big book about the history of cricket in the country because he knew what the heritage of the game meant over there. Maybe being a foreign coach helped him. Nobody could accuse him of being aligned to any of the regional factions that can get in the way of selection. And he was a good foil for Ganguly. Wright believes that the captain should run the show and supported Ganguly in public. India became a more professional outfit in areas such as fielding, and he left them in a better state than when he arrived. You can't ask any more than that. He is also in the Robin Smith category as far as the nice guys go. He is a ripper.

JOHN GEOFFREY WRIGHT

BORN	5 July 1954, Canterbury, New Zealand
TESTS	82
RUNS	5,334 in 148 innings at 37.82 with 12 hundreds/23 fifties
ONE-DAY INTERNATIONALS	149
RUNS	3,891 in 148 innings at 26.46 with 1 hundred/24 fifties

73

•••••••

MIKE GATTING

MIKE GATTING, SHANE WARNE . . . THERE IS probably only one place to start. I do wonder in what way my life would have been different if he'd managed to get a bit of bat on my first ball in the Ashes, or even if the one that came out of my hand like a dream had been my second, not my first against England. The result would have been the same, but not the sense of theatre. I was lucky enough to have a good Test career, but even with everything else that happened over the next 16 summers, I reckon I get asked about the 'Gatting Ball' as much as anything else. And don't think I'm complaining!

We have laughed and joked and talked about it many times since, and we have told the tale together at various functions and dinners. The way Gatting relates it is that I'd been out the night before with Merv Hughes, who had taken me under his wing on my first Ashes tour in 1993. He says that he was coming out of a pub just as the pair of us were going in, so he wasn't expecting too much when I came in to the attack the next day. It's just about plausible, but maybe the story has become a bit exaggerated with the telling. There is no harm done, and if Gatting can laugh about it, then we all can.

The following summer in England, he attempted to recreate the event for one of the Test match sponsors. England were using a machine called 'Merlin', a weird-looking, home-made contraption that somehow simulated leg-spin. They set it up to reproduce that same ball as a publicity exercise; this time it hit him on the pads.

More seriously, he still reckons that he could not have done anything differently. He thought he had the ball covered and didn't even realise that I had bowled him, because he didn't hear the death

229

rattle of the ball hitting the stumps. It only flicked the wood on its way through, and Gatting actually turned towards the square-leg umpire to check that Ian Healy had not dislodged the bails.

Perhaps my favourite part of the clip when it gets replayed from time to time is Gatting's expression as he realises what has happened. He opens his eyes wide and almost gives a little shake of his head as if to check that he isn't dreaming. In those days, there wasn't the same emphasis on video footage and analysing opponents to every last detail, so he wouldn't really have known what to expect from me. And I had been carted around a little bit in some of the warm-up games. If he was surprised, then I'm sure he wasn't the only one.

I don't mind admitting I was a bit taken aback myself. I was so nervous when Allan Border told me I was about to be called up to bowl. My priority was just to make sure it landed on roughly the right bit of the strip and take things from there for the rest of the spell. So my first thought when the ball left my hand was: 'Thank God for that.' It felt right straight away. A good leg-break drifts into the right-hander through the air. This is really helpful, because it means the batsman might be tempted to shape to play to leg and overbalances when it goes the other way. Batsmen also talk about a 'blind spot' when they momentarily lose sight. For all that, I really didn't expect it to do so much off the pitch or to beat Gatting's defensive push and hit the stumps.

Over the years, Old Trafford became a favourite ground of mine. Even in that game, I bowled balls that turned more sharply than the Gatting Ball, but nothing matches the sensation of doing something for the first time, and the media just jumped on the story straight away. I probably didn't appreciate at the time just how big a wicket it was. Gatting, as I later learned, could be a brutal player of spin bowling. He was feared on the county circuit, and it is a bit unfair that his name is synonymous, at least to Australians, with that one dismissal. In England, he is better known as the bloke who won the Ashes in Australia in 1986–87, the last time we were beaten by the Old Enemy until 2005. That would be a more fitting judgement, because Gatting was a good player and a good bloke. I can imagine him sticking out his beard and his chest and leading England by example.

That 1993 series proved an unhappy experience for them all round. He scored a half-century in the second Test but was dropped for the rest of the series, one of five changes made by England as they tried desperately to find a recipe for success. It seems incredible in these days of consistent selection that they even thought about dropping half the side, including somebody of Gatting's proven ability. He came back for the 1994–95 tour and scored a hundred in Adelaide. His experience shone through when he spent more than half an hour on 99. He never got flustered and just waited for the right ball to put away. Gat was really quick on his feet against spin and had a good defence. Against the quicks, he scored very quickly. He is a very good ambassador for the game today and one of the nice guys I played against.

MICHAEL WILLIAM GATTING

BORN	6 June 1957, Kingsbury, Middlesex, England
TESTS	79
RUNS	4,409 in 138 innings at 35.55 with 10 hundreds/21 fifties
ONE-DAY INTERNATIONALS	92
RUNS	2,095 in 88 innings at 29.50 with 1 hundred/9 fifties

74

·······

SHANE BOND

SHANE BOND WAS ONE OF THE best bowlers I faced, and if his career had not been so badly affected by injury, he would be a lot higher up the list. He does things a little bit differently, combining the sheer pace of an out-and-out fast bowler with the craft of an old-fashioned medium pacer. Getting up to and beyond 95 mph is well within his range, but he does more than simply fire the ball fast and straight. He can angle it in or swing it away and then, with his full length, reverse the old ball if the conditions are right. His variety means that you never know what to expect from him, which is a great disadvantage for a batsman who has split seconds to respond. Put all of that together and you can see why he is just very, very awkward to face.

Unfortunately, he only played two Test matches against Australia, and those at the very start of his career. At that stage, he was quick but raw. Over the years, we saw him more in one-day cricket, where he could be awesome. Like Brett Lee, his ability to bowl fast and full at the end of an innings made him very difficult to hit. He was the most economical bowler in the 2007 World Cup, and that is even before the wickets he bagged are brought into the equation. In fact, he is a great example of taking wickets being the surest way to slow the run rate. I don't know if it was coincidence, but he seemed to reserve many of his best performances for us, from the 2003 World Cup onwards. New Zealand have consistently been a good one-day side, and when people say they punch above their weight, I think that fails to do them justice, because they have always worked out really good plans and their teams have included some seriously good cricketers. Their own pitches suit the little medium-pacers who can wobble it around, and Bond gave them something on top of that foundation: the firepower to be able to cut through teams at the start and finish off proceedings.

Of all the New Zealand bowlers I faced throughout my career, Bond was by far the quickest and best of all the quicks. At his peak, he was probably up there with Shoaib Akhtar for out-and-out pace, whatever the speed gun said. And he got the wickets of good players – I remember in one-day games he made life really difficult for top-quality guys such as Ricky Ponting and Adam Gilchrist at a time when they were scoring runs for fun against everybody else. He was especially dangerous when you first went in, so we really made an extra effort to get through the first two or three overs. By then, batting was not exactly pleasant, but at least you were adjusted to the extra speed. I know that Stephen Fleming always kept a close eye on his fitness in the weeks before a key series. A bowler of Bond's calibre would be missed by any side, but New Zealand suffered particularly when he was injured, because they do not have the same depth of talent in their domestic leagues and the guy to come in would inevitably be a different, less-penetrating replacement.

Off the field, he is a really nice, placid guy. He always has a smile on his face. If you did not know who he was and struck up a conversation with him in a bar or restaurant, you would be amazed to see him hurling a cricket ball with such ferocity around batsmen's ears the following morning. Actually, Bond is one of the smartest bowlers when it comes to the short ball, which he uses very sparingly. And given his trouble with injuries, it might be surprising that he likes to bowl long spells. He is very hard-working, and once he gets on the field, he makes sure that he stays there whatever the conditions. That was another reason why Fleming loved to have him around.

His is actually a great story: of a bloke who missed out on cricket in the early part of his career to concentrate on his police training. He used to walk the beat in the main square of Christchurch. In those days, I don't think he realised his full potential, because he was happy to play cricket for fun and definitely saw the police force as his main employer. He would turn out between shifts and try to arrange holidays and days off around cricket. Maybe we should not concentrate on the time he lost because of injury, but appreciate that he could easily not have played for New Zealand at all – or for any of the English county sides who quickly recognised his value as an overseas player.

To me, it was a joke that Bond was stopped from playing international cricket when he joined the ICL. Nobody will convince me it is good for cricket that one of the most exciting bowlers in the world is not allowed to represent a country that is desperately trying to hang in and compete at a time when money is flowing to their rivals. People need to be sensible about this. And bear in mind that I am speaking as an ambassador for the Indian Premier League, the supposed rival of the ICL. The ICC looks pretty ridiculous in all of this. If keeping Shane Bond out is a way of promoting the long-term interest of the game, I'm afraid I am missing some of the argument – and I know for sure I am not in a club of one.

SHANE EDWARD BOND

BORN	7 June 1975, Christchurch, New Zealand
TESTS	17
WICKETS	79 at 22.39
ONE-DAY INTERNATIONALS	67
WICKETS	125 at 19.32

75

•••••••

MAHELA JAYAWARDENE

I THINK OF MAHELA JAYAWARDENE AS a baby-faced assassin. Nothing in his appearance or his gentle, unassuming manner would lead you to think that he now ranks among the toughest batsmen in the game. He has a soft, squeaky voice and doesn't look much older today than when I first saw him ten or so years ago. Since taking over the Sri Lanka captaincy full time, his personal game has kicked on to another level, and the strength of his leadership has left those people who wondered whether he would be up to the task of making difficult decisions eat their words. This could have been an awkward period for the team, with a few senior guys being phased out, but Jayawardene has relished the responsibility of being a senior figure on and off the field.

When I picked him as one of my players to watch in the 1999 World Cup, it caused a few raised eyebrows. He wasn't especially well known in England, but I just liked the look of him in Australia the previous winter during a very niggly tri-nation one-day series. His captain, Arjuna Ranatunga, seemed to be on a mission to create as much ill feeling as possible, and although Jayawardene didn't score a lot of runs, I just liked his calmness at the wicket. Sometimes you get feelings about players whether or not they score runs. With guys like that who are new or relatively new to the side, you are looking for potential, for signs that they will do well once they get their bearings at the top level. Jayawardene just looked at ease. He wasn't twitching or forever looking to pat down imaginary bumps in the pitch.

He has lived up to those expectations, and his leadership has been increasingly impressive. It was a major achievement for Sri Lanka to reach the World Cup final in 2007. His hundred in the semi-final against New Zealand was a top innings, and it took an even better century by Adam Gilchrist in the final to deny them a repeat of their 1996-final win, one of the lowest moments of my career. You can say that it helps a captain to have Muttiah Muralitharan in the side: throw him the ball, set a field and worry about rotating the seamers at the other end. But Jayawardene has not always had his big spinner available and has had to work out a Plan B.

Leading Sri Lanka must be very difficult because of the politics going on behind the scenes. I guess it is something that you just grow up with and learn to deal with, but whenever I look there seems to be an interim committee involved somewhere or other. How you can plan in those situations, I don't know. And then occasionally you see the president of the country getting involved. What it shows is the importance of cricket to life in Sri Lanka, which must create its own pressures. Jayawardene seems to be able to put all of that to the back of his mind and concentrate on the game.

Technically, I think he is a very sound batsman. I managed to get him out a few times, and his record against Australia is not as good as his overall figures, but part of that is down to the different types of pitches in our country. He has said himself on more than one occasion that something would not be quite right if your stats at home were worse than they are overseas. In Sri Lanka, he averages in the mid-60s, which is an incredible achievement over more than a decade. And I think it is wrong to say that he cannot adapt when he has scored two hundreds at Lord's, a ground where the slope means that batsmen need to adjust quickly. One thing about Jayawardene is his balance at the crease. He is quick on his feet, doesn't allow spinners to dominate and cuts really well against the quicks.

It is not that he particularly failed against us, more that he didn't go on after getting starts. If that suggests concentration is a problem, then remember that he scored a massive 374 against South Africa in Colombo a couple of years ago. Conditions there can be more difficult than anywhere else in the world because of the humidity, and just because the Sri Lankans are used to that sapping heat does not mean they find it comfortable. I think the team around that time, and especially Jayawardene, felt the benefits of having Tom Moody as coach, because he challenged them to go that bit further and had great experience of the world game himself. They became a tougher unit with Moody in charge, though ultimately it is the captain who sets the tone for his team on the field.

Jayawardene is now established at number four. I think that is his best position, especially with Kumar Sangakkara at three. In the early days, he said that he worried too much about little things if the runs were not coming, such as the finer points of technique. He came to realise that it usually came down to the basics, such as keeping a close eye on the ball as it was delivered. That, and confidence. The tireless work he does for a cancer charity in Sri Lanka has given him perspective on life, and because he realises that cricket is not the be-all and end-all, he is relaxed enough these days to play with freedom. We can all see the results.

DENAGAMAGE PROBOTH MAHELA DE SILVA JAYAWARDENE

BORN	27 May 1977, Colombo, Sri Lanka
TESTS	95
RUNS	7,478 in 160 innings at 51.93 with 22 hundreds/32 fifties
ONE-DAY INTERNATIONALS	283
RUNS	7,830 in 265 innings at 33.17 with 10 hundreds/48 fifties

76

·······

SHANE WATSON

I DON'T KNOW IF THE PUBLISHERS have any plans to reprint this book, but if we need to do a bit of revising in a few years' time, then I'm sure that Shane Watson will be far higher in my rankings. By then I reckon he could be the best all-rounder in the world. Yes, people in England might think I'm just one Aussie pumping the tyres of another. That is only part of it. Believe me, this guy has talent to burn. All he needs is a change of luck with his fitness to be able to show the world why we rate him so highly back home. Up to now he has given only glimpses of his enormous potential, but if people saw him in the IPL this year and then in the one-day series in the West Indies they will know he is ready to deliver consistently.

So far, Watson has been unlucky, pure and simple. To describe him as being 'injury prone' sounds as though he has a low pain threshold, but that is not the case. He is a very, very determined person. Freaky things have just happened. For example, he damaged a shoulder diving for a ball. There is no way you can legislate for something like that. True, he has also had issues with his back in the past because of his bowling, but he has strengthened the parts of his body that maybe needed a little bit of extra work and is now super fit and settled off the field, too. The foundations are all in place to allow him to take the game by the scruff of the neck.

One former Australia coach whose name I don't want to mention suggested that Watson think about packing in the bowling to concentrate on being a specialist batsman. A better piece of guidance from me is to not worry too much about that particular bit of advice. Watson can bowl. He can maybe work on doing a little bit more with the ball, such as nipping it or getting some swing, but he has a good action and enough pace to be more than just an option if all else fails. I think he will become a number four or five batsman and a fourth seamer in Test cricket for Australia, giving our side a really good balance, and if the selectors choose Mike Hussey to open and Watson at five, that would give the side even better balance.

When he first broke through in our domestic game, he batted at three and was timed at around 90 mph on the speed gun. He once scored three hundred and took seven wickets in a club game. He is also a brilliant fielder. Put that together and you have an obscene amount of talent, but whenever he has been on the verge of breaking through, something has gone wrong. The fact that the selectors have tried to find a way back for him each time says everything about how highly we value him. Unfortunately, he missed the 2003 World Cup, then the 2005 Ashes and after that the 2006–07 series against England. There was a lot of talk after 2005 about the need to bring in an all-rounder in the future to give us extra options. Watson actually got first call but another injury set him back. Andrew Symonds, another good cricketer but a different type of player and bloke, came in and took his chance. There is no reason why they should not play in the same side.

Watson has been opening the one-day innings for Australia and recently scored a run-a-ball hundred from that position. He could actually bat anywhere in the top six, because he has sound all-round technique and would grow into a specific role. I just think that to ask him to do that at Test level and to bowl as well could be too much, and something would be lost if he cut back on the bowling. His workload does need to be monitored, although quietly without a lot of fuss. I also think that his game is better suited to the middle order. He has loads of shots and loves to attack.

He was a great bloke to be able to call on for the Rajasthan Royals for all the reasons I have mentioned. Watson is a three-dimensional cricketer who can bat, bowl and field. He took four Man of the Match awards in the IPL before being named the official Player of the Tournament. That is a great tribute, given the number of proven world-class players who appeared in the competion. Watson was not one of the expensive buys in the first round of the auction, but he was great value, with nearly 500 runs and 17 wickets. The other thing was that his fielding and enthusiasm set a great example to the young Indian guys we had in our side. His approach to practice was first class. He just wants to improve, and I know that he has been as frustrated as anyone with his injuries. There is still plenty of time for him to fulfil his talent. The only thing he needs is to learn to chill a bit, and if things aren't quite right in preparation or in the middle during the game, to adapt. That will come with more experience. I have a soft spot for Natto, and I really do believe he will become the number-one all-rounder in the game in the next few years.

SHANE ROBERT WATSON

BORN	17 June 1981, Ipswich, Queensland, Australia
TESTS	3
RUNS	81 in 4 innings at 20.25
WICKETS	2 at 61.50
ONE-DAY INTERNATIONALS	70
RUNS	1,207 in 52 innings at 35.50 with 1 hundred/7 fifties
WICKETS	68 at 32.85

77

. . . .

V.V.S. LAXMAN

MENTION V.V.S. LAXMAN TO ANY AUSTRALIAN and they will inevitably think of Calcutta. I do. His 281 in that teeming city in 2001 ranks as one of the best innings ever played against an Australia side I was part of, and it might even top them all. I don't think I will ever forget the way he whipped balls that were spinning out of the rough through mid-wicket time after time on that scorching afternoon. But it is wrong to consider Laxman a one-innings wonder. While nobody can be expected to bat as well as that consistently, he had scored hundreds against us before that double and went on to do so again. He is unusual for an Indian batsman because his record is better in Australia than in any other country, including his own. And that is from a bloke you really don't think of in terms of averages and statistics. Better to just sit back, close your eyes and think about the brilliance of Laxman's strokes. Like Mark Waugh and Brian Lara, he really is a guy you would pay to watch.

I've never known a game turn around so completely as that one in Calcutta. We went into the contest having won 16 Tests on the trot and then established a first-innings lead of 274. There was some debate about whether we should enforce the follow-on, but although we knew that India had stacks of batting talent, they hadn't shown much evidence of being in great nick up to that point. We were on top of our game and looking forward to taking a 2–0 lead going into the final match in Chennai. Laxman did not worry us too much despite scoring a half-century in the first innings and timing the ball nicely. There was even talk that his place was in jeopardy; how ridiculous that seems now. Looking back, those first-innings runs were important to him. India moved him up from number six to three on the back of the innings, and he managed to pick up his timing where it left off.

The killer stand came with Rahul Dravid. They love their cricket in India and could probably quote you the figures. The pair of them batted through the fourth day and added 376. Laxman was just outstanding. He couldn't be anything other than elegant – you can see from his wristiness that Mohammad Azharuddin was a role model – and on this occasion everything clicked. He danced down the pitch and hit me into the leg side. I thought that if I kept spinning it across his body, he was bound to miss one or get a leading edge sooner or later. The chance never came. Dravid played solidly at the other end, but Laxman scored rapidly. That was why, ultimately, India not only gained a lead but had time to bowl us out on the final day, helped by some pretty tired and ordinary batting on our part. The rest of his team took confidence from his brilliance, and they went on to win the series 2–1.

He could not stay at number three for long, because Dravid was soon reinstated in the position he had made his own. But Laxman has batted in most slots during his time. I think that the first time I came across him he was opening. He is tall enough to be able to get over the ball in Australia, which helps to explain his success there. He also likes the ball coming onto the bat so he can play his shots. Jason Gillespie and Brett Lee played against him at Under-19 level and say that he was effective against us even then. One of his attributes is the ability to score off good balls. He also has the eye to be able to work straight ones either side of the pitch, though he does prefer to zip it through leg.

Our plan was to use the short ball, but he wasn't afraid when it whizzed past his ears – or no more so than anybody else. In 1998, he struck an incredible hundred at Sydney, scoring around 60 per cent of India's runs after being hit on the helmet early in the innings. He has always done well in Sydney, a ground that traditionally helps spinners. Because he likes to play his shots, it is obviously a good idea to keep him quiet with a consistent line and length. If he wants to take that on, he is taking a risk, and he cannot get away with it all the time.

After Calcutta, there was a lot of interest when he came over to Australia in 2003. I was not involved in that series, unfortunately, because I would have liked to have had another go at him. As a rule, I think aggression is the right policy against spin, and Laxman had the confidence to take me on. Anyway, our crowds were not disappointed because he again batted really well and scored hundreds at Adelaide and Sydney. This time he was the bloke in support as Dravid and Sachin Tendulkar scored doubles in the two matches. In time, I think their quartet of batsmen from recent years – throwing Sourav Ganguly into the mix – will be thought of as a group, like their four spin bowlers from the 1960s and '70s. But they all have their own individual strengths. Laxman at his best was the most elegant of the lot.

VANGIPURAPPU VENKATA SAI LAXMAN

BORN	1 November 1974, Hyderabad, Andhra Pradesh, India
TESTS	93
RUNS	5,785 in 158 innings at 43.82 with 12 hundreds/35 fifties
ONE-DAY INTERNATIONALS	86
RUNS	2,338 in 83 innings at 30.76 with 6 hundreds/10 fifties

78

·······

STUART CLARK

IF STUART CLARK HAD A DOLLAR for every time he'd been mentioned in the same sentence as Glenn McGrath, he would be the richest cricketer in Australia. It is such an obvious comparison, but the great thing about Clark is that he's not fazed by the link. In fact, he has never made any secret of the fact that he models himself on McGrath. His view is quite simple: he bowls at fast-medium pace, he is tall and he moves the ball off the pitch. When those are your assets, why would you try to do things any differently to a bloke of that type who was the best in the business? There is no way that Clark will end up with the same figures, because he was too late on the scene to have the time to tally up perhaps even half as many wickets as our great champion. But he has filled McGrath's role in the side more than adequately, and if people still look at him and wonder how he does it, then Clark will be quite happy.

People who do think along those lines are looking for something that isn't there. They are forgetting the golden rule of cricket: the game is best kept simple. That is how McGrath succeeded, and it is how Clark has gone about his business over the past couple of years. You run in, get close to the stumps, target the top of off stump, hit the pitch hard, draw the batsman forward, hit the seam and hope that it will deviate a little bit one way or the other. Do that often enough, and the bloke at the other end will come nibbling like a fish around a juicy hook. Clark has done well at international level because he realised that what was good enough to get him there in the first place is good enough to keep him there.

In his own way, he is an inspirational cricketer. You wouldn't know that to look at him or listen to him, because he just shrugs things off quietly and modestly. But he had to wait until he was 30 to make his Test debut, and he never stopped dreaming the dream. I think there is a lot to be said in picking a guy at that stage of his career rather than a youngster. There is no hard and fast rule, and it varies from player to player, but when Clark came into the Australia team, he was pretty much the finished article. Yes, there is always room for improvement, and you are always fine-tuning the odd technical thing, but he knew his game inside out. As long as your game is solid, the only question that remains is your ability to cope with bigger crowds and extra pressure. That is where selectors have to use their judgement, and in Clark's case he fitted in straight away. He has some very subtle changes, such as the leg cutter, which is probably the best in the world, he out thinks a lot of batsmen and his bouncer is deceptively quick.

I knew about him from state cricket and never had a problem when he came into the side for our tour to South Africa in 2006. Effectively he replaced McGrath while he was caring for his lovely wife, Jane, now sadly gone. The South Africans were the first to fall into the trap of underestimating Clark. Before the first Test at Cape Town they ordered the groundsman to water the pitch because they were worried that it would be too dry, crumble and turn. So when they batted conditions were perfect for a seamer like Clark, who promptly took three wickets in his first spell, five in the innings and walked away with the Man of the Match award on his debut. Forgetting McGrath for a minute, I think there is a good comparison between Clark and Paul Reiffel, another unassuming guy who did a great job for Australia in a similar quiet way in the 1990s. He was perfect in the role of third seamer but would never waste the new ball if he was thrown it, because he had such impeccable control.

When Clark came into the squad, it was interesting to hear our batsmen talk about him, especially Mike Hussey, who had also waited a long time for his opportunity and had faced him on many occasions. Hussey thought he would do a sound job straight away. During the 2006–07 Ashes, he bowled in the same attack as McGrath and Brett Lee, who gave us pace and swing, and they formed a really effective unit. Without ever taking five wickets in an innings, he picked up his twos and threes consistently. He is now a regular member of the attack and has shown that he can bowl in different conditions.

It looks as though he and Brett Lee will form the nucleus of the attack when Australia go to England in 2009 to try to retain the Ashes. They are a good pair, and the left-arm of Mitchell Johnson will give Ricky Ponting a different option. There are quite a few pace bowlers pressing for places at the moment, so we may see an interesting new face or two in the squad. Clark has done well in county cricket, so he will be an important figure and a senior player, despite having relatively few Tests behind him. With tours every four years, it might be his only chance in England. Overall, Australia can't afford to lose Clark before the South African series or the Ashes. He is a very important member of the Test side.

STUART RUPERT CLARK

BORN	28 September 1975, Sydney, Australia
TESTS	18
WICKETS	81 at 21.46
ONE-DAY INTERNATIONALS	33
WICKETS	45 at 29.88

79

·······

MARK BOUCHER

LIKE ALL GOOD WICKET-KEEPERS, MARK BOUCHER can be a niggly opponent behind the stumps. That is not an insult, simply a fact. He is probably no better or worse than most of his colleagues. Having a good quip at the right time is part of the job, although the words have more of an impact when they are supported by actions. Boucher doesn't have a problem on that score, because he has been one of the steadiest players in the South Africa side over the past ten years. I would describe him as being a solid all-round cricketer for the modern game. He is a very good number seven, will get you a few runs when you need them, values his wicket highly and does the bread-and-butter work behind the stumps without any fuss.

Boucher chose a great role model in Ian Healy, although I didn't realise that was the case until hearing an interview he did after passing Healy's all-time record of Test dismissals. It turned out that he used to watch him really closely as a kid when Australia were on TV. Boucher was very generous when he moved clear of Healy and then became the first man to take a combination of 400 catches and stumpings. He said that it was the sort of record that was bound to be beaten if somebody played for long enough, and because of that it felt almost a shame to overtake such a great technician as Healy. There is so much international cricket these days that aggregate figures are little use in comparing players from different eras. What you can say is that to claim so many victims – and Boucher is young enough to reach as many as 500 – means that you have to be the best in your country for a long time. Remember, there is only one place for the keeper in the whole XI.

As far as collecting wickets goes, Boucher has had very good attacks to keep to. Allan Donald and Shaun Pollock were the type of bowlers who found a lot of edges, and more recently the same applies to Makhaya Ntini. Boucher has not completed as many stumpings as either Healy or Gilchrist, which reflects the fact that South Africa have struggled to find a top-class spin bowler. Had they done so, I think, for a short time, they could have challenged us for the top spot. Paul Adams was effective for a period but largely because he was different, and his confidence and swagger didn't really reflect his ability. Once batsmen worked him out, he didn't have a comeback. Call me biased, but I think the true test of a keeper is the way he stands up to the stumps against spin. This can hardly be held against Boucher; his job was to keep to bowlers not to produce them.

South Africa obviously rated him highly, because they picked him very young, when he was only 20. I can understand the reasoning, because if you find a good wicket-keeper at that age, you shouldn't have to worry about the spot for the next decade, as long as there are players below Test level to keep the top man honest. It is the kind of job in which mistakes are magnified and can be costly, and in which experience does count for something. It says a lot for Boucher's mental strength and dedication that he came through the inevitable difficulties early on. I know that Bob Woolmer, when he was coach of South Africa, admired his work ethic, so Boucher had a good ally there. It was only later, when I was at Hampshire, that I realised his big rival at the time to succeed Dave Richardson was Nic Pothas, one of my county colleagues. Pothas is certainly good enough to have played at the top level.

We always felt we had the wood on South Africa during my time. They didn't beat us in a Test series, and we tended to win the big one-day games – or at least not lose them, given the incredible tied semi-final in the 1999 World Cup. Boucher was one of the players, along with Jacques Kallis, Lance Klusener and Shaun Pollock, who gave the side terrific depth and balance. Hansie Cronje was usually good for a few overs of medium pace as well. Personally, I didn't mind bowling to Boucher, because he liked to try to sweep me, which I thought gave me a chance. But on his day, late in an innings, he could smash 20 or 30 runs quickly enough to turn a decent score into something over par or kick-start an innings after it had stalled. The same holds true in Test cricket, where many of his best knocks have come with South Africa in trouble.

Away from the field, he has always struck me as being a good bloke. He has made a few comments about things that were said on the field, but he realises that sort of thing is part and parcel of the game. I know that Donald used to encourage him to gee up the rest of the side out there on long afternoons. Like Jonty Rhodes, another role model, he plays it tough but knows where the lines are drawn and keeps things in the right spirit. At one point, it looked as though A.B. de Villiers would take over as keeper, but I think that South Africa have done the right thing by allowing de Villiers to concentrate on his batting. He is good enough to be a specialist in the middle order, and I wonder if he could concentrate for long periods – as he did at Headingley against England in 2008 – with the added responsibility of keeping wicket.

MARK VERDON BOUCHER

BORN	3 December 1976, East London, South Africa
TESTS	116
RUNS	4,272 in 167 innings at 29.87 with 4 hundreds/28 fifties
DISMISSALS	421 catches and 20 stumpings
ONE-DAY INTERNATIONALS	263
RUNS	4,203 in 194 innings at 28.98 with 1 hundred/25 fifties
DISMISSALS	368 catches and 18 stumpings

80

· · · · · ·

DARREN BERRY

ONE OF THE BEST WICKET-KEEPERS IN my time, and maybe of all time, Darren 'Chuck' Berry is also a great mate and sadly one of a dying breed. The balance has shifted from specialist keepers and even keeper/batsmen towards the batting side of the job – I call the current day keepers such as the Gilchrists and the Sangakkaras batsmen first and keepers second. Everybody thinks they are out there in abundance. They're not.

Berry was so unlucky not to have played Test cricket. Ian Healy, another master gloveman, was around at the start of his career and Adam Gilchrist at the end. There was just no way past those two, and it is a shame that people outside Australia never saw Berry, especially standing up to the stumps. He was just a natural, with some of the best footwork and speed of hand you can imagine. There was nothing showy about his keeping; there didn't need to be, because he was always in the right position to do what needed to be done. If Healy hadn't been around, I think that Berry could have played 100 times for Australia and been recognised for the brilliant player he was.

Records only hint at his ability, although some of them are still really impressive. Nobody has completed more dismissals for Victoria over the course of a career; he once managed eight in a single innings. During one sequence, he went more than 2,000 runs over a number of digs without conceding a bye. His hands were very safe, but he was also an attacking keeper. He put more pressure on batsmen by standing up to the seamers. I remember a state game when he stumped David Boon down the leg side off Paul Reiffel – who was more than just medium pace – to the last ball before lunch. That gave us all something to talk about during the break. Batsmen could never afford to stand out of their ground with Berry breathing down their necks.

Another of his big advantages against the seamers was the ground he would cover going for catches. He went for everything, and pretty much got everything. That meant you could stand a bit wider at first slip, second slip could push out and so on. It was like having an extra fielder. He was always decisive as well, so there was never any confusion about balls going wide to your left at first slip. Even if he had to be fully horizontal, Berry would go for them and take them as though it was second nature. He was always consistent about that, unlike some keepers who might shape to go for a chance and then pull back, causing the confusion that leads to chances going down or being missed completely.

The only area of his game which he perhaps could have done more with was his batting, but even then he was no mug. He was a really gritty player who could be hard to chisel out when he really set his mind to the task. He scored four hundreds, and I think all four of them were against New South Wales. They were our big rivals, and games against them were fought as hard as anything I have been involved with outside Test cricket. In the 1990s, it tended to be the case that Victoria had most of the Australia bowlers and New South Wales the batsmen, but Berry still scored runs against the likes of Glenn McGrath and top spinners such as Greg Matthews and Stuart MacGill.

I know that he was frustrated that the call from Australia never came. You can have six batsmen in a side and four or five bowlers, but only one keeper. He was our equivalent of Bob Taylor, who missed out against Alan Knott for years in England, although Taylor at least had opportunities later in his career and did a really good job. At one point, Berry thought about going to Zimbabwe to live and qualify. It would have taken four years, but the attraction of proving himself at international level was strong. This was in the days when Zimbabwe had a half-decent team, with guys such as Neil Johnson, Murray Goodwin and the Flower brothers making them competitive. In the end, he decided against it and went on to break Dean Jones's appearance record for Victoria before retiring after captaining the side to the Pura Cup in 2004.

He was a really full-on competitor. If anything, he was sometimes a little bit too intense and a bit emotional, which could be his downfall. But nobody doubted his passion for the game. Nowadays, he is taking his first steps into coaching. As the assistant at Victoria, he is every bit as determined as he was for us in his playing days. He did some great work alongside me for the Rajasthan Royals in the IPL, and I don't think it will be long before he gets a senior coaching position somewhere, maybe with an English county. We have a similar outlook to the game in general. Neither of us likes to see things just drift along. He is really well organised, and his drills are done to the letter. Not surprisingly, he is especially good with young keepers. Berry did a lot of work with Pakistan's Kamran Akmal while he was playing for the Royals. Akmal really enjoyed being shown a few new things and will only improve as a result.

DARREN SHANE BERRY

BORN	10 December 1969, Melbourne, Australia
FIRST CLASS RUNS	4,273 at 21.58 with 4 hundreds/11 fifties
FIRST-CLASS DISMISSALS	552 catches and 51 stumpings

81

·······

GREG MATTHEWS

GREG MATTHEWS IS ONE OF THOSE guys who used to divide opinion.
I know the feeling. He's been away from the international game
for a few years now, so the name might not mean a lot to younger
readers. In some ways, he is like Phil Tufnell – a true character.
As an off-spinner and left-handed batsman – a pretty unusual
combination straight away – he was a true fighter who wasn't short
of talent. He was great for the game because he had an image that
helped to bring in crowds. And he loved cricket.

He still plays grade level for Sydney University and even now,
heading towards his 50th birthday, still reckons he is the best finger
spinner in the country. He could be right. He is waiting for the
selectors to call and always stresses that he hasn't retired. In fact, he
reckons what he has lost with his zip he can more than compensate
for with his experience and knowledge. Somebody asked him
whether his body would stand up to a whole four-days match with
New South Wales, and he pointed out that if the batsmen did their
job, he would only have to be involved for two or three of them.
That's what I meant when I described him as a character.

I will never forget how he helped me in Sri Lanka on my first
senior Australia tour in 1992. Having been catapulted into the Test
side and having taken a battering from the Indians at home, I was
feeling a bit down on myself and wondering whether I could cope
alongside some of the great Australia players. Matthews could sense
that things were not quite right, so he took me out to an Italian
restaurant after the fourth day's play in Colombo and gave me some
advice that was so simple but so true. The gist was that if people

did not think I was good enough to do the job, they would not have picked me. However obvious that sounds now, believe me it was just what I wanted to hear back then. I have since passed it on to young players who are new to a side.

During that same meal, he decided to nickname me 'Suicide' after one of the biggest records being played by the squad at the time, 'Suicide Blonde' by INXS. I had blond hair, and the next day when I was bowling at a crucial time in the match he kept yelling out 'Come on, Suicide' or 'Spin it up, Suicide' before every ball – you could probably hear him from the boundary. The little pep talk did the trick, because I took three wickets without conceding a run, we won a tight game and I felt that I'd made my first contribution to the side. Allan Border said a few nice things, but Matthews deserved all of the credit, and he was awesome that day. His bowling was brilliant and won us the game.

That was not an isolated case, because I know that he helped other young players when they came into the side, often with nothing more than a few words of encouragement. He never thought of any of us as rivals for his place and liked the idea of being a mentor, passing down his thoughts and ideas. Later, when he stepped down from state level, he set up coaching clinics, among other little ventures. It is quite hard to know his main line of work these days. He does a few bits and bobs for television and the media. Journalists like him because he has a lot of opinions, often from left field. As a rule, he isn't a great one for authority. I saw a website recently that named him captain of an all-time Australia Loose Guns XI. He would take that as a compliment.

Basically, Matthews was and still is an extrovert. He would play air guitar in the outfield. His dress sense is flamboyant, and people might still remember some of his haircuts; he had a Mohican before Kevin Pietersen was a twinkle in his mother's eye. People might also remember his ten wickets in the famous 'Tied Test' in Chennai in 1986. Even by Indian standards, that can be a tough place to play. Matthews did not just bowl and bowl and bowl, he never once took off his sweater. He was heroic in that game.

For all his bravado and little quirks, he was a good cricketer, one who never shrank into the background when things got tough. He batted against the West Indies when they had a bowling attack of Marshall, Garner, Holding and Walsh, and he featured in three Ashes series. One of his proudest moments was scoring a hundred against England in Sydney. I remember his darting footwork against England's spinner Eddie Hemmings, who seemed to get more and more annoyed and red-faced. Matthews followed that with 58 overs in the next innings. He was a really important player at number seven throughout the 1990–91 series. In fact, in his last Test against the West Indies a couple of years later, he scored 79 and then bowled 59 overs. That is a pretty impressive way to go – although, as Matthews will tell you, he hasn't actually gone. He was lots of fun and deep down loves the values of the game. He is a friend who really helped me at a tough time, and I will never forget that. Thanks, Mo, and 'spin up spinner'.

GREGORY RICHARD JOHN MATTHEWS

BORN	15 December 1959, Newcastle, New South Wales, Australia
TESTS	33
RUNS	1,849 in 53 innings at 41.08 with 4 hundreds/12 fifties
WICKETS	61 at 48.22
ONE-DAY INTERNATIONALS	59
RUNS	619 in 50 innings at 16.72 with 1 fifty
WICKETS	57 at 35.15

82

·······

CRAIG MCMILLAN

CRAIG MCMILLAN WAS ONE OF THE more underrated players in world cricket over the course of my career. The other way of looking at it is that he underachieved, but I think that misses the point about the way he played the game. He could be a match-winner, and that type of batsman is not going to pull it off every time. A side has to have balance, and if McMillan had reined in some of his shots, he would have lost the qualities that made him what he was, and the New Zealand batting unit would have lost something at the same time. This is a bloke who hit 26 runs in an over in a Test match, against Younus Khan, and struck a 67-ball hundred against Australia in a one-day international. His reputation in the game – certainly in our dressing-room – might have been higher than it was outside.

Whenever he came out to bat, we realised we were up against a guy who could turn the game around. Because of his inconsistency, we never knew what we were getting, and I think that made him interesting to the crowds. He could be fun to play against, because you knew he would never go for the draw and always wanted to be in the game. Like a lot of the New Zealanders under Stephen Fleming, he was extremely competitive on the field and knew what it meant to his country to beat Australia. To put it bluntly, he had balls. Away from the game, he was great company and liked to socialise.

The challenge for Fleming, which he quickly worked out, was how to build up McMillan's confidence. If he felt good, he could be dynamite. So, from the opposite point of view – ours – we always tried to knock his self-belief when he first came to the crease. The plan was simple: keep him under pressure at all times and avoid a loose ball at any price. You don't want to give anybody an easy boundary, but if you could keep McMillan quiet, he was more likely than most to go for a rash shot, because he started to feel uneasy. On the same tack, when he wasn't sure of his place in the side, he became less of a threat. Confidence can make the difference between success and failure.

He had a big reputation as a young player in New Zealand, and because there is not the depth of talent over there, he came into the Test side early. He impressed me straight away. I remember him whacking a straight six on his debut at Brisbane. The New Zealand plan in that match was to push forward to try to reduce the impact of my flipper, and he coped pretty well. In fact, that Test is a pretty good summary of his career: a good fifty in the first innings and a first-baller in the second. For all his inconsistency, I was happy to help sign him for Hampshire as an overseas player because of the contribution he would make in the dressing-room as well as on the field. There are so many commitments these days that players rarely last the whole season, and it is vital to find somebody with the character to fit in straight away.

I think of him as an all-rounder – not a fully fledged Freddie Flintoff, but a guy with a habit of breaking partnerships. He got Damien Martyn out a couple of times, as well as both of the Waughs. He was also very useful for a few overs in the one-day arena. The trick for the captain was not so much when to bring him on but when to take him off and make sure he didn't keep going for one over too long when the batsmen had sussed out his pace. His strike rate is really good for a bloke you would think of as a spare sixth bowler at best. That is probably because batsmen thought he was easy for runs and tried to go after him too early. He was lucky to have had Stephen Fleming as captain to get the best out of him.

He was only 31 when he retired, but he left after a good season because he wanted to spend more time with his family. A few months earlier, he had been one of the stars of the first World Twenty20 in South Africa. The format was perfect for his style of play, and he must have been glad that he jacked in the idea to stand down a year or so earlier to move into sales. It is a shame that twenty-over cricket didn't take off in such a big way three or four years earlier. McMillan would have given spectators around the world a better indication of his true talent.

CRAIG DOUGLAS MCMILLAN

BORN	13 September 1976, Christchurch, New Zealand
TESTS	55
RUNS	3,116 in 91 innings at 38.46 with 6 hundreds/19 fifties
WICKETS	28 at 44.89
ONE-DAY INTERNATIONALS	197
RUNS	4,707 in 183 innings at 28.18 with 3 hundreds/28 fifties
WICKETS	49 at 35.04

83

•••••••

PAUL REIFFEL

AFTER ENGLAND'S FINAL INNINGS IN THE final Test at the Oval in 1993, it just so happened that the four Australia bowlers found ourselves together, behind the rest of the group, as we walked off the field. You could probably say we dawdled a bit at the end of another hard day's work. As we trudged off, to the surprise of all of us, the crowd got to their feet and clapped. We all appreciated that moment, and it was fitting that Paul Reiffel was there with Tim May, Merv Hughes and me, because over the previous weeks his great efforts had been slightly overlooked. Whereas Hughes was a bloke everybody recognised and loved to hate, Reiffel just did his job in a quiet, unassuming way. In the dressing-room, we knew he was a really important factor in our success, even if his contributions did not always get the recognition they deserved.

People might be surprised to learn that his bowling average is as low as 26. Reiffel was easy to underestimate, but he had the ability to make the ball talk. He hit the seam as often as almost anybody and had good control of his line and length. He was not express pace but bowled a heavy ball, and he always asked questions of the batsmen. Ideally, he was a first-change bowler. He made a great third seamer, because you could guarantee that he would maintain the pressure after the new-ball attack. A lot of sides fail because they lack depth, but Reiffel was perfect for that particular job, and if there was anything in a pitch, he could be devastating thanks to his control. That also made him a really effective one-day player. In fact, his last one-day international was the World Cup final in 1999 when we beat Pakistan at Lord's. His wife was about to give birth

259

to their second child, and he just thought it was the right time to get out. Then when he retired from all cricket three years later, he was Victoria's leading wicket taker of all time.

By the time I started playing for the Vics, he was a regular member of the team. He could be quite sharp in those days, but injuries forced him to cut down on his speed as the years went by. At Test level, he was consistent enough to make a very significant contribution at some point in almost every major series. Having been left out of the original squad for the 1997 England tour, he received a late call-up when we were one down after the first game, and he helped to turn things around. The attack of Reiffel, Glenn McGrath and a young Jason Gillespie from that point onwards was one of the tightest I can remember for Australia. Reiffel took five wickets in the second innings at Headingley, a game we were especially pleased to win after England switched the pitch two days before the start of the match.

Maybe his greatest moment came in the Kingston Test in 1995. Whoever won that game won the series, and we were looking to topple the West Indies from their number-one spot. Looking back now, it was typical Reiffel. Given the new ball, he responded brilliantly with seven wickets in both innings, including both openers both times. He also sent back Brian Lara for a duck. Yet the game is remembered for other contributions, especially from Mark and Steve Waugh in a match-winning partnership. We had lost Craig McDermott and Damien Fleming to injury, but Reiffel quietly took responsibility and found an extra yard of his old pace. Once again, he was the unsung hero.

He was a very reliable fielder, and during the last couple of years of his Test career, he also did really well with the bat against England, New Zealand and South Africa. He would ice the cake for us, to use an old phrase, just rubbing it in on the opposition bowlers after they had got through our main batting. A lower-order batsman holding up an innings is one of the most frustrating things for a captain. Reiffel had a solid defence – as with his bowling, it was effective, no-frills stuff – and he thought that if he had made a few scores when he was younger, he might have developed as an all-rounder. By the end of his career, his batting average was up there with his bowling figure, but he never quite managed to make it to a first-class hundred.

PAUL REIFFEL

Since retiring, he has gone into umpiring, and I think the sooner the likes of Reiffel and Rod Tucker are fast-tracked to Test level and join the ICC panel, the better. In Australia, it is far rarer for ex-players to go into umpiring than it is in England. That may be because there are simply more former players in England, with eighteen first-class counties instead of six state teams. But Reiffel has shown very good judgement so far, and he would have the respect of all the players from every country, because he was always known as an honest, 100 per cent cricketer. That is what you want in an umpire – nothing flash, just somebody who makes the right decisions and quietly goes about his business.

PAUL RONALD REIFFEL

BORN	19 April 1966, Box Hill, Victoria, Australia
TESTS	35
WICKETS	104 at 26.96
RUNS	955 in 50 innings at 26.52 with 6 fifties
ONE-DAY INTERNATIONALS	92
WICKETS	106 at 29.20
RUNS	503 in 57 innings at 13.97 with 1 fifty

84

·······

SIMON JONES

PUTTING THE RESULT TO ONE SIDE – which is the best way for an Aussie – there were so many great human-interest stories in the 2005 Ashes. The return of Simon Jones was probably the happiest of all. Anybody with any feelings must have been delighted at the way he came back into the England side after the terrible injury he suffered in Brisbane in 2002 that threatened his career. More problems in the past three years mean that he hasn't actually played for England since 2005, although it has been great to see him back in the wickets with Worcestershire in 2008. Who knows what lies ahead now? I think the best way to look at Jones's career is not to wonder what might have been if he had stayed fit to play 50 or 60 matches, but to think how fortunate England were that he hit his peak in the month or so when they needed him most.

Jones was a significant player in that series. I've said elsewhere that the depth of the England bowling was new to us, and Jones fitted into the attack perfectly because he could swing the old ball at around 90 mph. He caused us all sorts of problems in the first four matches before he hurt his ankle and missed the decider at the Oval. I know that he tried desperately to make it through to the end of the series, but he had to pull out, allowing Paul Collingwood to come in and grab an MBE. Mention Jones and everybody thinks of reverse swing. Freddie Flintoff reversed the ball as well that summer, but Jones perfected the skill better than anybody, and we spent a long time in our camp talking about and working on the best ways to counter the threat. Although we had seen it before – the Pakistanis have been masters for years – we found it very hard to combat because of the sheer pace it was delivered at.

There are all sorts of theories about how and why the ball reverses, or 'goes Irish' as we call it in Australia. This isn't my area of expertise, but basically it seems to happen as a result of keeping one side of the ball dry and hoping that it becomes abrasive to change the weight balance on different sides of the seam. Jones got interested in it in a big way after he started messing around with different balls in the nets a few years before the 2005 Ashes. He began to experiment with Troy Cooley, who was England's bowling coach at the time and is now back in Australia doing a similar job.

For batsmen, facing reverse swing can be like playing Russian roulette, especially at the kind of speeds that Jones is capable of generating. You are programmed to note the ball in the bowler's hand and judge the way it will move by the position of the shiny side. With reverse, by definition, the ball swings the other way, so the batsman has to check his instinct. It can be even harder if the bowler conceals the ball in his run-up or manages to switch it in his hand as he approaches. Mike Kasprowicz, who played with Jones at Glamorgan, later explained to me that the Cardiff pitch is dry and slow so bowlers need to come up with different tricks to be effective. They were big buddies, and Kasprowicz also got the ball to reverse in 2005, but not at the same speed as Jones.

I guess the highlight for Jones was at Old Trafford when he took six wickets. The in-swinger he produced to get rid of Michael Clarke has been described as one of the balls of the summer. But it was a bittersweet game for Jones. Towards the end of that incredible final day, when 20,000 or so people were locked out an hour before the match because the ground was already full, he suffered a bad cramp attack and was not on the field when our last-wicket pair of Glenn McGrath and Brett Lee were staving off the final 24 balls to get a draw. I thought it was a tribute to England's determination throughout the series that instead of moping around after a lost opportunity, they went straight to Trent Bridge and beat us in another tight game.

Jones had a few more great moments over those crazy weeks. His very first ball got him a wicket, Damien Martyn, in the dramatic first session at Lord's. He also made an impact with the bat at Edgbaston when his last-wicket stand with Flintoff in the second innings gave England just enough runs to go on and win. I liked the way he went for his shots, and with Flintoff going great guns at the other end, it gave the crowd a big lift. Jones is an aggressive cricketer with the physique of a bodybuilder, and he has a very good strike rate for England. Usually, his type of bowler takes the new ball, but as first or second change he gave the attack extra depth.

Off the field, he was good company. The Glamorgan lads are noted as being one of the best bunches on the county circuit. I liked the story about Jones and Kevin Pietersen going into an Australia theme bar in Birmingham after their win at Edgbaston wearing head bands to make themselves look like Dennis Lillee. He is one of those blokes you want to see do well.

SIMON PHILIP JONES

BORN	25 December 1978, Swansea, Wales
TESTS	18
WICKETS	59 at 28.23
ONE-DAY INTERNATIONALS	8
WICKETS	7 at 39.28

85

• • • • • • •

CHRIS GAYLE

IN MY EXPERIENCE, A LOT OF the West Indian players who give the impression of being laid-back, happy-go-lucky characters are the most determined competitors of all. Chris Gayle belongs in this camp. He is famous for being the coolest cricketer in the world, as judged by Chris Gayle, although there is a lot of competition for that tag even in his own dressing-room. Many of the West Indians like to chew gum, look out from behind their shades with their earphones in and move with the rhythm of their music – sometimes I wonder whether there actually is any sound coming from their iPods. But behind Gayle's appearance lies a guy who is deadly serious about his cricket. You can see when he has captained the West Indies that he has a feel for situations. He just knows the game, and you don't get that knowledge without making a few mental notes throughout your career. I think he is a lot smarter than people give him credit for. And when he complained about some of the players the selectors gave him for the recent one-day series against Australia, it sent out another signal that he cares deeply about his side.

He is certainly one of the great entertainers in the game today. From the style of his batting to those little groovy jigs when he takes a wicket, he is a bloke spectators cannot afford to lose from their sight. He is a modern-style opener, in that he doesn't mind taking on the new ball. I would put him in the Virender Sehwag and Michael Slater category, though maybe he's not quite of the same quality. When you consider Gayle, you have to remember his very handy off-spin and some of the brilliant catches he takes in the slips, as

265

well as his captaincy. We think of him as a batsman rather than an all-rounder, but the options he offers in the other areas mean that he becomes a very important package to his team.

When I played, our tactic was to work on him with the short stuff and be as consistent as we could – just give him nothing to hit and frustrate him. I actually enjoy bowling to guys with that approach, because I know it is always me or them. Gayle is tall, so he can give the bat a good swing, and he likes to flay the ball through the off side. The key is not to worry if you get hit for a couple of sixes or a few fours and to remember the old cliché, one of the truest in cricket: it only takes one ball – one moment of overambition from the batsman – to get a wicket. Another thing we talked about at meetings was to make sure that with Gayle more than most we stuck to our plan. It is interesting to note that he hasn't got out to spin too often in Test cricket. That is because he scores his runs quickly at the start of the innings but gives chances along the way.

He would be more effective with a regular opening partner, but the West Indies have never found a solid, reliable bloke who can go out there and work as his foil. It has left them susceptible, with Gayle, who can be brilliant or who can go early, at one end and somebody at the other who is always playing for a place. Of course, when he pulls it off, he is electric, and it is worth remembering that he has a triple-hundred in Test cricket to his credit, albeit on one of the flattest pitches in the world in Antigua. Generally, his conversion rate from 50 to 100 has been pretty ordinary.

His game is perfect for one-day cricket. With only two fielders on the boundary, he has even more scope to bat the way he likes in the initial stages, and his bowling also comes into its own. He has the calm temperament to be able to come on at the death, and he can make inexperienced batsmen panic. It is easy to think you should be scoring more quickly against him, because he is not thought of as a front-line bowler, but that doesn't do justice to his ability. There is an easy comparison with Carl Hooper, who took on a similar role in one-day matches. Although Gayle does not turn the ball a long way, he varies his pace cleverly, has a good yorker and because he is a batsman first and foremost he usually has a good idea what the batsman at the other end is planning.

CHRIS GAYLE

He is quite unusual in that his figures in one-day cricket are currently better than they are in the Test arena. As far as the batting goes, that may be because fields are not as attacking in 50-over matches. Captains are reluctant even to begin with a cordon of slips, and when they do post men there, they usually start to come out as soon as a couple of balls go through extra cover or mid-wicket. You want to tie down batsmen, but the best way of containing an innings is to take wickets. On the bowling front, I can see why Gayle takes wickets, because batsmen are looking to take risks. I would not describe him as all that penetrating in Test cricket, but he is more than handy for a few overs to try to put on the brakes or split a partnership.

CHRISTOPHER HENRY GAYLE

BORN	21 September 1979, Kingston, Jamaica
TESTS	73
RUNS	4,804 in 131 innings at 38.12 with 7 hundreds/29 fifties
WICKETS	63 at 40.26
ONE-DAY INTERNATIONALS	184
RUNS	6,487 in 181 innings at 38.84 with 15 hundreds/37 fifties
WICKETS	149 at 32.38

86

·······

IAN BISHOP

THERE ARE PEOPLE WHO THINK THAT Ian Bishop could have been the greatest of all the West Indian fast bowlers of the 1980s and '90s if he hadn't suffered a run of terrible injuries. I didn't have the 'pleasure' of facing Joel Garner or Malcolm Marshall, but I came up against Curtly Ambrose at his peak, so I know that any claims on behalf of Bishop represent incredibly high praise. Having batted against him, I know where they are coming from, although personally I couldn't put him above Ambrose, a towering figure in every way. Whatever, it is always sad when bowlers who could have been truly outstanding have their careers cut short through no fault of their own; Bruce Reid and Shane Bond are another couple who immediately spring to mind. In all three cases, they played for long enough to show their undoubted ability, and we can only speculate what might have happened if they had played more.

Bishop had a lovely high action, he was tall enough to get good bounce, he was genuinely fast and he managed to swing the ball away. You don't need a lot more than that little combination to be a very difficult opponent. Although his approach looked pretty smooth, he twice had to overcome serious back trouble to get his career back on track. But he was still the quickest West Indies bowler in terms of appearances to notch up 100 Test wickets. His strike rate was good, even though he didn't always have the advantage of the new ball. He was only 30 when he had to pack it in, and his name tends to be forgotten these days alongside some of those who went on for longer. Courtney Walsh would stand at the other extreme. He bowled consistently well with few problems for the best part of two decades.

I played against Bishop in two series, both in Australia. The first time, in 1992–93, he took the new ball with Ambrose, and there was talk among some of the West Indians that they could be a similar combination in style to Garner and Mikey Holding. With Ambrose, there is his obvious similarity in height to Garner, and Bishop, I suppose, had that same light-footed tread as Holding when he ran in. Comparisons like that never do anybody any favours, but I remember the game in Perth when Ambrose took seven wickets in the first innings, with the most destructive spell of bowling I ever saw, and Bishop followed it with six in the second. He was very, very quick on that occasion and actually sent back our two most solid players, David Boon and Allan Border, in the same over. To make the achievement even more amazing, he bowled both of them, sending Boon's off stump cartwheeling and then getting Border with an inside edge.

He had spent more than two years out of cricket between that series and the next time the West Indies came over in 1996–97. The balance of the world game had swung towards us during the period in between, but they were still a strong-looking side. We took a 3–1 lead and won the series, but after bowling as first or second change at the start, Bishop finished by resuming his new-ball partnership with Ambrose. He chipped in with wickets rather than blasting through as the spearhead, and I think that his pace was perhaps slightly down on four years earlier. He could still be very awkward, though, especially in Perth on a pretty ordinary pitch at the end of the series.

What strikes me about his record is his consistency on different pitches. He was just as effective away from home as he was in the Caribbean. Actually, his figures against Australia are very slightly better than overall, which is a huge tribute considering the quality of our batting during the series he played. I took performances all over the world into account when I picked my 100. Bishop was not one of those bowlers who needed conditions to be in his favour before he was effective.

These days, he is making a good living as a shrewd commentator. One of the ironies about the injuries he suffered during his playing career is that they opened up time for him to become involved in the media. He is a cricket man through and through who has cared for the game deeply, man and boy. Like most of us, he used to listen to the radio commentaries from abroad when his team was touring, noted down all the scores and then went out to relive the games in a garden or park.

It is great that he is now back helping the West Indies. But he does get annoyed when the young West Indies bowlers today forget the basics of line and length – Bishop's generation used to hate giving away easy runs. There are so many really good players with things to offer, and Bishop recognised the problems with cricket in the Caribbean early on. I remember almost a decade ago he was saying that they needed systems in place to support the players and make sure that the brightest kids were coming through with the best coaching available. People thought the conveyor belt of fast bowlers and gifted batsmen would keep on turning, but Bishop knew that the West Indies would struggle as soon as it slowed down and then stopped. They are making up for lost time now, and it looks as though things are in place, thankfully. World cricket needs a strong West Indies.

IAN RAPHAEL BISHOP

BORN	24 October 1967, Belmont, Port of Spain
TESTS	43
WICKETS	161 at 24.27
ONE-DAY INTERNATIONALS	84
WICKETS	118 at 26.50

87

·······

GARY KIRSTEN

OVER THE COURSE OF ALMOST EVERY Test series Gary Kirsten played in, at least a couple of his innings had a serious bearing on the outcome of a game. He could either lay a foundation, quietly and unspectacularly, for a major first-innings score or drop anchor second time around to get South Africa out of trouble. In between, he would chip in with runs, so it was not a case of feast or famine. He always did his bit, often more. But because he didn't dominate like a Virender Sehwag or Michael Slater, he perhaps hasn't had the wider recognition he deserves. I suppose you can call him a players' player in that sense. On the circuit, we all knew his value just as much as the South Africans did. And he has definitely been one of their most effective batsmen since coming back into international cricket.

The Australia bowling attack was constantly frustrated by Kirsten. He had a happy knack of playing and missing. I would put him in the top three for that in my time, but after a while I realised that it wasn't simply down to luck. What Kirsten did really well was to play the line of the ball. That way, if it moved even a small distance, he made sure that he wouldn't make contact and nick to the wicket-keeper or slips. A lot of the time, being a left-hander, the ball would be slanting away from him in any case. The batsmen who give the edges are the ones who follow the ball after it pitches. That is the instinctive thing to do, and remember, we are talking split seconds here. But Kirsten had such good concentration and awareness of the position of his stumps that he rarely lulled himself into making a misjudgement.

He also made sure that he thought about the next ball rather than the last. As slip fielders, we were always kept interested, but Kirsten never worried when he heard the anguished gasps from our cordon that always followed what we thought of as a close shave. And there wasn't a lot of point telling him in our polite way that he was having all the luck going. He just settled in his stance again and ploughed on regardless.

South Africa had a top-class side in the second half of the 1990s, and Kirsten was their rock at the top of the order, a very reliable foil for whoever his opening partner happened to be. Because South Africa never found anybody as effective to go out alongside him, he was always the senior figure, but responsibility never became a burden.

We were fortunate to have some good pace bowlers while I played for Australia, including Merv Hughes, Craig McDermott, Glenn McGrath, Jason Gillespie and Brett Lee. They all did a bit with the ball, so they were used to batsmen playing and missing. When it happens regularly, it can become frustrating, and the temptation is there to try something different. Kirsten could take bowlers away from their plans like that. The atmosphere at the Wanderers ground could be very hostile – in the stands and on the pitch. But Kirsten himself is a lovely, level-headed bloke with a good sense of humour. He is just a very solid all-round citizen.

He once batted for more than 14 hours against England, the second longest innings of all time, and his final Test innings helped to deny New Zealand a series win. Years earlier, he made his initial appearances against us, and I'd like to think he found it a pretty tough baptism. Even still, he looked calm at the crease. He did not make any big scores, but he generally saw off the new ball and made his 30s and 40s. By the time he came over in 2001–02, he had already demonstrated so many examples of his stamina. In the second innings at Sydney, he batted more than seven hours, spanning five sessions, to score one hundred and fifty-three after we had built up a lead of four hundred on first dig. Eventually, he dragged a wide one from Stuart MacGill onto his stumps. I think a lot of batsmen with their side so far behind would have capitulated early – we were already 2–0 up, and this was the last game in the series – but Kirsten still had enough pride to keep going and make us work as hard as he could. You do not have to blast the ball to all parts to be an inspirational teammate.

I am not surprised that he has decided to go into coaching. He is the kind of guy who will get on well with anybody. He knew his own technique so well that if something went wrong he could break it all down and put it back together, with the glitch sorted out, whatever that happened to be. Because he wasn't the most orthodox batsman, he will appreciate that players find their own methods, and I do not imagine him being much of a tinkerer – one of those coaches who feel they have to suggest changes to justify their positions. He can do a really good job with India because there are some talented young cricketers coming through and interest in the game is getting stronger and stronger, as I saw during the 2008 IPL.

GARY KIRSTEN

BORN	23 November 1967, Cape Town, South Africa
TESTS	101
RUNS	7,289 in 176 innings at 45.27 with 21 hundreds/34 fifties
ONE-DAY INTERNATIONALS	185
RUNS	6,798 in 185 innings at 40.95 with 13 hundreds/45 fifties

88

. . . .

MUSHTAQ AHMED

FOR A PERIOD OF A FEW weeks, Mushtaq Ahmed got me into a bit of trouble with my own team. Bowling spin can be a lonely job, because there is usually only one of us in a side, and we tend to get to know each other well on the circuit. I am a big one for sharing ideas and learning from other players. The trouble when Pakistan came over in 1995 was that Mushtaq learned things too quickly for our own good. It came about after a long chat when I showed him how I bowl my flipper, and he gave me his 'wrong-un'. I thought that would be a good swap from my point of view, because even now he probably bowls the wrong-un (better known in England as the googly) better than anybody else in the world. Unfortunately, by the time he came into the side, Mushtaq had got his head – or more to the point his fingers – around the flipper and kept using it to dismiss our batsmen! They couldn't believe it when they found out it was a ball that he'd picked up from me. It was probably just as well that we managed to win the series and that I took a few wickets myself along the way.

When I was coming into the game, Mushtaq was probably the top wrist-spinner in the world. His googly to bowl Graeme Hick in the 1992 World Cup final was one of the greatest balls I had ever seen. He filled the gap left by the great Abdul Qadir, who kept the torch burning during the 1970s and '80s. You can see the rubbery Qadir's influence on the way that Mushtaq bounces in with his arms whirling.

Mushtaq could also be a frustrating batsman at number ten or eleven because he liked to give the ball a hit and sometimes got away with edges when he ought to have been on his way. When we get together, it isn't usually long before he reminds me of his pulled innings in Karachi in 1994. He remembers it because he put on a few runs with Inzamam for the last wicket so that Pakistan sneaked home for the win – probably the worst ending to a game in my career. I tell him that I remember the partnership as well – for the three good lbw appeals I had turned down. And I always rib him about my sixes off his bowling in Hobart a year or so later. Spinners always like to have a bit of fun when they cross swords in the middle. I guess if we can't read each other's bowling, then nobody can.

Given how long he played the game, it amazes me that he didn't play more Test matches, even taking into account the occasional madness of the Pakistan selectors. An attack based around Wasim Akram, Waqar Younis and Mushtaq was as devastating as anything in the world. I know that Saqlain Mushtaq came onto the scene and caused trouble with the doosra, and that they played together at times, but if it came to a choice between one or the other, I thought that Mushtaq was the more effective as a wicket taker. Yes, he took a bit of punishment from time to time – unfortunately, that goes with the territory – but the moment a batsman starts to take you on is often the moment to start licking your lips. Perhaps one of Mushtaq's weaknesses was that you could get hold of him. He was a bit like Stuart MacGill, as he saw himself as a genuine wicket taker and didn't worry too much about economy rates. Because his googly was so effective, we generally reckoned to play him as an off-break bowler if we were unsure of a delivery, knowing that a leggie would turn past the edge.

Mushtaq is always great fun to be around. He took wickets all over the world, and it is good to hear that he wants to stay in the game as a coach now that he has finally packed it in. The more spinners involved in coaching, the better as far as I'm concerned. And he will be great with young players. You could see – and hear – the enthusiasm he had for the game by the way he appealed. Down at Hove with Sussex, he reminded me of one of the seagulls squawking away overhead. He would probably have had a bit more success if he had been playing Test cricket these days, because umpires are more willing to give batsmen out lbw when they play with their bats behind the pad. Mushtaq's wrong-un with the ball coming into the right-hander would have been even more effective.

It was funny to read in a magazine recently that Mushtaq sees his golden days as the period from 1992–98. He knows better than anyone else, of course, but I bet there were a few batsmen in English county cricket who were pleased they didn't come across him back then – because they found life hard enough, thanks very much, in the years after he joined Sussex. He loved playing there on the south coast, and I'd say he was the biggest reason for their success. It is a classic case of a captain, Chris Adams, being able to bring on his 'gun' bowler early – and the great thing about a spinner is that he can stay on. Mushtaq took bags of wickets, but he worked really hard for them. He loves the game and that rubs off on everybody around him. No wonder he is so popular at the club. Indeed, his recent announcement that he was retiring due to a persistent knee injury brought forth an outpouring of warmth and emotion at Sussex. To my mind, he goes down as one of that county's greatest players – and deservedly so.

MUSHTAQ AHMED

BORN	28 June 1970, Sahiwal, Punjab, Pakistan
TESTS	52
WICKETS	185 at 32.97
ONE-DAY INTERNATIONALS	144
WICKETS	161 at 33.29

89

....

JACK RUSSELL

NOT MANY PLAYERS IN MORE THAN a century of cricket have actually changed the game. Jack Russell belongs in the list of those who have. He is not an obvious member of such an illustrious group, but I reckon that wicket-keepers now look differently at one-day cricket because of his approach to the task. They had stood up to medium pace and even quick bowlers before, but I don't think anybody had done it so routinely as Russell, although I would also put Chuck Berry in that category. Those two changed the thinking of batsmen in the middle overs by standing up to the stumps. Maybe it doesn't sound significant, but it meant that batsmen could not stand out of the crease because of the risk of a stumping. And Russell, with his quick hands and feet, was a master at positioning himself to whip off the bails. Whereas a lot of keepers break the wicket straight away, he had the composure to hold the ball until the batsman lifted his back foot out of the crease to regain balance. Russell really was a master of his craft. I would rank him up there with Darren Berry as the best pure gloveman I played with or against.

I first came across Russell during my year in club cricket in Bristol in 1989. That was one of the best summers of my life, although I wouldn't be surprised if my liver is still recovering. Russell was legendary in the west of England. Even people who had never met him knew of his eccentricity – he would only eat Weetabix that had been soaked in milk for the right period of time, and he lived on one cup of tea after another. Best of all, he guarded his privacy so well that nobody at the county club knew his address.

If somebody wanted to go to his house, he would pick them up and blindfold them in case they remembered the route. This bloke takes the word 'slightly' out of the old saying that keepers are slightly mad.

A decade later, when I first came over to play for Hampshire, he was one of the major figures at Gloucestershire as they took a grip on one-day cricket. They switched their focus from the four-day game and soon started to win trophy after trophy. Looking down the list of names in that side, there were no out-and-out stars, but they all knew their roles to the letter and would choke teams in the final stages of a match with their brilliant fielding. Russell ran the show from behind the stumps. Everything went back to him before going on to the bowler to start again with the next ball. They were a really slick machine, with Russell barking out encouragement to the bowler and the fielders as well as providing the odd comment for the ears of the batsman. You couldn't fail to be aware of his presence breathing down your neck.

There was nothing showy about his keeping. The ball went softly into his gloves, and he always took it without a fuss. He made fielders look better than they were when he collected a throw on the half volley. Some keepers can't quite pick those balls up and settle for just stopping them, rather than completing the whole catch, and then having a moan at the thrower. He holds the record for the biggest total without conceding a bye, but the incredible thing is not the sheer size of that score – 746 by Northamptonshire – but that he was heading towards 40 years of age at the time. That tells you everything about his fitness and concentration, especially as he was forced to retire a year or so later because of a back injury.

Only his batting prevented him from playing more times for England. He was a brave and – needless to say – unorthodox guy at the crease who had the same attitude as the military heroes he likes to paint today. Yielding ground was against his nature, and his best innings usually came when England were in trouble and needed him to stick around. He was unlucky to play at the same time as Alec Stewart – or, to be more accurate, when England did not have an orthodox all-rounder. It meant that Stewart had to take on the two roles to balance the side. Had Freddie Flintoff been around then, Stewart could have concentrated on his batting and Russell would have kept wicket more often. It meant, for example, that I never played against him in a Test match. There are still people who think he was treated shabbily by the selectors.

I know that he was disappointed not to have spent more time keeping wicket to leg-spin. He has said that he envies the likes of Ian Healy, Moin Khan and Nayan Mongia, of India, for having had that opportunity. He kept to Mike Atherton and Ian Salisbury on limited occasions, but that is not the same as being in the same team with a Mushtaq Ahmed or an Anil Kumble. And I know he was worried that bowling attacks of medium and fast-medium trundlers with a bit of finger spin would remove the emphasis on skilled, specialist glovemen. He saw the day when the keeper became simply another fielder. Personally, while I can see the importance of runs, I would far rather have a keeper/batsman than a batsman/keeper. I really hope that things never go as far as he fears. It is impossible to know how many runs Russell saved England by holding catches that an inferior gloveman but better batsman would have missed.

ROBERT CHARLES RUSSELL

BORN	15 August 1963, Stroud, Gloucestershire, England
TESTS	54
RUNS	1,897 in 86 innings at 27.10 with 2 hundreds/6 fifties
DISMISSALS	153 catches and 12 stumpings
ONE-DAY INTERNATIONALS	40
RUNS	423 in 31 innings at 17.62 with 1 fifty
DISMISSALS	41 catches and 6 stumpings

90

·······

INZAMAM-UL-HAQ

INZAMAM WAS A HUGE GREAT BEAR of a man who looked as though he was batting with a toothpick. The stumps always seemed very small when he was at the crease – that's if you could see any of them behind his frame. Whatever his figure, Inzamam was a fine player who scored more than 20,000 runs in Test and one-day cricket over a period of more than 15 years. Anybody underestimating him at first sight soon realised that his appearance really was deceptive.

He was one of the most identifiable batsmen in the world, but he was comfortable in his big-boned frame. The part of Pakistan he comes from, Multan, is extremely hot – certainly not a place where people rush around doing exercise for the sake of it. I don't think he did a lot of running when he was a kid, and he didn't catch the bug as he grew older. He was a really good slip fielder, probably because he didn't fancy patrolling the covers for too long. But when he did, he had a rocket arm. Away from the game, he comes across as being very relaxed and just as easy-going. He even speaks slowly, but he is good fun to be around and is the sort of guy who can make you laugh.

The other unusual thing about Inzamam was his running between the wickets. He was very sensitive about people criticising this aspect of his game, but it is amazing that he seemed to have as many problems with it at the end of his career as he did at the start. Experience did not do a lot for him there. He took a while to turn and was a bit stop-start. Also, there always appeared to be communication problems between him and his fellow batsman. As an opposition player, you could certainly create pressure on the field and play on his weakness.

He was a strong player against pace but didn't do as well in Australia or South Africa as in other parts of the world. On his last couple of visits to Australia, he had a terrible time and only scored two runs in four Test innings. There was no doubt about his bravery, because he was a really good hooker and puller. Our approach was to tie him up with line and length and see if he had a rush of blood, maybe going for a big shot or a suicidal run. Our plan was generally to give him a bouncer, followed by a yorker or vice versa when he first came in and then to get spin on early. The best line to bowl to him was slightly outside off stump – anything on middle he liked to whip through the leg side. He could also be quite slow to get his bat down early on, so lbw was another good option.

He was prone to come down the track and have a swing, as though the shot was predetermined. Other spinners such as Anil Kumble also had success against him. Inzamam was especially vulnerable early on, as his feet took a while to get moving. The straight ball to him could be as good as any. Once he was in, he started to play more confidently. He played the pull against spinners, which my mate Ian Chappell reckons is a shot that has gone out of the book since batsmen began wearing helmets and developed confidence to sweep.

The only hundred he scored against us has been a bit overlooked. It was in Hobart in 1999, but people now remember the game – at least in Australia – for the brilliant partnership between Justin Langer and Adam Gilchrist in a fourth-innings chase that really proved to us that we could win from any position. The Pakistan batsmen, unusually for them, had been accused of indecision in their first innings, so a few of them, Inzamam included, went along at their natural tempo in the second. He actually ran a lot of runs that day – there were plenty of threes I remember – and it took a brilliant overhead slip catch by Mark Waugh off a full-blooded cut to get him out.

He developed into quite a good captain for Pakistan and managed to bring most of the team together for most of the time, which was a big achievement. It helped to have a solid batting unit, with Younus Khan, Mohammad Yousuf and him in the positions between three and five, and Shoaib Akhtar could be a major threat with the ball when everything was right. I think that Inzamam's calm approach helped him as captain, and he was loyal to his players. But he went too far at the Oval in 2006 when his team refused to leave the dressing-room after one of the players was accused of ball tampering. Having made the point, he should have brought them back on instead of forfeiting the Test, which created a lot of unwanted publicity for cricket.

INZAMAM-UL-HAQ

BORN	3 March 1970, Multan, Pakistan
TESTS	120
RUNS	8,830 in 200 innings at 49.60 with 25 hundreds/46 fifties
ONE-DAY INTERNATIONALS	378
RUNS	11,739 in 350 innings at 39.52 with 83 fifties

91

·······

GRAEME HICK

EVEN NOW, GRAEME HICK SPLITS OPINION up and down England. At Worcester, they see him as an amazing talent who was destroyed by the system. But critics believe he had plenty of opportunities that he failed to take due to character flaws. Personally, I think the answer lies somewhere between those two extreme positions, but trying to decide exactly where is the difficult part. When I came to England for my first Ashes tour in 1993, we identified Hick as one of our most dangerous opponents. And then, two Tests into the series, he was dropped. That was an incredible decision, especially as he had carted me all around Worcester only a few weeks earlier to score a big hundred. Yes, he probably did underachieve during his Test career, but he could not have played the kind of innings he produced on that occasion at New Road without possessing great natural ability.

Guys in our squad on that tour knew him from a long time back. Steve Waugh thought he was the best teenager he'd seen when he toured Australia with the Under-25 team a few years earlier. Hick had also spent a year at Queensland playing alongside Ian Healy, who rated him very highly, too. At Worcester in 1993, he just looked so strong, big at the crease and in total command of his game. It was his 69th first-class hundred, and he hadn't even reached his 27th birthday. Maybe a clue to his problem is revealed by that statistic. During a long qualification period for England, he piled up century after century in county cricket, and it could be that weaknesses were not spotted until too late, when they were ingrained in his technique. Expectations were huge by the time he made his Test debut. He was not used to having to dig his way out of tight corners.

I never had much joy against him. In seven Test matches, I can only remember getting him out once. The pace bowlers had a better record against him. When I remember Hick in 1993, it is impossible not to think of Merv Hughes at the same time. Hughes gave him a real going over in that series. It was typical of him to pick on one of England's best batsmen, and as soon as he detected a slight bit of weakness in character, he just went for the jugular. He thought that he could intimidate Hick, and he was probably right. People had already picked up on a weakness he had against the short ball, which was a running theme of criticism from his debut against the West Indies in 1991 onwards. I was playing club cricket in England that summer, and I remember the media harping on and on about it. Name me any batsman who didn't struggle against Curtly Ambrose at some point.

The weird thing is that I've seen Hick pull and hook like the best of them. Somehow, Hughes got on top of him, and Hick seemed to forget his plan. He got out to him three times in four innings before the selectors decided to make a change, although it is worth pointing out that Hick scored sixty-odd in his last innings and had scored around one hundred and forty runs in all – not a contribution that will ever win a series but not exactly outright failure either. I think Hicky got confused about whether to duck or hook and was caught in between. Four months earlier, he had scored a big hundred against India in Mumbai. He was caught in a vicious circle, because as soon as things started to go wrong, the critics pored over his technique and developed all sorts of theories about where he was going wrong. That probably undermined his confidence. I wonder if anybody from England ever went up to him, quietly, and said: 'You're a great player, Hicky – just go out there and do it your way,' and backed him 100 per cent.

He was back in the side when England came to Australia in 1994–95, but he suffered again when Mike Atherton declared in Sydney when he was ninety-eight not out, two short of a first hundred against us. We were amazed in the field at Atherton's decision. In fairness, Atherton came to recognise his mistake, but I can see where he was coming from, because he needed to give his bowlers time to bowl us out in the final innings. I'd guess the line of communication had broken down between the batsman and captain. A lot has been written about it, far more than the game itself. We could sense the tension around the dressing-room, and when England came out to field, they looked downbeat and nervous instead of pumped up and ready to go for victory.

Atherton has gone down as the villain, but maybe the way Hick played in those final minutes says something about him. He was batting well, but once he got into the 90s he started to look scratchy and nervous. Temperament is so important in playing at the top level. Scoring a hundred in an Ashes match is a big achievement – Hick, as it turned out, never managed to complete that task, although his record against us was better than his overall figure. He will go down as one of the great county players, but something in his make-up repressed him from hitting the same heights for England. It's a shame, because Graeme is a wonderful guy and an amazing player. It's a real pity he never performed consistently well on the big stage.

GRAEME ASHLEY HICK

BORN	23 May 1966, Harare, Zimbabwe
TESTS	65
RUNS	3,383 in 114 innings at 31.32 with 6 hundreds/18 fifties
ONE-DAY INTERNATIONALS	120
RUNS	3,846 in 118 innings at 37.33 with 5 hundreds/27 fifties

92

......

MONTY PANESAR

MONTY PANESAR IS ONE OF THE jewels of the game today. He is brilliant for the profile of cricket, especially in England. Everything you see with Panesar is natural, from the smooth rhythm of his approach to the commitment of his appeals and excitement when he takes a wicket. Kids playing at school and in the streets imitate Panesar, and in the grounds he is probably as popular as Freddie Flintoff. Being in England with Hampshire, I could see how 'Monty Mania' was sweeping the country a couple of years ago. None of this has affected his bowling or the size of his head, and while his fielding is still a bit short of the mark, he never, ever looks to hide. That is why people like him: he's a trier. However, I think Monty has stalled at the moment. I want to see improvement and different plans and strategies.

Australian crowds were really looking forward to seeing Panesar during the last Ashes series. It is a shame they had to wait so long. Everybody in the game knew that Duncan Fletcher had his favourites as coach, and Ashley Giles belonged in that group. Ashley is a great bloke who came through a lot of flak to forge a good Test career, and his job in holding up an end in the 2005 series was part of a plan that brought success. Time moves on, and it was wrong of Fletcher to think that England could simply pick the 2005 bunch in different conditions and ignore what had happened in the previous year. Similar thinking lay behind the decision to recall Geraint Jones when Chris Read, a better wicket-keeper in any case, had done a good job at the end of the 2006 season.

Panesar is a proper attacking spinner who will win matches for England as a strike bowler. There shouldn't be an argument about that, because he has done so already. When he finally came back into the side at Perth, he took five wickets in the first innings and eight in the match. We still won to go 3–0 ahead, but Panesar added a cutting edge to the attack. Now that Giles has unfortunately retired because of injury, Panesar is the undisputed number one. England just have to let him bowl. There has been criticism that he can be a shade too quick, which stops him getting the bite he needs from the pitch. But he has to be allowed to find his own way. Spinners tend to reach their peak slightly later than pace bowlers, and Panesar has not yet been three years in the Test team. He will always turn the ball because of the revolutions he puts on it, and a strong action means that nothing can go seriously wrong. As he plays in different conditions, he will learn the best way to be successful; at least I hope he learns from the different conditions. If not, he will stay as he is and not improve.

His career is really interesting. Basically, he seems to have learned the game in a park outside the formal coaching system, and he has improved by bowling and bowling and bowling. It sounds like an Australian story in which a guy comes from one of the remote bush towns with a method that holds up when he goes up a level. The fact that Panesar could do that should tell him to keep trusting his instinct – it has certainly paid off so far. He is a very modest bloke who always seems surprised that he has progressed so far in the game. He has never looked overawed to me. In fact, for a young spinner, he seems to have great mental strength as well as stamina to be able to bowl long spells with good control.

We finally had a chat at the end of the 2006–07 series in the dressing-room at Sydney. It wasn't really like the usual conversations in which a couple of bowlers trade information about batsmen and grips on the ball. I got the impression that he had prepared what he wanted to ask, and it was quite funny when I found out that he'd asked Mike Hussey, an old mate of his from Northamptonshire, whether he thought I would talk to him. Again, I wondered how this apparent insecurity sat with his confidence and consistency with a ball in his hand. Then I realised: he is simply a really polite kid who was brought up to take nothing for granted.

We were together for maybe 30 minutes or so, and he went away with a few ideas that he said were new. I talked about having plans for different batsmen and something I believe in a big way that always sounds odd on the surface: what matters about a ball is not where it lands, but how it gets there. The way it travels from A to B determines where it will go when it hits the pitch and the variety comes from the pace and angle of delivery, use of the crease and the amount of spin imparted on the ball. I reckon his mindset is such that he will be trying to pick brains for the rest of his career. But it won't be long before other spinners seek him out for the secrets of his own success.

MUDHSUDEN SINGH PANESAR

BORN	25 April 1982, Luton, England
TESTS	29
WICKETS	101 at 31.99
ONE-DAY INTERNATIONALS	26
WICKETS	24 at 40.83

93
· · · · · · ·

ARJUNA RANATUNGA

THROUGH GRITTED TEETH, I HAVE PUT Arjuna Ranatunga in my
100. When I picked my top 50 for *The Times*, there were a few
accusations that I'd gone for my mates instead of being objective.
Well, I hope this choice ends that criticism once and for all, because
everybody knows that I don't like Ranatunga. When I went over to
Sri Lanka after the tsunami to help out with Murali's great work,
I met Ranatunga again, and we got on reasonably well. We even
wagged. And then he bagged me in the newspaper almost the next
day. You can't be mates with everyone, and if there was any way
I could knock him down to number 101 for the purposes of this
book, I'd be delighted to do so. But having taken on the task, I
want to do it seriously, and the fact is that Ranatunga helped to put
Sri Lanka on the cricket map. And you know what? Deep down,
I'll quietly admit that I rated him as a cricketer.

Our differences are pretty well documented. Maybe we've kept
people entertained down the years with our comments. I don't
know about him, but personally I have meant every word that I've
said, even the ones that landed me in trouble. The basic problem I
had with Ranatunga was his attitude towards the game. He didn't
play cricket in the right spirit and tried to manipulate the laws and
regulations without actually breaking them. Off the top of my head,
I can remember occasions when he led his team off the field because
he was unhappy with an umpiring decision, ordered an umpire
where to stand behind the wicket, called for a runner by faking
injury to disguise his own lack of fitness – he looked as though he'd
swallowed a sheep – and told his teammates not to shake our hands

after a match. Time after time, he took the mickey out of the game and got away with it because the authorities were too frightened to stop him.

Our games against Sri Lanka were always more fractious than they needed to be with Ranatunga in charge. There is a difference between playing competitively and taking liberties. The trouble was that tension rubbed off on decent people who also became embroiled in situations that they would normally cross the road to avoid. There was just no need for it. There must be something in Ranatunga's make-up that means he needs confrontation to thrive. He was described as a little Napoleon early in his captaincy career, and I think he took it as praise. We found out that he loved it in the middle when we sledged him, so we tried to keep quiet – but he was so irritating it was hard to keep our mouths shut. He had the ability to get under everybody's skin, and from talking to players from other countries, I know it wasn't just Australia who disliked his approach. I have not heard a good word for him from a single international player outside Sri Lanka. Alec Stewart, for example, noted that Ranatunga was masterful at getting in the way of fielders or the wicket-keeper when a throw was coming in. But the bloke always had a way of making sure that the opposition were painted as the villains.

Putting all the baggage aside, he was quite a talented batsman, especially against spin. His great moment, I suppose, was being there at the end when Sri Lanka beat us in the World Cup final in 1996. He used his feet and swept as well as many batsmen I came across. One-day cricket was his forte – especially when he could convince the umpire into allowing somebody to do his running for him – because he worked the ball around neatly and was brave in the way he went about his shots. He was unorthodox and struck the ball into different areas, hitting inside out over cover, for example.

The other way of interpreting opponents' dislike of Ranatunga was that he did his job. He wasn't out there to win a popularity contest or give out prizes. He saw his role purely and simply as to help Sri Lanka win games of cricket, and he wanted to make himself into the hardest opponent he possibly could. A lot of the Sri Lanka players did not like him personally, and I know they had reservations about some of his antics, but they respected him as their leader, because he always stuck by them. He was always a tremendous supporter of Murali when accusations were flying about his action, and he strengthened his side as a cricketing unit. A few things went their way in 1996, but it was still a great achievement to lead them to that win, and it had an amazing impact in generating interest in the game in Sri Lanka.

Statistically, his record is not especially impressive, but he had a long Test career, and his record against Australia was good. He was no coward. He didn't like to back down with the bat any more than he did with his leadership. We thought he was vulnerable as a left-hander to the ball swinging away from around the wicket. And there is no doubt that his fitness counted against him, because he couldn't take quick singles, and there was always an easy one to him in the field. It was funny to see him puffing and panting after a chase. He once said that he based his game and attitude on Allan Border. Border would be horrified to know that.

ARJUNA RANATUNGA

BORN	1 December 1963, Colombo, Sri Lanka
TESTS	93
RUNS	5,105 in 155 innings at 35.69 with 4 hundreds/38 fifties
ONE-DAY INTERNATIONALS	269
RUNS	7,456 in 255 innings at 35.84 with 4 hundreds/49 fifties

94

·······

DEVON MALCOLM

DEVON MALCOLM WAS BORN WITH THE gift of being able to bowl fast. It took him a while to find that out; he didn't start playing cricket seriously until he left Jamaica, came to live in England and played for his college team in Sheffield – apparently most of the side were teachers rather than pupils. I can imagine him being much the same then as when I faced him in the mid-1990s and finally when he ended his career on the county circuit: tall, gangly, fast and either brilliant or frustrating. Even when he ran in at the age of 40, he could look as raw as a kid on his debut. He could be dynamite, or he could spray the ball all over, leaving you to check with *Playfair* that he really had played for England. In fact, he made more than enough Test appearances to be able to say that he had an international career, and from an Australian point of view, we were always happier to see him out of the side than in it. Preparing to face Malcolm was close to impossible, because we never knew which side of him we would see on any given day. When on song, his pace, swing and control were tough to face.

Malcolm was just a joy to be around. Sheer passion for the game kept him going long after his England days came to an end. And the crowds loved him. There was something of the everyman about his approach. You could see it best in the way he batted – uncomplicated is as good a word as any. There was no messing around. If he blocked one, you knew that next ball he would swing his arms and try to whack you as far as he could. And if he did manage to clobber one, the chances are that he would defend against the next. The plan had a nice simplicity about it. I remember he hit me for a couple of pretty big sixes in a game at Sydney. But I also have a very happy memory of his batting: he became my hat-trick victim in Melbourne in 1994.

You couldn't dislike Malcolm. He was a nice, gentle bloke off the field with a really big heart. He was sensitive about the way he was treated by England, which wasn't always very well. He had a great physique to be able to bowl at pace: tall, loose-limbed and just naturally fit. You could probably say he was the Steve Harmison of his day. Just as he could bowl really fast, he had a rocket throw from the boundary. There was a danger that you'd see this collection of arms and legs loping around the boundary and think there was an easy second run – and you'd end up diving into the crease to beat an Exocet missile fizzing to the keeper. His problem was always focusing on the ball, because he was very short-sighted and couldn't play without glasses or contact lenses.

The selectors didn't know what they had in him. Sometimes he thought they were tougher opponents than the opposition batsmen. Too often they worried about his bad days instead of remembering the devastation he could cause if his action was working well and his radar was in sync. He was actually a more intelligent bowler than some people gave him credit for, including one or two within the England set-up. The key was to make sure the rest of the attack supplied a balance. He had a good partner in Angus Fraser to make sure that things were kept tight at the other end. Fraser was a good operator, especially in helpful conditions, because he had control over line and length, and we were always far happier to see him with another medium-fast bowler in tandem. There were plenty of those in England, but not many with Malcolm's pace. In 1994–95, they picked Martin McCague at Brisbane when Malcolm had chickenpox, supposedly as a like-for-like replacement, but he wasn't in the same league and soon left the tour injured, overwhelmed by the pressure of Test cricket.

Not long afterwards, Malcolm helped England to win in Adelaide. We were 2–0 up, but were bowled out for 156 in the second innings. Malcolm took six wickets in the match, and in the second innings he forced Michael Slater to mis-hook and beat Steve Waugh for pace, bowling him between bat and pad. By then, Waugh had become recognised as a bloke who was a very difficult batsman to knock back. Then, later in the series, Malcolm broke Slater's thumb. Because he went slightly wide of the stumps in his delivery, his stock ball angled in towards the right-hander. It looked as though it was following you, so his bouncer, when it was directed well, could be hard to avoid.

His greatest day came against South Africa shortly before the 1994–95 tour to Australia when he took nine wickets in the second innings. We had come across him before, most recently at the Oval in 1993 when he dismissed all of our top six over the course of the two innings. But that performance served to remind us of his ability, and while it was asking a lot to expect him to reach that height again – very few bowlers bag nine in an innings even once in their career – he continued to have his moments. Quite a few of the very quick men disappear as quickly as they arrive, like meteors burning in the sky. But Malcolm kept on going and finished his career with more than 1,000 first-class wickets, a wonderful achievement for that type of bowler and a damning indictment of those who thought he didn't know what he was doing.

DEVON EUGENE MALCOLM

BORN	22 February 1963, Kingston, Jamaica
TESTS	40
WICKETS	128 at 37.09
ONE-DAY INTERNATIONALS	10
WICKETS	16 at 25.25

95

·······

MOIN KHAN

HE WASN'T THE BEST WICKET-KEEPER I saw, and he didn't rank
alongside Flower, Gilchrist and Stewart as a batsman, but Moin
Khan was still an easy pick for my 100. I put him on my list
instinctively and thought about it more closely later. Like a few
others, his value goes beyond his figures. He was a true fighter on
the field, a bloke you would want to have in your team. They called
him the 'Karachi Streetfighter', and given that Javed Miandad went
by the same nickname a decade earlier, it was not a tag given
lightly. I never played against Miandad, but I imagine we might
have had a love-hate relationship. He would have got under my
skin, and he'd certainly have taken on my bowling, because his
opinion of spin bowlers was very, very low. At the same time, I'm
sure I would have admired his determination, even if it was only
in a grudging way.

My first proper contact with Moin came in Lahore in 1994. I
bowled more than 40 overs in the innings and took a few wickets,
but Moin stuck it out even though he didn't seem to read everything
and came out with a really gutsy hundred. That was a very peculiar
week or so, because Wasim Akram and Waqar Younis both pulled
out shortly before the start of the game with injuries. The politics
of Pakistan cricket went over my head at that stage of my career,
and I still didn't understand all the ins and outs by the time I retired
13 years later. There were always personal issues of some sort or
another, but you could never afford to underestimate the team that
took to the field because of the sheer talent of their players. Moin
seemed to be one of the more consistent performers over the years

and just got on with his job on the field. That innings in Lahore has stuck with me.

He could be a real nuisance to bowl to, because his technique was very unorthodox. In that sense, he was simply another wicket-keeper. he found his own way to cope and did not waste too much time worrying about whether it looked pretty or not. If Pakistan needed quick runs, he would have a hit. If they needed him to hang around, he would defend as resolutely as any of the blokes above him in the order. He was a bit like our own Ian Healy: a great bloke to have when you wanted to get out of a mess. With Moin, the Pakistan side always looked to have a bit more backbone, and I know that Inzamam-ul-Haq in particular liked to have him there in the ranks.

For almost all of his career, he faced a challenge from Rashid Latif for the one place in the side. Moin is a generous guy and said that the competition was good for the team. He thinks that the two of them used to stay on for extra practice not because they needed it, but to show each other how much they wanted the place. Personally, I would have gone for Moin ahead of Latif and not had any worries about his attitude, as he was the best player. At least Moin is consistent, because he believes that Kamran Akmal, his successor in the side, has suffered through not having a similar threat for his place. It is an interesting theory, and there is always a difficult balance between being comfortable and playing in a relaxed frame of mind, and feeling complacent.

Depending on the make-up of my side, I would consider him for a Rest of the World XI to face Australia in one-day cricket. He would slog, sweep, drive and even had the 'ramp' shot, crouching down and spooning the ball on the rise over the head of the wicket-keeper. He played some superb little cameos against us. I remember the World Cup game in 1999 when he whacked 31 from, I think, 12 balls at the end of the innings to change the nature of the game. You wouldn't know from looking at the scorecard all these years on, but it was a match-winning innings of its kind. Glenn McGrath suffered more than anybody, and Moin was arguably the best keeper/batsman in the whole tournament.

His keeping was more than adequate, as it had to be with guys such as Saqlain Mushtaq and Mushtaq Ahmed in the side. And he was a right little chirper behind the stumps. You would hear him shout after every delivery 'Well bowled, Mushy, very well bowled, *shabash, shabash.*' Every Australian who ever played against Moin knows at least one word of Urdu: '*shabash*' means well done or very good. And off the field he was always a very jolly sort of bloke. He has moved into coaching, and I wouldn't be surprised if he is around for a long time because of his sound attitude to the game.

Given the turnover of captains, it was inevitable that anybody in the Pakistan side for more than a year or two at a time would skipper the side at some point. Moin had a couple of goes at the job but was probably not really cut out for the task. He was a combative guy but maybe a little bit overcautious. As a rule, I think that keepers make great number twos, as they have a perfect view of the batsman in front of them. But they have enough to concentrate on as it is without having to think of bowling changes and field placements.

MOHAMMAD MOIN KHAN

BORN	23 September 1971, Rawalpindi, Pakistan
TESTS	69
RUNS	2,741 in 104 innings at 28.55 with 4 hundreds/15 fifties
DISMISSALS	128 catches and 20 stumpings
ONE-DAY INTERNATIONALS	219
RUNS	3,266 in 183 innings at 23 with 12 fifties
DISMISSALS	214 catches and 73 stumpings

96

. . . .

SOURAV GANGULY

SOURAV GANGULY MIGHT NOT BE MY cup of tea as a bloke, but what he has done for Indian cricket has to be respected. He is a feisty sort of character, not short of self-confidence or unaware of his standing in Indian life. He is regarded over there, especially around his teeming home city of Calcutta, as one of the greatest ever Indian captains. They won more games under him than anybody else, so I guess the statistics back that up. Personally, I'm not so sure. I think he had some outstanding players and solid characters in the team. Do you need to be a great leader to win games with Sachin Tendulkar, Rahul Dravid and Anil Kumble in the ranks? Tactically, he was not among the best leaders I came up against, and his man-management skills left a bit to be desired. And yet for all that, I didn't hesitate to include him in my 100.

Supporters know him as the 'Prince of Calcutta'. The story is that he gave himself the nickname and it stuck. There is something princely about his attitude and the wristy way he bats. I think that every bowling attack in the world, even Bangladesh, has tried to get him with the short ball or has placed a couple of gullies for those left-handed slashes that he likes. They might be obvious weaknesses, but he also has a knack of finding gaps. After a while, I had to half-acknowledge that nobody could be so streaky so often and that he actually had skill.

When I played, I liked the fact that Ganguly was a fighter. Whatever happened, whenever he was hit, he gritted his teeth and fought back. With his confidence, he always backed himself to come good in the end. He toured Australia very early and suffered badly because he was just not ready. Sometimes young players are exposed too early, but when he got his second chance a few years later, he took it and stayed in the side for a decade. He might have been born with a silver spoon in his mouth – I can quite easily believe the story that he had a servant to strap on his batting pads when he was a kid – but that never prevented him from putting in the work he needed to succeed. I would not say that he toughened up India, but they probably became harder to beat away from home.

My own tactic was simply to try to tie him down. He didn't like blocking, and I knew that if I plugged away accurately for long enough, he would try something a bit risky. In one way, it was easier bowling to left- rather than right-handers, because they could not pad up into the rough, as it was outside their off rather than leg stump. Kicking the ball away left them vulnerable to a leg-before decision. Towards the end of games in particular, the ball could turn in sharply and spit from the footmarks, although there wasn't a lot of nip in the surfaces in India. I knew that Ganguly would use his feet to try to get after me. He became one of my favourite dismissals when Adam Gilchrist stumped him from a wrong-un at Adelaide in 1999, because I did not get that many wickets with the wrong-un. The ball kept a bit low, but I did genuinely beat him on the outside edge, and he hadn't long celebrated a half-century.

Maybe his strength is in one-day cricket, where there are strict rules on the use of bouncers. He can be really effective when he opens because he can punish anything wide, and if he slashes hard enough, there is very little chance of those edges going to hand and sticking. He can also play some glorious-looking drives with perfect timing, like most of the Indian batsmen. There are some big, big one-day scores in his book, and his medium-pace bowling, shuffling in off a run at least 20 yards too long, can be quite deceptive. He puts it on a length and wobbles it enough to make you check before hitting through the line.

Off the field, we have enjoyed the odd beer and a chat. As you would expect given his background, he is an intelligent bloke, with some interesting ideas on all sorts of subjects. But he did have the knack of rubbing up opponents (and even teammates when he went to Lancashire) the wrong way without seeming to try very hard. If this was part of a deliberate strategy, then he got it bang on at times.

When we arrived in India in 2000 in the middle of our really good run, he said that we had only beaten weak teams in the past. Funny, that, as India were one of them. He would also be late for the toss and then walk off on his own without waiting for Steve Waugh, our captain. To be a minute or so behind because an issue crops up is one thing, but more than that is just taking the mickey. He will say that the results are in the book and, yes, India did beat us in that series – thanks, I would say, to a great stand between Laxman and Dravid at Calcutta and Harbhajan's bowling rather than any tactical genius on Ganguly's part. On this, as on practically everything else, Ganguly splits opinion.

SOURAV CHANDIDAS GANGULY

BORN	8 July 1972, Calcutta, India
TESTS	106
RUNS	6,792 in 180 innings at 42.71 with 15 hundreds/34 fifties
WICKETS	32 at 51.31
ONE-DAY INTERNATIONALS	311
RUNS	11,363 in 300 innings at 41.02 with 22 hundreds/72 fifties
WICKETS	100 at 38.49

97

·······

SHAHID AFRIDI

THEY CALLED HIM 'BOOM BOOM' IN Pakistan, but the way that Shahid Afridi went about his batting, he could just as easily have been 'Boom Bust'. It was impossible for a guy with his approach to be consistent, and I don't think the rest of his team expected it. That wasn't his role in the side. In one-day cricket – his main format – his job was to go out there, usually at the start of the innings, and get them off to a lightning start. He could make somebody such as Adam Gilchrist look like a tortoise, and there isn't really much mileage in making the obvious point that if Afridi had been a bit more selective in deciding which balls to hit, he would have been more successful. That wasn't him. You could hardly keep your eyes off him when he was in full flow. In fact, you couldn't keep your eyes off him when he was struggling, because he would still look to play big shots and could have connected at any minute. For entertainment value, he has to be in my 100.

He didn't need 20 overs to change a game – if he did bat for that long, then the game was practically Pakistan's already. Anything in his arc would be whacked straight, high and long. His best shots were the most orthodox, such as the drive. He once hit Andrew Symonds for a six estimated as being one hundred and fifty metres long in a one-day game at Perth. Tom Moody, who knows the ground as well as anybody, said that it should have counted as 12. Afridi could be frustrating to bowl to, because not everything came off the middle of the bat, and with only two fielders on the boundary for the initial overs, it was impossible to plug all the gaps. You knew that he would have a go and give chances along the way. There was no need to be too clever when bowling to him. You just needed to tie him up so that he couldn't swing his arms.

His strike rate of well over a run per ball is the best in the history of one-day cricket, and only Sanath Jayasuriya has struck more sixes. He hit the fastest hundred in one-day internationals from 37 balls against a Sri Lanka attack including Chaminda Vaas, Jayasuriya and Muttiah Muralitharan. Amazingly, it was his first innings at that level, and he was only 16. In Pakistan, they tend to see him as an unfulfilled talent. I don't know how you could possibly live up to a start like that, but, as I have said, you have to accept that he is not going to pull it off every game. Let's be honest, he is not the only Pakistan cricketer in history who has been inconsistent. His great strength – apart from his physical power – is his conviction. He has a way of playing, and he backs himself 100 per cent.

I am not sure the selectors have ever known what to do with him in Test cricket. He obviously has so much talent, but his style isn't really suited to the five-day game. I can remember an innings he played against us at Sydney in 2005 when he whacked a six and a four and was caught on the deep square-leg boundary from his ninth ball – that isn't really what you are looking for from a Test number six. Having said that, his record is better than you might expect. He has scored a hundred against India as an opening batsman, and those games are as tough as the Ashes. For a period of a couple of years or so when Bob Woolmer was the coach, Afridi made some good contributions. Woolmer was happy to take his talent for what it was, made him feel important to the side and didn't ruin him by trying to make too many changes. He knew that Afridi gave the team something that nobody else could.

They had so much talent during that period and all-rounders in Abdur Razzaq, Shoaib Malik and Afridi to give them options. Wicket-keepers Moin Khan and more recently Kamran Akmal have been decent batsmen. They had the potential to win a World Cup but underperformed against us in the final at Lord's in 1999, having beaten us earlier in the tournament. I like to think that we were more ruthless on the day and simply didn't allow them to play.

As a wrist-spinner, Afridi has quite a few variations, and it is a sign of his improvement that some people now consider him a bowling all-rounder. His quicker ball is about as fast as Glenn McGrath's stock delivery, but I think that he needs to give it a little bit more spin and air to be really effective at Test level. He is certainly a good option for a captain to have up his sleeve, and we will never know how good he could have become if he hadn't been such a dominant batsman and had concentrated on the bowling side of his game instead. He is an aggressive competitor and doesn't mind having a word with the batsman. In fact, he seems to be a passionate bloke all round who doesn't find it easy to back down. I rate him as a cricketer.

SAHIBZADA MOHAMMAD SHAHID KHAN AFRIDI

BORN	1 March 1980, Khyber Agency, Pakistan
TESTS	26
RUNS	1,683 in 46 innings at 37.40 with 5 hundreds/8 fifties
WICKETS	47 at 34.89
ONE-DAY INTERNATIONALS	265
RUNS	5,479 in 249 innings at 23.51 with 4 hundreds/29 fifties
WICKETS	239 at 34.90

98

·······

GRAHAM THORPE

GRAHAM THORPE WAS ONE OF THE best all-round England batsmen I came across. He could attack or defend, depending on the situation, but he didn't get stuck in one mindset or the other. He impressed us from the start when he scored a hundred on his debut at Trent Bridge in 1993. I lost count of all the batsmen who faced us in that series, but Thorpe was definitely one of the better picks. He had been on the fringes of the side for a few years and had a lot of talent, but a few people wondered about his temperament and commitment to the team. There didn't seem to be much obvious evidence of any issues, either in that match or throughout his career. What I did see, straight away, was a young player with the character to succeed. He looked after his game, making sure it was all in order, and he didn't allow much to distract him. He was a very solid performer for England and tried to hold things together during their dark days. He then became a key player for his mate Nasser Hussain when they started to turn things around.

He had a good, tight technique and could play off either foot. He was happy to take on the short ball but was also quick to get forward if the ball was there. Yes, he had a cocky side, but I think a lot of that was simply down to confidence in his own ways. I liked his attitude and approach. We actually thought there was a bit of the Australian in him, and I know that he liked the way we went about our business as a team. I guess he showed that when he came over to New South Wales to help out with coaching recently. He was quite happy to get involved in any chirping that went on in the middle while England were fielding and used to thrive on being the target himself at the crease. He enjoyed the challenge that came about from difficult situations. At the same time, he made sure that he never got too high when things went well on the field or too low if he got a really good ball that he knew he couldn't do very much about.

We used to try to keep him tight on off stump. He liked to play shots outside that area, like a lot of left-handers do, because they get plenty of balls angling away from their bodies. But he was quite good at moving across and working the ball into the leg side, another of his productive shots. With experience, nudging singles and finding gaps became one of his specialities, especially in one-day cricket. Glenn McGrath thought he was prone to get caught at mid-on or chop the ball onto his stumps, but his concentration was always good and his weaknesses very slight. I don't remember him hitting a six against us, because he looked to keep the ball along the ground. And on one occasion he scored a hundred against Pakistan in Lahore with only a single boundary.

His record against Australia was almost exactly the same as his figures overall, but although he scored his fair share of runs, I was quite happy to bowl to him. The good thing about left-handed batsmen for a wrist-spinner is that they can't just push their pad into the rough, because they leave themselves open to lbw decisions. There were plenty of times when I thought I was having the better of our little battle, the game within the game, but he would hang on. He played with very soft hands rather than lunging at the ball. I remember one of his best innings against us, at Edgbaston in 1997, when he put on nearly 300 with Hussain. He was generally a safe slip fielder, but he made a costly error later in the series when he dropped our tall opener Matthew Elliott at Headingley in a tight situation. Elliott and Ricky Ponting turned around our innings, and we won the game. As slips fielders, we all drop some.

I don't know how much he was restricted by back trouble, but he made the most of his talent and enjoyed a long international career. Sometimes a player who does really well straight away fails to live up to their promising start, but Thorpe's hundred at Trent Bridge was no flash in the pan. He immediately gave some backbone to a side that had lost seven Tests in a row. There was a bit more to him than some of the blokes we came across, and if the stubborn streak in him rubbed the establishment up the wrong way off the field, then it was a handy quality on it.

Although I rated Thorpe as a batsman, I thought that the selectors were right to leave him out for the 2005 Ashes. The striking thing about the England team from the start of that summer was their self-belief. In the past, they had talked about competing against Australia; this time they made no secret of wanting to win. It just struck me that Thorpe was one of those who had lost to us too many times in the past and was scarred by the experience. Ian Bell did not have a particularly good series, but young players bring something to the dressing-room. There was no sense of 'here we go again' from England after we won the first Test at Lord's. Overall, I still rate Thorpe highly enough to include him in the top 100.

GRAHAM PAUL THORPE

BORN	I August 1969, Farnham, Surrey, England
TESTS	100
RUNS	6,744 in 179 innings at 44.66 with 16 hundreds/39 fifties
ONE-DAY INTERNATIONALS	82
RUNS	2,380 in 77 innings at 37.18 with 21 fifties

99

·······

ANDREW CADDICK

IF ABILITY WAS THE SOLE REQUIREMENT to become a major world-class player, then Andrew Caddick would have been near the top of the tree. But there is more to it than that, as we've seen with plenty of players down the years. Caddick could be deadly when conditions suited him, but to me he did not do it often enough for somebody with his natural talent. He still had his days, of course, and his new-ball partnership with Darren Gough was really important to England during the two or three years when they fought back from the depths. Previous captains had struggled to get the best out of Caddick, but Nasser Hussain was prepared to put up with all the baggage, stay focused on the good things about his bowler and not worry about the rest.

I tend to think of them as 'Gough and Caddick' rather than the other way around. Gough was definitely the leader of the attack, the bloke you would go to first if you were desperate for something to happen. But they offered good balance. Caddick, tall, gave bounce and seam movement from just short of a length at one end, while Gough was shorter, skiddier and pitched it up a little bit further to swing. The trouble, speaking as an outsider looking in, was that they didn't always seem to bowl for each other. It looked as though there was a competitive edge, most of it from Caddick's viewpoint. That can be healthy up to a point if players are lifting each other to greater things, but the first and biggest task is to play as a team and beat the opposition. I just think that in Caddick's case there were times when he could have given a little bit more to his side.

It is a tribute to him that he is still bowling for Somerset. Not only that, he is up there among the best English bowlers on the county circuit and was put on standby for a Test recall in 2007 at the age of 38. Bearing in mind that pitches at Taunton do not give a lot of help to bowlers, his record there is tremendous. He might have lost a yard of pace, but he will put the ball in the right spot and do something with it for as long as he decides to keep on playing. Maybe in some ways he is better suited to domestic cricket, because he can be the big fish in the pond.

At international level, I thought that his head went down too easily. Our approach was to try to work him over in his first spell, because the effects would still be there when he came back for his second and third of the day. He did not seem to be very good at drawing a line under something that went wrong. It needled him throughout the day. Of course, it worked the other way as well. When he started well and picked up a couple of early wickets, he would be all over you like a cheap suit, chipping in with a few words and making life pretty tough. Our job, pretty obviously I guess, was to make sure he didn't get into that position.

Cricket would be a very dull game if every side was packed with 11 players of the same type. Actually, that would not work as a dynamic in the dressing-room. You need different characters, and to put this in perspective there are no stories about a nasty, unpleasant side to Caddick. He has a reputation as being a really helpful guy, but he just has an unfortunate knack – and I'm sure it isn't deliberate – of saying the wrong thing at the wrong time. I guess it comes down to a basic insecurity, which you could see on the field whenever he was hit to the boundary and started to tie his shoelace or scrape at the footholds, as if to find a reason outside his own control that the ball he had delivered was not too clever.

I know that Hussain used to build him up. He made him feel like a hero for taking responsibility – and never told him that Gough was the real 'gun' bowler. If Caddick did something Hussain wasn't too pleased with, he tried not to put him down in front of the rest, because that would be seen as humiliating. Captaincy is all about getting the best out of individuals, and from that point of view, I would have liked the challenge of having him in my side to try to work him out.

ANDREW CADDICK

On a personal level, I never had any issues with him. I did not get to know him as well as some of the other England players – Gough, for example – but when we did chat, he seemed to be a thoroughly decent, uncomplicated bloke. And he left Test cricket on a high with seven wickets in the second innings when England beat us at Sydney in 2003. Unfortunately, he then suffered injuries to his foot and back. By the time he was fit again, the bowling attack had been rebuilt with the next Ashes series in mind, and we all know what happened there.

ANDREW RICHARD CADDICK

BORN	21 November 1968, Christchurch, New Zealand
TESTS	62
WICKETS	234 at 29.91
ONE-DAY INTERNATIONALS	54
WICKETS	69 at 28.47

100

·······

JAMIE SIDDONS

IT IS A REAL SHAME THAT people in England never saw Jamie Siddons in action. He was a superb cricketer, a wonderful-looking batsman who played strokes gracefully and an outstanding fielder wherever he stood. Mark Waugh and Siddons are the best two all-round fielders I played with. Siddons had a rocket arm, held blinding catches at slip and stopped everything at cover. When I made my Victoria debut, he was one of the main guys in the team, a batsman we all looked up to. He was dynamite against spin, as I found when he moved to South Australia. I've tried to be as objective as I can about these 100 names, but I'm bound to be biased in favour of batsmen who did well against me. It is natural to rate them higher. Unfortunately, Siddons never had the rub of the green when he needed luck to be on his side to take the next step into the Test side. Instead, he is recognised – in general, not just by me – as one of the best three or four men never to have played for Australia.

The closest he came was on the tour to Pakistan in 1988, but he picked up a really nasty stomach bug. He lost something like 20 kilograms as a result, and at one point his life was in danger. It took him more than a year to recover, and he lost the momentum of a big-scoring summer the previous year. There can be so much fortune in cricket, and it is about who gets the breaks at the right time. If things had worked out better on that trip, who knows? At least he managed to play in a one-day international on that tour before he got ill. Even that was eventful, as it was moved from Karachi to Lahore because of rioting. He made a brave recovery from his illness but suffered another blow a few years later after he left the Vics when Merv Hughes hit him with a bouncer, breaking his cheekbone and denting his confidence probably even deeper. I guess the plain fact is that Siddons happened to be around during one of our golden periods for batsmen.

Although fast bowlers will say that batsmen have bats and helmets to protect themselves, there is no fun in seeing a decent bloke go down. Merv had a lot of respect for Siddons, as we all did. Siddons is one of those guys who tells you things as he sees them. Before concentrating on cricket, he played Aussie Rules at the highest level, and you don't see many shrinking violets in that sport. He didn't stand on ceremony, and if he thought somebody wasn't pulling his weight, he would say so. Some years before my debut, he told Hughes that he was being too nice to his new mates in the Australia team when he bowled against them for our state team. Siddons came from a similar background, so he could get away with a comment like that. I don't know whether it was a deliberate gee-up or an honest opinion, but apparently Hughes was back to his nastiest straight away.

Instead of playing for Australia, Siddons just stacked up runs in state cricket year after year after year. Only Darren Lehmann and Jamie Cox have scored more at that level. One of his great innings for Victoria came when I was on the fringes of the side, a hundred in the Sheffield Shield final against our big rivals, New South Wales. That innings got a lot of attention in Australia, because it was a low scoring game, and he was there to see us home at the end – it was a genuine match-winning knock. He went to Adelaide straight after that, so we ended up playing against each other far more often than we stood together. Lehmann reckons he only ever saw him drop one catch; that is one more than I can remember.

Outside the game, Siddons was very much a country guy. At the end of the season, he was happy to go back to his home town of Robinvale, a quiet spot on the Murray River in the north-east of Victoria. He would chill out around the barbie or sip a few cold beers on a houseboat, watching the world slowly go by around him. It was no hardship for him to miss the bright lights and pace of city life, and if he had any offers from English counties, he probably thought that he'd be happier at home. He would have made a great overseas player, because he could have played the full season, and I think he would have found a lot of the bowling to his liking, especially in the days before two divisions.

Behind his laid-back approach, he was serious about cricket, and I reckon he will have a good career now as a coach. He was our assistant in the 2005 Ashes and has now taken on one of the hardest jobs in the world, with Bangladesh. I hope the people there back him for the long term, because he has sound ideas about the way the game should be played and the facilities that need to be put in place to bring the whole structure – from the Test side downwards – up to the required standard.

JAMIE DARREN SIDDONS

BORN	25 April 1964, Robinvale, Victoria, Australia
ONE-DAY INTERNATIONALS	1
RUNS	32
FIRST-CLASS RUNS	11,587 at 44.91 with 35 hundreds/53 fifties

POSTSCRIPT

Shane Warne's Dream Test Match

I SHOULD STRESS STRAIGHT AWAY THAT I have not picked what I think to be the greatest teams from Australia and the Rest of the World – rather they comprise the best players I never played with or against. It is so difficult to compare players of different eras. The game changed even while I was playing. As a rule, I believe that a great player in one generation would be able to adapt to any other, but whether Don Bradman would have averaged almost 100 in modern-day Test cricket, I really don't know. One has to consider the ground, plus how fielding standards are so much higher these days. Then again, bat technology is better, so that is an advantage. We will never know, and that is a good thing. What would there be left to talk about if we did?

Greatest Australia XI

Arthur Morris
Bill Lawry
Ian Chappell (captain)
Donald Bradman
Greg Chappell
Keith Miller
Richie Benaud
Rod Marsh (wicket-keeper)
Bill O'Reilly
Dennis Lillee
Jeff Thomson

A lot of my Australia team is based on players I have been lucky enough to meet over the past couple of decades. And my childhood is also a big influence on my selection, for both sides. I think of them as backyard teams, because I used to imitate a lot of these players with my brother Jason after watching them on television. We would relive the real games and pretend to be all of the players in turn, adopting all of their different mannerisms and techniques. If I was Abdul Qadir, I would bounce in to bowl. He was a very easy guy to impersonate. Looking back, I can't think why I didn't end up bowling that way in real life. Garth le Roux was another bowler we really enjoyed watching. This was in the days of Kerry Packer's World Series. I remember going along to Waverley Park in Melbourne with Jason to watch one of the games. Le Roux was a big, bulky South African fast bowler, and, like Qadir, his action was good fun to copy.

I would love to have played with some of the Australians in my side. Arthur Morris was our main opening batsman from the 1948 'Invincibles', one of our all-time great teams. He is a bloke I have got to know from being around cricket, especially at Sydney, and he's been great company down the years. He always sees the positive things about our players. In my side, he is opening with Bill Lawry, a hilarious bloke, one of our best-loved commentators and a Victorian. These days, he has a reputation as having been a bit of a blocker when he played in the 1960s, and he doesn't mind playing along with it. But I've also heard that he was a very aggressive batsman when he wanted to be. Bradman is a 'must have'. I'd love to have seen him bat, and one of the biggest thrills of my career was being invited to spend some time with him on his 90th birthday, along with Sachin Tendulkar.

Ian Chappell is the captain. Everybody who played under his leadership has so much to say about him, his tactical brain, communication with players and the way he went about his captaincy. He always backed his players. I have learned more from him than from anybody else in cricket – about the realities of the game and how to deal with match situations rather than the technical, high-left-elbow stuff you get from the coaching books. His brother, Greg, was thought of as being our greatest batsman since Bradman and has to be in there as well. My all-rounder is Keith Miller, a larger-than-life personality and colleague of Morris in the 1940s and '50s. I just love his attitude to cricket and life. As a fighter pilot, he survived the war and lived every day afterwards as though it was his last. He defined pressure as 'having a Messerschmitt up your arse', not someone trying to get you out.

Rod Marsh is the wicket-keeper. He did some great work in preparing future Australia players at the Academy in the 1990s and was unbelievable behind the stumps. He also got on with it when he had the bat in his hands. I've gone for Dennis Lillee and Jeff Thomson as a pair to share the new ball. They were great backyard players, Lillee with his deep, dark stare and classic appeal, and Thomson with his slingy action and incredible pace. Their battles with the top West Indian batsmen, such as Viv Richards, in the 1970s were just electric. They would be able to relive those days as opponents in my dream game here. My Australia spinners are Bill O'Reilly and Richie Benaud, both leggies. Bradman said that O'Reilly was the best he saw. He went into journalism after his playing days, and I still have a copy of a really nice article he wrote about my first Test match. I'd been carted around the field by Ravi Shastri and Sachin Tendulkar, but he said that I would have a good future and could bamboozle batsmen. That meant so much to me at the time. Benaud is one of the great men of Australian cricket. He hardly needs an introduction, but like Chappell he has always been around the games in his role as a commentator, and their advice and friendship have meant a lot.

Greatest Rest of the World XI

Gordon Greenidge
Barry Richards
Viv Richards
Graeme Pollock
Garry Sobers
Imran Khan (captain)
Ian Botham
Alan Knott (wicket-keeper)
Malcolm Marshall
Garth le Roux
Abdul Qadir

There is a more modern look to the Rest of the World team. My World openers are Barry Richards and Gordon Greenidge. Richards is recognised as one of the lost talents from the apartheid era. I saw him at the Junction Oval in a friendly game around 1989. I can't recall the teams, but I do remember him driving a Victorian left-arm spinner called Paul Jackson through one of the windows. Graeme Pollock is another South African batsman who makes the team. Again, I was lucky to see him, in a benefit game for Mike Whitney. He scored 60 or 70 and looked to be such a powerful player. He had more of a Test career than Richards before the ban came into force.

My team has a great balance, with three all-rounders filling the spots from five to seven. Sobers has to play. I would love to have been in the same side as him to see what made him tick. He could do everything: bowl with the new ball or send down a few chinamen. My mate Sir Ian 'Beefy' Botham has to be included as well. A good rapport between the sides would be assured, because Botham and Miller would be able to hold the bar up together in the evening – I'm not sure I would be able to follow their pace. Imran was a great captain for Pakistan and managed to bring the side together. He was also a fine swing bowler and batsman. As with Botham, I didn't miss his career by too much.

Alan Knott strikes me as a bit of an Ian Healy type as a wicket-keeper. His batting could be unorthodox – I loved the way he used to lift the short stuff over the slips to third man – but he was a great keeper with smart footwork and soft hands. I think he would enjoy keeping to Qadir. One of the most interesting nights of my life was at Qadir's house when we sat on the floor and flipped an orange to each other with different grips and forms of spin and discussed tactics and how to sum up batsmen. That was an education and a very good night between two spinners.

ACKNOWLEDGEMENTS

THANKS TO EVERYONE WHOM I HAVE played with and against. It was a pleasure and real honour to play cricket for Australia.

To make so many friends from both my own and opposition teams shows that no matter what happens on the field, friendship is the most important thing. I hope the game of cricket continues to grow and the standard does not drop. Enjoy the contents of this book, and I hope everyone continues to play the game in the right spirit.

I would especially like to thank my managers Michael P. Cohen and James Erskine, together with Nick Canham, at MPC and my assistant Helen Nolan for everything they do for me – it's very much appreciated. Special thanks to Iain MacGregor for his continued support and to all the crew at Mainstream Publishing – particularly Gill McColl and Paul Murphy – for their invaluable help.

To my children Brooke, Jackson and Summer: you guys are my life, and I love you very much!